Higher Education in a Global Society

Higher Education in a Global Society

Edited by

D. Bruce Johnstone
University at Buffalo, The State University of New York, USA

Madeleine B. d'Ambrosio
TIAA-CREF Institute, USA

Paul J. Yakoboski
TIAA-CREF Institute, USA

In association with TIAA-CREF

Edward Elgar
Cheltenham, UK • Northampton, MA, USA

© TIAA-CREF 2010

All rights reserved. No part of this publication may be reproduced, stored in a retrieval system or transmitted in any form or by any means, electronic, mechanical or photocopying, recording, or otherwise without the prior permission of the publisher.

Published by
Edward Elgar Publishing Limited
The Lypiatts
15 Lansdown Road
Cheltenham
Glos GL50 2JA
UK

Edward Elgar Publishing, Inc.
William Pratt House
9 Dewey Court
Northampton
Massachusetts 01060
USA

A catalogue record for this book
is available from the British Library

Library of Congress Control Number: 2009940655

ISBN 978 1 84844 752 3

Printed and bound by MPG Books Group, UK

Contents

List of figures and tables	vii
List of contributors	viii
Foreword by Roger W. Ferguson, Jr.	xix
Introduction *Paul J. Yakoboski*	1 |昨

1	The significance of globalization to American higher education *D. Bruce Johnstone*	14
2	The realities of mass higher education in a globalized world *Philip G. Altbach*	25
3	Higher education crossing borders: programs and providers on the move *Jane Knight*	42
4	International research collaborations *Elizabeth D. Capaldi*	70
5	Offering domestic degrees outside the United States: one university's experiences over the past decade *Mark S. Kamlet*	83
6	Creating successful study abroad experiences *M. Peter McPherson and Margaret Heisel*	109
7	Creating an international experience on the domestic campus *Kathleen M. Waldron*	124
8	The centrality of faculty to a more globally oriented campus *Patti McGill Peterson*	134
9	Internationalizing the scholarly experience of faculty *Diana Bartelli Carlin*	148
10	Bringing international students to campus: who, what, when, where, why and how? *Charles E. Phelps*	162
11	Reinventing higher education in a global society: a perspective from abroad *Gowher Rizvi and Peter S. Horn*	184

12 American higher education in an increasingly globalized
    world: the way ahead   200
    D. Bruce Johnstone

Index   215

Figures and tables

FIGURES

5.1	Educating global citizens: degree programs outside of Pittsburgh, 2000–present	86
5.2	CERT locations	88
5.3	Software Engineering Institute (SEI) – current partner affiliations	90

TABLES

3.1	Evolution of international education terminology	43
3.2	Framework for cross-border education types of mobility	48
3.3	Typology of cross-border program mobility	51
3.4	Typology of cross-border provider mobility	53
3.5	Different perspectives on rationales and impacts of program and provider mobility	57
3.6	Rationales and expectations of different stakeholder groups	61
10.1	Leading places of origin for international students	165
10.2	Post-secondary schooling participation	167
10.3	US citizens as percent of earned doctorates in the US, by field and country of origin	170
12.1	Internationalization of higher education: learning from each other	208

Contributors

AUTHORS

Philip G. Altbach is J. Donald Monan, S.J. University Professor and director of the Center for International Higher Education in the Lynch School of Education at Boston College. He was the 2004–06 Distinguished Scholar Leader for the New Century Scholars initiative of the Fulbright Program. He has been a senior associate of the Carnegie Foundation for the Advancement of Teaching, and served as editor of the *Review of Higher Education* and the *Comparative Education Review*, and as an editor of *Educational Policy*. He is author of *Turmoil and Transition: The International Imperative in Higher Education, Comparative Higher Education, Student Politics in America*, and other books. He co-edited the *International Handbook of Higher Education*. His most recent book is *World Class Worldwide: Transforming Research Universities in Asia and Latin America*. Dr. Altbach holds the B.A., M.A. and Ph.D. degrees from the University of Chicago. He has taught at the University of Wisconsin-Madison and the State University of New York at Buffalo, and was a post-doctoral fellow and lecturer on education at Harvard University. He is chairperson of the International Advisory Council of the Graduate School of Education at the Shanghai Jiao Tong University, and is a Guest Professor at the Institute of Higher Education at Peking University in the People's Republic of China. He has been a visiting professor at Stanford University, the Institut de Sciences Politique in Paris, and the University of Bombay in India. Dr. Altbach has been a Fulbright scholar in India, and in Malaysia and Singapore. He has had awards from the Japan Society for the Promotion of Science and the German Academic Exchange Service (DAAD), and has been Onwell Fellow at the University of Hong Kong, and a senior scholar of the Taiwan Government.

Elizabeth D. ("Betty") Capaldi is Executive Vice President and Provost at Arizona State University. Dr. Capaldi provides leadership to all of the university's campuses and academic programs fostering excellence in teaching, research and service to the community. She guides the university's mission in providing educational excellence and access and directs the university's efforts in strategic redesign of its academic mission to achieve the vision of The New American University. Prior to her arrival at ASU, Dr. Capaldi served as the Vice Chancellor and Chief of Staff of The State University of New York, where her responsibilities included strategic planning coordination of the activities of the vice chancellors to build quality in the 64 campuses of The State University of New York and service as the main liaison between system administration and the campuses. She served as Provost and Professor of Psychology at the University at Buffalo SUNY prior to moving to Albany. Dr. Capaldi came to the University at Buffalo SUNY from the University of Florida, where she served as Provost and Professor of Psychology. Dr. Capaldi received her bachelor's degree from the University of Rochester in 1965 and her Ph.D. degree in experimental psychology from the University of Texas at Austin in 1969. She has contributed over 65 chapters and articles to the scientific literature, co-authored three editions of an introductory psychology textbook and edited two books on the psychology of eating. She is Past President of the American Psychological Society (2000–01) and of the Midwestern Psychological Association (1991.) In recognition of her work, Dr. Capaldi has been elected to Fellow Status in the American Psychological Association, the American Psychological Society, and the American Association for the Advancement of Science.

Diana Bartelli Carlin is a professor of communication studies at the University of Kansas who served as dean of the Graduate School and International Programs from 2000 to 2007 and as the Council of Graduate Schools dean in residence and director of international outreach from 2007 to 2008. During her tenure as dean, the University of Kansas received a Paul Simon Award for Campus Internationalization from NAFSA (the Association of International Educators) and a NASPA (Student Affairs Administrators in Higher Education) best practices award for the Global Awareness Program, which provides a means for students to receive transcript certification for study abroad, international coursework, and co-curricular international activities. A joint degree program in engineering with a Korean University and a dual degree program with a French business school were established. Carlin served as chair of the NAFSA task force on the Bologna Process and its impact on U.S. higher education. She has presented programs on Bologna for professional associations in the U.S. and for international meetings and is the co-author of "International Student Adjustment Issues," in Norman Evans and Maureen Andrade's edited volume, *International Students: Developing a Critical Resource*. She is currently president of the KU chapter of Phi Beta Delta. Carlin regularly includes international units in several of her communication courses.

Madeleine B. d'Ambrosio is Vice President, TIAA-CREF Institute. She joined TIAA-CREF in 1975 as an Institutional Consultant. She spent nine years counseling colleges, universities and other not-for-profit institutions on all aspects of their employee benefit programs. From 1984 until 1994 as Vice President, Institutional Counseling, she had management responsibilities for the design and administration of institutional benefit plans and the counseling and financial education of participants. During this time d'Ambrosio introduced TIAA-CREF Financial Education Seminars, including a special financial education program for women. In 1994 she was named Vice President of Education and Financial Support Services responsible for training, financial guidance and advice for participants, FINRA and SEC compliance, and further development of educational seminars on topics important to the financial well-being of individuals and families. In 1998 Ms. d'Ambrosio was appointed the first Executive Director of the TIAA-CREF Institute. She received her B.A. degree from Manhattanville College and is a Certified Employee Benefit Specialist.

Roger W. Ferguson, Jr. is President and Chief Executive Officer of TIAA-CREF. Dr. Ferguson joined TIAA-CREF from Swiss Re in April 2008. At Swiss Re, he was head of financial services, a member of the executive committee and Chairman of Swiss Re America Holding Corporation. Previously, he served as Vice Chairman of the Board of Governors of the U.S. Federal Reserve System. He was a voting member of the Federal Open Market Committee, served as Chairman of the Financial Stability Forum, and chaired Federal Reserve Board committees on banking supervision and regulation, payment system policy and reserve bank oversight. In 2001, Dr. Ferguson led the Federal Reserve's immediate response to the terrorist attack on September 11. Prior to joining the Federal Reserve Board, Dr. Ferguson was an Associate and Partner at McKinsey & Company from 1984 to 1997. From 1981 to 1984, he was an attorney at the New York City office of Davis Polk & Wardwell, where he worked on syndicated loans, public offerings, mergers and acquisitions, and new product development. Dr. Ferguson holds a B.A., a J.D. and a Ph.D. in economics, all from Harvard University. He is President of the Board of Overseers of Harvard University and a member of the Boards of Trustees for the Institute for Advanced Study, Carnegie Endowment for International Peace, and the New America Foundation. He is on the Board of Directors of the Partnership for New York City, and a member of the Council on Foreign Relations, the Economic Club of New York, and the Group of Thirty. Dr. Ferguson is also a member of President Obama's Economic Recovery Advisory Board.

Margaret Heisel is Director of the National Center for Capacity Building in Study Abroad, an organization based in Washington, DC, and jointly sponsored by the Association of Public and Land-grant Universities (A.P.L.U.) (formerly the National Association of State Universities and Land Grant Colleges (NASULGC)) and the Association of International Educators (NAFSA.) The Center focuses its efforts on the needs of colleges and universities as they ramp up programs to serve their students interested in new formats for learning about the global dimensions of issues such as health, environmental concerns, emerging communication modalities and other rapidly changing fields. The Center also develops strategies for addressing the needs of students from groups who have been less represented in the traditional study abroad population in the past and identifies opportunities for study in destinations less frequented historically, such as Latin America, Asia, and Africa. Dr. Heisel earned a Ph.D. in Spanish and Latin American Studies at the University of Kansas. She served as a faculty member and Assistant Dean of the College of Liberal Arts and Sciences at the University of New Orleans, and has taught language and literature courses at Middlebury College and the University of the Pacific. She has extensive experience as an administrator at the University of California Davis, and the University of California Office of the President, where she was Deputy Vice Provost for Academic Affairs. She has worked in international education, selective undergraduate admissions, K-14 outreach programs, community college transfer programs, and multi-campus collaborative instructional programs. In California, she collaborated with colleagues within the ten-campus University of California system and across the State's educational segments to address statewide issues of student achievement, educational quality, learning outcomes, and articulation of courses and curricula.

Peter S. Horn graduated from Vassar College with an honors degree in political science in 2008. His research interests include international relations, access to higher education and affirmative action. A member of the Johan Bruyneel Cycling Academy, Horn currently lives in Belgium.

D. Bruce Johnstone is Distinguished Service Professor of Higher and Comparative Education Emeritus at the State University of New York at Buffalo. His principal scholarship is in international comparative higher education finance, governance, and policy formation. He directs the International Comparative Higher Education Finance and Accessibility Project, a nine-year examination into the worldwide shift of higher education costs from governments and taxpayers to parents and students. During a 25-year administrative career prior to assuming his professorship at the University at Buffalo, Johnstone held posts of vice president for administration at the University of Pennsylvania, president of the State University College of Buffalo, and chancellor of the State University of New York system, the latter from 1988 to 1994. Johnstone was the Distinguished Scholar Leader in 2007–08 of the Fulbright New Century Scholars Program (a group of 12 American and 32 international scholars examining higher educational access through international perspectives.) In the 2006–07 academic year, he was a part-time Erasmus Mundus lecturer in higher education administration at the Universities of Oslo and Tampere. He has written or edited many books, monographs, articles, and book chapters and is best known for his works on the financial condition of higher education, the concept of learning productivity, student financial assistance policy, system governance, and international comparative higher education finance. Johnstone holds bachelors (in economics) and masters (in teaching) degrees from Harvard, a 1969 Ph.D. in education from the University of Minnesota, and several honorary doctorates.

Mark S. Kamlet has been Provost of Carnegie Mellon University since 2000, and was reappointed in 2005, at which time he was also named Senior Vice President. Kamlet has worked with the deans and department heads to strengthen the university's academic programs, retain and recruit world-class faculty, enhance its many research programs, centers and institutes, and create new academic and research initiatives leveraging Carnegie Mellon's talent and expertise. Kamlet joined Carnegie Mellon's central administrative team after an eight-year tenure as dean of the H. John Heinz III School of Public Policy and Management. Under Kamlet, the Heinz School's endowment increased more than 80 percent and its research funding grew by nearly 400 percent. Kamlet became a member of the faculty in 1976 and was named a professor in 1989 with a joint appointment in the Heinz School and the College of Humanities and Social Sciences (H&SS.) Before becoming dean of the Heinz School in 1993, Kamlet was associate dean of H&SS and head of its Department of Social and Decision Sciences. With his research focusing on the economics of health care, quantitative methodology and public finance, Kamlet has authored more than 75 published papers and two books. He received the outstanding publication award from the Association of Public Policy and Management for his work on the federal budgetary process. Kamlet served on a U.S. Public Health Service panel to produce national guidelines on applying cost-effectiveness analysis in health care; and on three National Institute of Health (NIH) consensus panels to make recommendations on national policies relating to prenatal genetic testing, neonatal screening, and end of life care. He serves on the Institute of Medicine's Health

Promotion and Disease Prevention Board, and the Institute of Medicine's Committee on Poison Prevention and Control. He received his bachelor's degree in mathematics from Stanford University in 1974. Kamlet earned master's degrees in economics (1976) and statistics (1977) and a Ph.D. in economics (1980) from the University of California at Berkeley.

Jane Knight focuses her research and professional interests on the international dimension of higher education at the institutional, system, national, and international levels. Her work with United Nations agencies, universities, foundations, and professional organizations in over 60 countries of the world helps to bring a comparative, development and international policy perspective to her research, teaching and policy work. She is the author or editor of many publications on internationalization concepts and strategies, quality assurance, institutional management, mobility, cross-border education, trade, and capacity building. Her latest 2008 publications include *Higher Education in Turmoil: The Changing World of Internationalization* (author), *Financing Access and Equity in Higher Education* (editor), and *Higher Education in Africa: The International Dimension* (co-editor.) She is an adjunct professor at Ontario Institute for Studies in Education, University of Toronto, and a Fulbright New Century Scholar 2007–08. Formerly she was Head of International Affairs in the Office of the President at Ryerson University. Prior work experiences with the Education Planning and Policy Unit of UNESCO, Paris, and with a development NGO in India, plus her involvement in many Canadian International Development Agency (CIDA) supported projects, help bring international policy and developing country perspectives to the study of international education. Jane Knight serves on the Board and Advisory Committees of several organizations including the East-West Centre, Hawaii; University of Free State, South Africa, and the Observatory of Borderless Education, United Kingdom. She is currently engaged in international research projects on Regional Education/Knowledge Hubs; Comparative Approaches to Regionalization of Higher Education in Africa, Asia and Latin America; and 21st Century Universities.

M. Peter McPherson is president of the Association of Public and Land-grant Universities (A.P.L.U.) (formerly, the National Association of State Universities and Land Grant Colleges (NASULGC).) A.P.L.U. is dedicated to advancing research, learning and engagement, and has been at the forefront of educational leadership nationally for more than 120 years. McPherson is the former chair of the Board of Directors of Dow Jones and Company. He is the founding co-chair of the Partnership to Cut Hunger and Poverty in Africa; chair of the Board of IFDC, an international center dealing with soil fertility and agricultural development; and chair of the Board of Harvest Plus, an organization working on breeding crops for better nutrition. McPherson also recently completed the chairmanship of a commission created by Congress to consider ways to greatly increase the number of students who study abroad. Prior to joining A.P.L.U., McPherson was president of Michigan State University from 1993 to 2004. From April to October 2003, he took leave from that position and served as the Director of Economic Policy for the Coalition Provisional Authority of Iraq. Before Michigan State, McPherson held senior executive positions with Bank of America from 1989 to 1993. From 1987 to 1989, he served as Deputy Secretary of the U.S. Treasury, focusing on trade, tax, and international issues. He was Administrator of the U.S. Agency for International Development (USAID) from 1981 to 1987. During that time he was also the Chairman of the Board of the Overseas Private Investment Corporation. From 1977 to 1980, he was a partner and head of the Washington office of Vorys, Sater, Seymour and Pease. Prior to that, he was a Special Assistant to President Gerald Ford. McPherson received a B.A. from Michigan State University, an M.B.A. from Western Michigan University and a J.D. from American University.

Patti McGill Peterson is Senior Associate at the Institute for Higher Education Policy (IHEP), whose mission is to increase access and success in postsecondary education around the world through research and special programs that inform key decision makers who shape public policy. From 1997 to 2007, Dr. Peterson served as Executive Director of the Council for International Exchange of Scholars (CIES) and Vice President of the Institute of International Education (IIE.) CIES, a division of IIE, coordinates international educational exchange with approximately 150 nations and has administered the Fulbright Scholar Program since 1947. Dr. Peterson was Senior Fellow at Cornell University's Institute for Public Affairs from 1996 to 1997. She holds the title President Emerita at Wells College and St. Lawrence University, where she held presidencies from 1980 to 1996. Her faculty appointments have included The State University of New York, Syracuse University and Wells College. She served as Chair of the U.S.–Canada Commission for Educational Exchange, the National Women's College Coalition, the Public Leadership Education Network and is a past President of the Association of Colleges and Universities of the State of New York. She was a member of the American Council on Education's Commission on National Challenges in Higher Education, as well as its Commission on Governmental Affairs, the Board of Overseers of the Nelson A. Rockefeller Institute of Government and the Ford Foundation's International Fellowship Program. Her current board memberships include the University of Wisconsin's Board of Visitors, the Council for International Educational Exchange and the Roth Endowment. She also serves as a board member and independent chair of the John Hancock Mutual Funds. Dr. Peterson holds a B.A. degree from The Pennsylvania State University and an M.A. and Ph.D. from the University of Wisconsin and did post-graduate study at Harvard University.

Charles E. Phelps received his B.A. in Mathematics from Pomona College in 1965, an M.B.A. (Hospital Administration) in 1968 and Ph.D. (Business Economics) in 1973 from the University of Chicago. Phelps began his research career at the RAND Corporation in 1971. During his time there, he helped found the RAND Health Insurance Study and served as Director of RAND's Program on Regulatory Policies and Institutions. In 1984, Phelps moved to the University of Rochester, with appointments in the Departments of Economics and Political Science. From 1984 to 1989, he served as Director of the Public Policy Analysis Program. In 1989, Professor Phelps became chair of the Department of Community and Preventive Medicine in the School of Medicine and Dentistry of the University of Rochester. During these years, Professor Phelps has published 36 peer reviewed articles covering the fields of health economics, health policy, medical decision analysis, cost-effectiveness analysis of various medical interventions, and other related topics. He also wrote a leading textbook in the field, *Health Economics* (Addison Wesley), now entering its fourth edition (2009.) In 1991, Professor Phelps was elected to the Institute of Medicine of the National Academies of Science, and also as Fellow of the National Bureau of Economic Research. In 1994, Professor Phelps was appointed as Provost (Chief Academic Officer) of the University of Rochester, a position he held until August 2007. At that time, he was named University Professor and Provost Emeritus, positions he now holds. He is currently on sabbatical leave at the Center for Advanced Study in the Behavioral Sciences at Stanford University.

Gowher Rizvi is Vice Provost for International Programs and Professor of Global Studies at the University of Virginia. Previously he was Director of the Ash Institute for Democratic Governance and Innovation at Harvard University's John F. Kennedy School of Government. Before joining the Institute, he was the Ford Foundation's Representative in New Delhi, having previously served as the Foundation's Deputy Director for Governance and Civil Society, as a program officer in the Foundation's Asia division, and as the Asia Society's director of contemporary affairs. Rizvi came to the Ford and Asia foundations from Oxford University where he held several positions. The founder and editor of *Contemporary South Asia*, an academic and policy studies journal, Rizvi is the (co-)author or editor of several books including *South Asia in a Changing International Order*, *South Asian Insecurity and the Great Powers*, *Perspectives on Imperialism and Decolonization*, *Indo-British Relations in Retrospect*, and *Beyond Boundaries*. A Rhodes Scholar, he received his D. Phil. from Trinity College, University of Oxford.

Kathleen M. Waldron is a University Professor at The City University of New York. Dr. Waldron served as President of Baruch College of The City University of New York, one of the most selective public colleges in the northeast, from August 2004 to August 2009 and led the College to achieve national rankings in its business and public affairs programs and a place in The Princeton Review's list of the top 10 percent of colleges in the country. With 16,000 undergraduate and graduate students, Baruch is the most diverse college in the United States and is home to the nationally renowned Zicklin School of Business. Prior to joining Baruch College, Dr. Waldron was Dean of the School of Business, Public Administration and Information Systems at Long Island University from 1998 to 2004 and from 1984 to 1998 served in various managerial positions at Citigroup, including head of strategic planning for the Global Wealth Management Division. She was president of Citibank International in Miami from 1991 to 1996 and served on the boards of Accion International, Accion USA, Shands Hospital and the Florida Bankers Association. She holds a doctorate in Latin American history from Indiana University and was a Fulbright Scholar in Caracas, Venezuela, in 1980–81. Dr. Waldron is a director of the Tinker Foundation and a member of the Association for a Better New York Steering Committee, the Financial Women's Association, the Academy of Management and the Latin American Studies Association. She also is a member of the Commission on International Initiatives of the American Council on Education. Dr. Waldron is the recipient of the Ellis Island Medal of Honor, the Women's Club of New York Award, and the Feminist Press award. She has lived and traveled extensively in Latin America and has published articles on Latin America.

Paul J. Yakoboski is a Principal Research Fellow with the TIAA-CREF Institute. He conducts, manages and communicates research on issues such as income and asset management in retirement, defined contribution plan design, the preparation of higher education faculty for retirement, managing faculty retirement patterns, options for funding retiree health care, and research on issues related to strategic management in higher education. He is also responsible for the development and execution of Institute symposiums on such issues. In addition, Yakoboski serves as director of the Institute's Fellows Program and editor of the Institute's *Trends and Issues* and *Advancing Higher Education* publication series. Prior to joining the Institute, he held positions as Director of Research for the American Council of Life Insurers (2000 to 2004), Senior Research Associate with the Employee Benefit Research Institute (1991 to 2000) and Senior Economist with the U.S. Government Accountability Office (1989 to 1991.) He is a member of the American Economic Association and serves on the editorial advisory board of *Benefits Quarterly*. He previously served as Director of Research for the American Savings Education Council (1995 to 2000.) Between 1986 and 1988 he served as an adjunct faculty member at Nazareth College (Rochester, NY.) Yakoboski earned his Ph.D. (1990) and M.A. (1987) in economics from the University of Rochester (Rochester, NY) and his B.S. (1984) in economics from Virginia Tech (Blacksburg, VA.)

CONFERENCE PANELISTS AND MODERATORS

Molly Corbett Broad, President, American Council on Education

Claude R. Canizares, Vice President of Research and Associate Provost, MIT

Elizabeth D. Capaldi (see list of authors)

Ronald A. Crutcher, President, Wheaton College

Madeleine d'Ambrosio (see list of authors)

William W. Destler, President, Rochester Institute of Technology

Roger W. Ferguson, Jr. (see list of authors)

Dan Guaglianone, Executive Director, Recruiting and Staffing, Merck & Co., Inc.

Bob Kerrey, President, The New School

Leo M. Lambert, President, Elon University

James T. McGill, Senior Vice President, Finance and Administration, Johns Hopkins University

M. Peter McPherson (see list of authors)

Constantine Papadakis, former President, Drexel University

Andrew A. Sorensen, Distinguished President Emeritus, University of South Carolina

Graham Spanier, President, The Pennsylvania State University

Garrick Utley, President, Neil D. Levin Graduate Institute of International Relations and Commerce, The State University of New York

Kathleen M. Waldron (see list of authors)

Eileen B. Wilson-Oyelaran, President, Kalamazoo College

Mark S. Wrighton, Chancellor, Professor of Chemistry, Washington University in St. Louis

Mark G. Yudof, President, University of California

Fareed Zakaria, Editor, *Newsweek International*; CNN Host

Foreword

Roger W. Ferguson, Jr.

The "Great Recession" that began in late 2007 offered important lessons on the range of challenges we face as a global society and evinced the need for a renewed commitment to higher education in the U.S. and around the world.

TIAA-CREF has long recognized the connections between intellectual capital and socioeconomic progress. We understand that the future of the global economy depends on an educated workforce, one that possesses not only a greater capacity for knowledge but also greater powers of critical thinking and creativity, and a deep sense of moral and ethical values.

Through the TIAA-CREF Institute, we seek to provide the leaders of higher education with an objective source of insights, and a trusted, independent forum for the exchange of ideas. In November 2008, the Institute convened "Higher Education in a Global Society," a major conference of university presidents, chancellors, academic deans, researchers and other leaders, to discuss the critical role of higher education in creating cross-cultural understanding, promoting international collaboration, and strengthening the global economy. More than 150 individuals shared their views, experience and expertise, and we are grateful for their participation.

The chapters in this book, written by a distinguished group of higher education scholars and leaders, capture, synthesize and build upon those conference discussions. We hope that this volume will be helpful as you shape the future of your institution and, indeed, as you define the way higher education meets the needs of a changing world.

In the coming years, the profiles and responsibilities of academic institutions will continue to grow; I can assure you that TIAA-CREF will continue to evolve in a way that is consistent with our mission, which is to say, in a way that best serves you. On behalf of my colleagues at TIAA-CREF and the TIAA-CREF Institute, thank you for your interest in the Higher Education Leadership Conference Series, and thank you for the opportunity to be of service.

Introduction
Paul J. Yakoboski

Individuals, groups, businesses and institutions now function in a global environment that impacts and influences almost every aspect of their activities. Higher education is no exception as it now functions in a global environment of consumers, employees, competitors and partners. In fact, it could be argued that higher education has in many ways been a force for globalization and a model for adapting and responding to the resulting trends, but nonetheless it remains challenged in some ways in responding to the new global reality.

Against this backdrop, in November 2008 the TIAA-CREF Institute hosted the Higher Education Leadership Conference, "Higher Education in a Global Society." The conference brought together presidents, chancellors, other senior campus officials, higher education researchers and thought leaders, and the senior management of TIAA-CREF to examine emerging issues, challenges and opportunities for advancing higher education across borders, with the realization that now is the future for creating cross-cultural understanding, building global collaborations and strengthening worldwide economies.

As noted by Roger Ferguson, President and Chief Executive Officer of TIAA-CREF, during his keynote address, the recent crisis in the financial markets highlights the sweep of globalization and the complex challenges confronting our society. He maintained that a better-educated global workforce is essential as we contemplate the future of the global economy and worldwide standards of living. He further argued that a better-educated workforce requires a global investment in human capital. This may necessitate more aggressive enrollment policies for higher education, particularly to increase enrollments in developing countries. It will also require more dynamic international cooperation and collaboration that do not presume a zero-sum game among countries; the academy can lead the way in fostering more expansive thinking in this regard. Finally, this calls for a broader definition of higher education, one that focuses on developing critical thinking and creativity as much as intellectual capacity and which also provides significant opportunities for lifelong learning.

While the demands upon and need for higher education have never been greater at both the individual and societal levels, the avenues for pursuing the mission of higher education have greatly expanded due to globalization. Many American colleges and universities are establishing a presence abroad and expanding their mission on a global scale. For other institutions globalization means recruiting international students, offering student exchanges, providing study abroad programs, and facilitating faculty collaboration and dual degree programs.

This volume was inspired by the conference presentations and dialogue. Several chapters are authored by conference speakers as the direct product of particular sessions. Other chapters provide a conceptual framework for considering the various global aspects of higher education or focus on issues addressed by conference sessions or issues raised during discussion periods, and were authored by thought leaders from the higher education community.

Several common themes emerged from the presentations and dialogue during the conference and are further explored throughout this volume:

- Students need an international experience to be effective citizens and workers in the emerging global order. But there are multiple means for colleges and universities to provide such experience.
- Challenges facing the world call for international research collaborations. But such collaborations need to be entered into with due diligence by institutions and then be led by the academics rather than administrators.
- Higher education in the rest of the world is catching up to the standard set by the U.S. system. But to U.S. institutions that think strategically, the focus on higher education abroad presents genuine opportunities to better fulfill their missions and to do so on a global scale.
- It is imperative for higher education to clearly articulate to domestic constituencies the benefits for students and society at large of investments in global initiatives.

THE LEADERSHIP IMPERATIVE ON CAMPUS

An unprecedented rate of change in the world makes it imperative for campus leaders to quickly understand and strategically respond to the implications of globalization. Fareed Zakaria, Editor of *Newsweek International* and CNN Host, maintained during the conference opening keynote that higher education is America's best industry and in no other field is the U.S. advantage so overwhelming. He argued that U.S. higher education is a brand with extraordinary value in the rest of the world, and higher education leaders must consider how best to leverage this brand in the global marketplace. Mr. Zakaria also stated that U.S. higher education must meet the challenge of explaining why global initiatives and engagement are good for America, and why investment in great universities is a value proposition for the country.

Peter McPherson, President, Association of Public and Land-grant Universities (A.P.L.U.), observed that internationalizing a campus requires the president to make it a priority and there are, of course, other competing initiatives for the short list of priorities. He argued that, for the benefit of the students, internationalization should make that list. He also asserted that metrics are needed to track progress in achieving greater internationalization. Leo Lambert, President, Elon University, built on this by outlining the importance of building internationalization into the strategic plan of a college or university covering curriculum, faculty, staff, students and facilities.

In Chapter 1 of this volume, Bruce Johnstone discusses the concept of globalization as it applies to higher education, the positive and negative implications for higher education, and whether globalization can be managed for the greater good through policy. As a former state college president, state system chancellor, and scholar of international comparative higher education finance and governance, he addresses what an increasingly globalized world says to leaders of American higher education. First, manage through fiscal austerity. But beyond that stress second and even third language facility, reward faculty and staff who reach out to students and scholars from abroad, recognize that international students need care and support that costs money, provide financial and staff support to study abroad programs, support real curricular and departmental restructuring that leads to new levels of international and global scholarship and learning, and recognize that real scholarly collaboration comes only from faculty.

In Chapter 2, Philip Altbach discusses the "massification" of higher education throughout the world. He explains how the emerging mass higher education systems have an inherent logic that will characterize key elements of academe in all countries and in all academic systems in the coming decades. According to Altbach, topics central to the phenomenon of mass higher education in the 21st century include: the challenge of funding; new sectors of higher education, including private higher education, for-profit higher education, and new vocational institutions; distance learning as a means of coping with demand; the differentiation and complexity of academic institutions; the managerialization of academic institutions, and the creation of the "administrative estate"; the nature of the academic profession; and the diversity of students and student culture.

In Chapter 3, Jane Knight discusses the emergence of alternative cross-border activities to provide education in response to increasing demand around the world. Cross-border education refers to the movement of people, programs, providers, knowledge, ideas, projects, values, curriculum, research and services across national boundaries. The key element is the movement from student mobility to program and provider mobility. Knight then examines the complex world of cross-border education that is emerging while noting the challenges and failures that have occured in establishing branch campuses and operations abroad. Recognition, accreditation, and intellectual property rights to course design and materials are examples of issues that arise. Knight explains that an examination of the rationales and impacts related to the increase in cross-border education requires consideration of the diverse and often contradictory perspectives and expectations that different groups of stakeholders may have in both receiving and sending countries. Views vary according to the drastically different perspectives of a student, a provider, a governmental or non-governmental body, and whether the perspective is that of the exporting or importing country. Knight also discusses emerging second generation cross-border education strategies – regional education hubs, economic free zones, education cities, knowledge villages, gateways and hot spots.

INTERNATIONAL PARTNERSHIPS AND INITIATIVES

Partnerships and collaborations with foreign universities and governments, particularly with regard to research, was an ongoing area of discussion during the conference. Molly Corbett Broad, President, American Council on Education, opened a discussion on international research collaborations by noting that in the face of stagnant or declining federal support for research, U.S. colleges and universities are open to and looking for partnerships around the world, while other parts of the world are increasing their R&D and expanding their higher education systems as a focused economic development strategy. She also noted that star academics and researchers tend to cluster and therefore many foreign-born American scientists return to their homeland once that country develops a significant strength in their particular area of expertise. Broad maintained that increased research capacity around the world has the potential to facilitate growth and development around the world, and key to realizing this potential is opening borders to more collaborative research.

Claude Canizares, Vice President of Research and Provost,

Massachusetts Institute of Technology, reported during the conference that MIT has established an ad hoc faculty committee to assess overarching principles, guidelines and approaches, given that the nature and environment of international research collaborations is changing. Since these collaborations are important to both the student and faculty experience, MIT is trying to understand the drivers of successful collaboration, and also the limitations as well as opportunities in these initiatives. Canizares asserted that faculty-led initiatives should not be controlled from the center and that, while institutional collaborations are entered into by some layer of administration and may require commitment of central resources, they still must be faculty driven. He noted that cultural differences need to be recognized and addressed in research collaborations and that expectations need to be matched on both sides with a clear agreement on how to manage intellectual property rights.

Mark Yudof, President, University of California, voiced a cautious perspective on international research collaborations. He argued that U.S. colleges and universities, at least the publics, sign too many collaborative agreements with an end result of nothing to show for it. He emphasized the challenges posed by international laws governing mutual engagements and by comparative laws across countries addressing particular issues. He noted that it makes little sense to enter into a research collaboration agreement unless the country involved has a functioning legal system that protects patents and copyrights; otherwise it is a very difficult environment in which to realize innovation. Yudof reiterated the position that if the initiatives are to be solid, then academics have to be in charge of the process with assistance from department chairs and deans.

Elizabeth D. Capaldi was a session panelist and also authored Chapter 4 in this volume. Capaldi sees international research collaborations continuing to increase because of the growing quality and capacity abroad to make them desirable. Furthermore, global challenges in health, the environment, and international relations, among other areas, demand it. Capaldi raises several issues to consider and address with international research collaborations. While such collaborations need to be faculty driven, she worries about faculty establishing collaborations on their own because of the complications inherent in the laws and regulations across countries governing credit, financing, use of animal and human subjects, and so on. She warns that managing funding for such research is also challenging given that sources often include both foreign corporations and governments (and even domestic corporations in some cases.) She notes the inherent logistical difficulties in conducting research internationally, as well as the cultural differences that must be recognized and addressed. In addition, Capaldi stresses recognition that foreign institutions do not tie education to research as do U.S. universities; research abroad is typically driven by a desire to achieve quick, direct economic results. At the same time she believes an imperative for U.S. colleges and universities is to better connect basic research with economic development, so U.S. institutions can learn from foreign institutions in this regard.

Given their demographics, China and India are two countries where interest levels are high for international collaborations. The conference featured presentations on the current state of higher education in each. Devesh Kapur, Director of the Center for the Advanced Study of India, University of Pennsylvania, argued that higher education in India is plagued by limited public resources, extremely centralized regulation, a dearth of quality institutions, increasing faculty shortages in elite institutions due to weak Ph.D. programs, entrenched mediocrity in most faculty, and an exceedingly weak research culture. On the last point, he noted that there is almost no research occurring in higher education institutions as research has been segregated into specialized centers since the 1950s. He further explained how the weakening of the traditional higher education sector has led to the emergence and growth of a surrogate system in India in which private providers are increasingly dominant, corporations are establishing their own schools to provide workforce training, and the elites are sending their children overseas for higher education. Kapur maintained that the quality of private institutions in India is extremely weak.

Zhang Li, Director-General and Professor, National Center for Educational Development Research, Ministry of Education of the People's Republic of China, discussed the status of higher education in China and priorities in China's plan for higher education. He first noted that China's modern higher education system is only a little over 100 years old. Zhang explained that the purpose of higher education in China is focused along three dimensions, the first being that it should ensure that China can compete in a global economic environment while promoting sustainable development. Second, it should adapt to new needs of public affairs and promote cultural development at the regional and community levels. Finally, it should promote the economic livelihood of individuals as well as their life-long development. With these objectives, China's higher education system has developed extensively since the turn of the 21st century. With a gross enrollment rate of 23 percent, the system has moved from educating the elite to educating the masses. Zhang outlined what he saw as current shortcomings in China's higher education system, including decreased per capita budget appropriations, wide gaps in higher education development across different regions of China, low quality of management and faculty in some new local universities, and problems from an examination-oriented education.

Not all initiatives abroad are research based; many center on academic programs. In Chapter 5, Mark Kamlet discusses fundamentals for establishing successful academic programs in foreign countries that he has learned as provost at Carnegie Mellon over the past several decades as that institution moved from one that "was in many ways a regional university" to one that currently offers over twenty degree programs in locations outside its Pittsburgh home, with over a dozen outside the U.S. He notes that becoming globally engaged in this manner has had very positive benefits, as hoped and intended, for the home campus. While not emphasized by Kamlet, one takeaway from his chapter is the importance of an institutional willingness to experiment with educational technology and pedagogical methods.

A recurring theme throughout Chapter 5 is that establishing academic programs in foreign countries involves a myriad of complex institutional interactions – legal, tax, human resource, regulatory – that must be addressed if such initiatives are to be successful. Kamlet explains that over time Carnegie Mellon has evolved groups within its central administration with a wealth of expertise and experience on these matters. Given that there are economies of both scale and scope in developing such expertise, and that academic departments and colleges should not be expected to have such expertise, he argues that it is most efficient for central administration to handle these aspects of establishing academic programs abroad, leaving academic, curricular and student-related matters to the academic departments and colleges. Central administration and academic departments will then be "interwoven in the context of any given effort." He also cautions that is more expensive, sometimes significantly so, to offer degree programs outside the U.S. Finally, Kamlet notes that, with a few exceptions, Carnegie Mellon's initiatives in offering degrees outside Pittsburgh involve professional masters programs. He explains this is driven by differences in quality metrics across program types. While the key metric of a professional masters program is career "value added," it is academic excellence of the students and sophistication of the curriculum for undergraduate and Ph.D. programs. Nonetheless, undergraduate and Ph.D. programs offered abroad can be successful with great effort under the right circumstances.

PROVIDING AN INTERNATIONAL PERSPECTIVE FOR STUDENTS

Providing students with an international perspective and understanding through higher education is an increasing imperative for colleges and universities. Daniel Guaglianone, Global Leader, Recruiting and Staffing, Merck & Co., observed during the conference that global work teams are common and people are needed who can function in that environment. The four items Guaglianone considers crucial in a global work force are superior functional discipline skills, multiple language capability, understanding of cultural differences, and an awareness of one's ethnocentric behaviors and the ability to control those. Ronald A. Crutcher, President, Wheaton College, shared findings from an Association of American Colleges and Universities' project confirming views such as Guaglianone's are common across employers.

However, as observed by Constantine Papadakis, then President of Drexel University, it is unrealistic to expect university faculty to teach all such skills, but international programs with meaningful experience abroad can produce students with a global view regarding their profession and an understanding of what it takes to work in a global environment.

There are various strategies to achieve this objective and these were critically examined during the course of the conference. A common approach is providing students with a study abroad experience. For example, Eileen Wilson-Oyelaran, President, Kalamazoo College, noted that 80 percent of Kalamazoo students study abroad, many where English is not the primary language. Kalamazoo College has for 50-plus years considered its mission to include ensuring that students are able to cross personal boundaries of language, race and ethnicity, and to cross cultural, academic and structural boundaries as well. She also observed that students want not only to study abroad but also to have foreign internships and service-learning experiences that will enhance their résumés. During a separate session Papadakis and William W. Destler, President, Rochester Institute of Technology, discussed their institutions' international internships where undergraduate students live and work in a foreign country.

Peter McPherson maintained during the conference that higher education is ahead of employers in understanding that an educated individual must have a sense of the world. He and Margaret Heisel argue in Chapter 6 that more research is needed regarding the academic value added of the study abroad experience. In addition, their chapter focuses on various aspects of the study abroad experience – its increasing prominence with foreign universities, the profile of students studying abroad, the types of study abroad, and the challenges and opportunities that lie ahead for this aspect of U.S. postsecondary education and for the students who will be entering colleges in the coming years. They also discuss the creation of the Center for Capacity Building in Study Abroad and its efforts to address these challenges and identify issues needing further research.

But study abroad is unrealistic for many students for various reasons. In addition, before there is even the opportunity to travel abroad, Papadakis advocated a well-diversified campus that blends foreign students with American students in an environment that broadens global perspectives. So just as important is creating an international experience on campus by engaging both students and faculty, and there are various strategies and avenues for pursuing this.

Kathleen Waldron, University Professor, The City University of New York, and President of Baruch College at the time of the conference, was both a conference panelist and the author of Chapter 7. Baruch College is the most ethnically diverse college in the United States, with 40 percent of students having been born outside the U.S. and 60 percent speaking more than one language (over 100 languages are spoken on campus.) But for reasons such as economics, family obligations and cultural restrictions, study abroad is not a realistic option for most Baruch students. In response, Baruch undertook a reassessment of its international activities to address the goals of study abroad at a non-residential urban public institution. As Waldron details in this volume, Baruch leverages the international experience available on campus and in New York City to promote initiatives with different international groups and cultural institutions as part of the academic program. Specifically, its Global Student Initiative seeks to build on Baruch's inherent international diversity to prepare students for work in the global economy through the Global Student Certificate Program. Students achieve the learning outcomes of study abroad while in residence at Baruch. Waldron maintains that it is the responsibility of the president to provide resources and to develop measures of success and accountability for internationalization programs. She also emphasizes that such programs on campus need to be institutionalized and strategic so that they do not fade when key faculty leave the school.

This latter point – the importance of engaged faculty to the ongoing success of internationalization efforts – was elaborated on at various points during the conference and is specifically addressed in this volume by Patti McGill Peterson in Chapter 8 and Diana Bartelli Carlin in Chapter 9. Peterson argues that internationalization efforts have frequently fallen short of the goal because faculty have remained on the periphery, often because of their lack of interest and motivation. She maintains that faculty have been neglected and ignored rather than encouraged and enabled to rise to the opportunity of this complicated task. She notes that internationalization efforts will require many faculty members to move beyond that which they were explicitly trained to do and to challenge their immersion in their "discipline." Faculty engagement will require adaptation of tenure, promotion, leave, compensation policies and departmental practices to this objective. And beyond the opportunity for international research collaborations, there needs to be the opportunity for teaching one's discipline to students in another cultural context.

Carlin reiterates that internationalized faculty are the key to creating a truly internationalized education for students. She highlights what she sees as the barriers to faculty international activity – lack of incentives for faculty and, in fact, the presence of disincentives regarding compensation, tenure and career advancement; lack of institutional funding; lack of support for faculty interested in internationalizing their courses; attitudinal barriers to institutionalization among faculty; and a disconnect between faculty and international offices along with their senior international administrators due to decentralized campus structures. Carlin then moves on to present and discuss an array of facilitators and programs to overcome these barriers to faculty involvement in internationalization. A primary point of emphasis is the necessity of a college or university having a systematic knowledge of the international activities of its entire faculty, something best achieved by a comprehensive annual survey. This then serves as a tool for promoting internationalization by identifying disciplines, programs and individuals (faculty with international activities, visiting scholars, and so on) that can be leveraged as resources (some likely unknown or unrecognized without such a survey), as well as areas in greatest need of assistance. She gives various examples of how this knowledge of existing internal expertise can then be leveraged. Carlin also discusses the importance of internationalizing faculty before they are faculty, that is, while they are graduate students, and strategies for doing so.

Another element of internationalizing the domestic campus is the recruitment and integration of foreign students. A strong presence of foreign students can serve to enhance domestic students' cultural understanding, increase enrollment and tuition revenue, and serve international economic needs. Two million students worldwide currently study outside their home countries and this number is expected to reach approximately eight million by 2025. Graham Spanier, President, The Pennsylvania State University, stated during the conference that he considers it desirable to recruit more international undergraduates to the U.S. He noted that most international students in the U.S. are graduate students; at Penn State they account for two-thirds of the international population. But he further observed that international undergraduates tend to be more integrated into campus life, and the relationships formed with domestic undergraduates contribute toward building goodwill and lasting respect among young adults. President Wilson-Oyelaran noted that foreign students develop a much deeper understanding of the U.S. when they are fully integrated into the campus fabric.

Andrew A. Sorensen, Distinguished President Emeritus, University of South Carolina, observed that American institutions now face a new environment where they often must compete with universities in other countries for the best students. He noted that the U.S. share of students who left their home country to study abroad fell from 38 percent to 22 percent between 1985 and 2005. Previously foreign countries would often pay the expenses of faculty and students who came to the U.S., but the expectation now is that U.S. colleges and universities will bear increasing shares of these costs. Sorensen argued that U.S. institutions must be more aggressive in competing for foreign students (and foreign faculty, as well.) For public universities, he noted, this means addressing the challenge of convincing legislatures that this is money well spent.

As part of his conference presentation, Mark S. Wrighton, Chancellor, Washington University in St. Louis, described the model developed by Washington University of strategic partnerships abroad with a network of 24 premier and developing foreign universities with the aim of recruiting several students annually from these partner institutions. These students are fully supported by Washington University. He argues that the benefits to domestic as well as foreign students justify the investment in a diversified student body. Key faculty members are also tapped to serve as ambassadors to the partner institutions, with the objective of building strong ties in collaborative education and research.

In Chapter 10, Charles Phelps, University Professor and Provost Emeritus, University of Rochester, elaborates upon the benefits of an internationally diversified student body and reviews the demographic trends in student movements. He then focuses on how to recruit, retain, educate, support, and celebrate international students. In the process he touches upon a variety of issues, many of which would not be readily top-of-mind to administrators and institutions with limited experience regarding international students: language competency, financial aid, travel and visa pitfalls, necessary and appropriate on-campus support, nurturing a sense of community, addressing ethnic tensions, understanding and adhering to U.S. academic norms, and special issues that arise in the sciences with foreign research assistants. He then discusses the potential of leveraging these individuals once they are graduates of the institution.

CONCLUDING THOUGHTS

There was a consensus during the conference that the U.S. system remains the world leader in higher education, but the rest of the world is catching up. Rather than being threatened by such developments, U.S. colleges and universities are viewing them as opportunities to better fulfill their missions of advancing knowledge through research and educating the next generation of workers, educators and leaders throughout the world, and in the process promoting the economic growth and social progress and stability of the world.

In Chapter 11, Rizvi and Horn argue the need for colleges and universities, both in the U.S. and around the world, to rethink their roles and purposes given the realities of the new knowledge-based global society and then to reinvent themselves accordingly. They argue the enduring value to society and individuals from the learning and critical thinking skills traditionally found in a liberal arts-based education and the importance of internationalizing higher education so it can continue to fulfill its purpose. They outline numerous avenues, many discussed in detail in previous chapters, which must be simultaneously pursued to achieve this internationalization. Rizvi and Horn argue that a primary challenge will be devising curricula that will be "innovative and imaginative, reflect the changed circumstances of the 21st century, and have a pedagogy centered on students." In their view, such curricula must move beyond a focus on traditional academic disciplines. But, in addition to addressing excellence, society must also address access and ensure that all academically qualified individuals, irrespective of socio-economic background, have equal access to such excellence. They argue that no country can afford to forgo the potential economic resource that is a college-educated individual; therefore, financial constraints should not and can not be a barrier to access. They further argue that all students benefit from socio-economic diversity in higher education through improvements in learning outcomes.

In Chapter 12, Bruce Johnstone shares his thoughts from the perspective of both a scholar of international comparative higher education and someone who has served as a university vice president, college president, and public system chancellor. He notes that today's global economy favors nations, such as the U.S., with advanced technologies and advanced systems of higher education. He feels that such nations have a responsibility, however, to assist the spread of knowledge and expansion of higher education elsewhere. He argues that U.S. higher education is far less internationalized than it should be and needs to be. He maintains that our weakest link in this regard is the lack of second language facility among American undergraduates and faculty to a degree allowing study and research in another language. He argues furthermore that global awareness must be strengthened through the core undergraduate curriculum and also through upper-division majors and graduate programs. Johnstone explains how the financing of higher education in the U.S. can create disincentives for institutions to provide students with opportunities for significant foreign study and experience as part of their education. In his view, higher education budgets "must recognize the appropriateness of curricular and scholarly activities that are international." He further explains that, while the world is learning and adopting from the U.S. system of higher education, there are numerous areas where U.S. institutions could and should learn from the practices of foreign universities and systems.

1. The significance of globalization to American higher education

D. Bruce Johnstone

Globalization, along with its related parts of speech, "global" and "globalized," has entered the lexicon of journalists, academics, and policy analysts, multiplying like organisms on a Petri dish. While such terms crowd out some old words like "international" and "internationalization," they also add new and richer connotations that suggests their origin in much that is new to the decades before and after the turning of the 21st century: new technology, the ubiquity of the computer and digitization, the Internet, the lowering of trade barriers, and the ascendancy of market capitalism.

Like many such terms, however, globalization is also almost certainly overused, or at least used with insufficient appreciation of its normative connotations: that is, its disparate and densely packed political and ideological critiques, especially against trade, capitalism, privatization, liberal (that is, market-oriented) economics, and the international organs of expanding free enterprise and trade, such as the International Monetary Fund and the World Bank. Much of this normative critique is, well, critical. "Critical" is academic shorthand for the social criticism of (most) international trade and more generally of markets, economic competition, multinational corporations, privatization, and capitalism – at least of the Anglo-American variety, which is thought to encourage all of these aforementioned proclivities in supposed excess, in contradistinction to Nordic, or welfare state, or "soft" capitalism, or simply to garden variety socialism.

This discourse is of some interest to me in my capacity as a scholar of international comparative higher education economics and finance, even though my disagreement with most such critical views places me, somewhat uncomfortably, in the conservative wing of my academic field. So in this chapter, I will employ the term globalization in its more ideologically neutral sense, even while acknowledging that globalization is far more than simply a new term for internationalization, and acknowledging also that there has been a genuinely transformative process of some kind going on (greatly accelerating in the past decade or two) that is affecting economies, societies, cultures, and institutions, which has profound (if not always clear) implications, both positive and negative, for higher education in the United States and other nations.

IN THE EYES OF ITS MANY BEHOLDERS

Let us begin with some definitions. The British political scientist and globalization theorist David Held describes globalization as "the widening, deepening, and speeding up of worldwide interconnectedness" (Held et al., 1999, p. 2.) Jamil Salmi, a leading higher education specialist with the World Bank, described globalization as "the process of growing integration of capital, technology, and information across national boundaries in such a way as to create an increasingly integrated world market, with the direct consequence that more and more countries and firms have no choice but to compete in the global economy" (Salmi, 2000.) The Spanish sociologist and communications theorist Manuel Castells, as reported by South African higher education scholar and activist, Nico Cloete (and introducing a more complex and decidedly critical spin), described the principal effect of globalization as turning the "semi-insulated world society of nation-states into an open network society, a society that exhibits a 'placeless space' of information flows." Castell's fascination and concern is for the clash between this networked, placeless economy and the concept of culture, as globalization forces the state to look outward, toward competitors and markets, rather than inward toward its own people, history, and cultures (Cloete et al., 2000.) Malaysian higher educational policy scholar Morshidi Sirat views globalization as "a socio-economic and technological process, which tends to blur or diminish geopolitical borders and national systems" (Sirat, 2006, p. 6.) And the Australian comparative education scholar Simon Marginson describes the elements of globalization distinctive to worldwide higher education as: "(1) the open information environment with instant messaging and data transfer created by communications technologies, so that higher education and knowledge are becoming thoroughly networked on a worldwide scale; and (2) the domination of Anglo-American economic and cultural contents in many sectors, including higher education." He goes on to write that "Globalization is associated with a global market of doctoral universities led by the Ivy League, the one-way influence of American institutions on the rest of the world, and a brain drain from emerging nations" (Marginson, 2006, p. 6.)

Although some commentators interchange "globalization" and "internationalization," these terms, while clearly associated, carry very different, and in some ways almost contradictory, connotations. International connotes between nations, implying relationships that are within the policy grasp of nation states and indeed are built on nation state interconnectedness. Internationalization is what universities promote and stand for: either importing students, scholars, ideas, and modes of operation or exporting the same, abetted by governmental policies. Globalization, on the other hand, is more *supranational*: diminishing and erasing national borders and even the very significance of the nation state. Internationalization or internationalism celebrates and trades in national and regional cultures. Globalization or globalism thins cultures, or at least those cultures that cannot withstand the emerging domination of modernism, liberal democracy, and the hegemony of the English language. In fact, Marginson (2007, p. 215) believes that internationalism and globalization may be pulling in two different directions, with globalization likely to overwhelm genuine internationalism.

Implied in these densely packed and nuanced connotations is the question of whether this globalization (by almost any definition) is a function of technology, the modern age, and something inevitable about human and institutional behavior – that is, above and beyond policies, and especially beyond the capacity of governments to resist – or whether globalization can be successfully resisted, or diminished, or at least steered by conscious policy into a force with more potential for broad social good rather than the mixed benefits that so many observers see. Those who view globalization as mainly beyond the reach of policy (except to ineffectively resist) view technology as a major driver, facilitating the vastly faster and cheaper flows of information, knowledge, and capital made possible by telecommunications that can send billions of digitized bits of information (or billions of dollars' worth of borrowing and lending) per second by optical fiber or microwave for fractions of pennies per mile. From these electronic miracles of telecommunications, computers, and capital-intensive production methods, the production of goods and even of services (for example, banking and education via telephone call centers and Web-based distance learning) becomes less place-bound and increasingly predisposed to locating anywhere that governments are reasonably stable, labor is cost-effective, contracts are enforceable, and tax and regulatory climates are accommodating to business.

However, these forces of globalization are not beyond the reach of nations and policies to enhance or retard. Clearly, governmental policies, either bilaterally or through multilateral agreements and entities, have greatly promoted the expansion of trade in goods, services, and commodities. Such trade expands jobs and profits on the exporting sides and similarly expands access to affordable goods and services on the importing side, sometimes simply providing cheaper goods and commodities and sometimes providing goods and/or raw materials otherwise unavailable without the advantage of trade. The classical Ricardian principle of comparative advantage, then, accelerated by the liberalization of trade, the telecommunications capabilities of the information age, and the ability of modern air, sea, and truck transportation to reach markets virtually anywhere in the world has increased the wages and profits of exporting countries as well as the purchasing power of importing countries. In the midst of a serious economic downturn, when protectionist sentiments rise, it is as well to remember that while US manufacturing has suffered plant closings and job losses aplenty to the foreign relocation of production and to cheaper competing imports, the United States remains the largest exporter in the world of goods and services, which our trading partners pay for with the dollars they earn by their exports to us. Furthermore, the United States has had the benefit of the billions of dollars' worth of low-costs goods (and increasingly, of low cost services) from Asia, which markedly lowers our cost of living. Additionally, the use of the foreign-held dollars has helped to make up for our deplorably low rate of domestic savings.

At the same time, there are admittedly winners and losers from increased globalization, and the gains and losses, while in the aggregate almost certainly favoring the gains, are unevenly (and some would say inequitably) distributed, both by country and by individuals within countries. The winners have been consumers generally, enterprise owners and the new labor forces especially in East and South Asia, owners and executives of multinational corporations, owners and developers of new technology, holders of reserve currencies, and the most highly educated in most countries, especially those in engineering, science, management, and finance. Some of the losers have been workers in high-wage countries whose jobs have been lost to foreign competition, whether on account of lower wages or of technological superiority; exporters of commodities (other than oil and gas) for whom the terms of trade have generally worsened; almost all of the so-called heavily indebted low-income countries, which have little or no reserve currencies and little way to earn the goods and services they need to import; and indigenous languages and cultures everywhere losing out to the lure of modernism and the hegemony of the English language.

To summarize, in the globalized economy, the wealth of a country flows less from tillable land, natural resources (with the exception of oil), and industrial assets and more from amenities (both natural and man-made that attract visitors and their money), capital, and knowledge. Thus, while natural resources, physical infrastructure (such as transportation, power generation, and telecommunications), and a cost-effective labor force are not unimportant, the wealth of nations in the new global economy increasingly comes from:

1. knowledge, the commercialization of which is protected by patents and copyrights, and licensing agreements;
2. universities and centers of research, which can constantly replenish knowledge;
3. scholars and scientists, who are able to create, apply, and manage the application of this knowledge to worldwide markets;
4. an educated and adaptable labor force, which is trained to produce the goods and services of this knowledge economy;
5. a system of education and training, embracing basic, secondary, higher, postsecondary vocational, and lifelong learning, which includes traditional and non-traditional forms and which has strengths in science and technology;
6. a political and legal infrastructure, including a stable and honest government, a predictable and incorruptible judiciary, a stable currency, and a benign regulatory and tax climate.

GLOBALIZATION AND HIGHER EDUCATION

The process or phenomenon of globalization profoundly affects higher education in many ways. On the downside – at least to faculty and staff, college and university leaders, and students – it almost certainly contributes to the difficulties in most countries, including the United States, of taxation and the support of public sectors generally, contributing to the increasing financial austerity of colleges and universities. To parents and especially to students, globalization may therefore seem complicit with rapidly rising tuition fees as well as the shift in financial assistance from grants to loans, leading to alarmingly high levels of student indebtedness. To those on the ideologically critical side, globalization may also seem to enhance the influence on education and educational policies of business and of the socially and financially conservative political right (even in the United States.) And in the developing countries of Africa and Latin America, most of which as yet have been unable to benefit economically from cost-effective manufacturing and assembly, globalization contributes to a worsening of their terms of trade, to a stagnation of most local economies, and therefore to the growing austerity in public sectors generally and in higher education especially. (Many critical academics also decry the growing and already excessive influence of Anglo-American culture and academia.) On the other hand, higher education's revenue needs are voracious, and many will contend that the constraint on taxation that is almost assuredly worsened by globalization and by the increasing ease of moving taxable assets (including residences of the wealthy) to lower tax jurisdictions, is an appropriate check on politicians and on the tendency of public sectors and taxes, unchecked, to grow at rates in excess of taxpayers' incomes.

However, on the upside and strengthening the position of colleges and universities, globalization greatly enhances the importance of higher education, both to individuals, for the sake of greater earning power, enriched lives, and enhanced status, and to the larger society, for the sake of greater global competitiveness and economic prosperity as well as a better functioning and more just government and a more vigorous civil society. In the United States, for example, enrollments continue ever upward, increasing by 23 percent in the 14 years from 1992 to 2006 and expected to increase another 9 to 16 percent by 2017, by then reaching between 19.4 million and 20.6 million (NCES Projections of Education Statistics to 2017, Figure C.) Spending by the more than 4000 degree-granting colleges and universities in 2007 (not considering the billions more spent on the expenses of student living) was expected to total $373 billion, (NCES Digest of Education Statistics 2009, Table 26.) Furthermore, this increasing demand, both public and private and reflected in surging enrollments and participation rates as well as in such indicators as the explosive growth of private higher education, is a worldwide phenomenon. The number of students in some form of higher, or postsecondary, education worldwide has risen in the past century from an estimated 500,000 in the early 1900s to well over 100 million in the early years of the 21st century, and a 2006 estimate projected that the number might reach 120 million by 2010 (Schofer and Meyer, 2005; Daniel et al., 2006.) Thus, globalization and the accompanying increase in global economic competition as well as the superior bargaining position of the more knowledge-based economies have clearly heightened both the private and the public need and demand for higher education.

This increasing public and private importance of, as well as demand for, higher education in the United States (as well as in most of the rest of the world) has had, for US higher education, a kind of bi-modal impact. On the one hand, the global preeminence of America's top research universities has never been greater. With all due allowance for the impossibility of ranking such a complex and elusive quality as university excellence, as well as the foolishness of the world's increasing preoccupation with rankings and league tables, US research universities in 2008 took 17 of the top 20 spots in the Shanghai Jiao Tong (2008) listing and 14 of the top 20 in the *Times Higher Education Supplement* (2008) "World University Rankings." This position, based (however imperfectly) on such metrics as citation indices and peer scholar opinions, is reflected in the ability of US universities to attract top students as well as top scholars from all over the world.

At the same time, there is also great interest throughout most of the world in our so-called non-university institutions, especially in our community colleges. The US community college model – combining as it does the advantages of accessible, short-cycle, community-oriented, vocationally-relevant, and relatively low-cost instruction with an especially cost-effective first two or three years on the way to the baccalaureate and beyond – is attracting great attention from other countries (as well as attracting increasing numbers of international students to US community colleges.) Thus, the United States is not only drawing students from around the world – which, of course, is partly attributed to the two-century-long mystic of America and the dream of American opportunity, reinforced by the draw of financial assistance and the international power of English language higher education wherever it is offered – but is also drawing attention to the American model of higher education and its seemingly effective sector diversification.

What is attractive to governments and higher education observers around the world, then, seems to be:

- The scholarly emphasis of the top American research universities, which is a function not just of our wealth and the long-standing reputations of the most eminent and venerable institutions (acknowledging that academic reputations are built over many years), but also of the American curricular and course-based model of advanced scholarly training, the rigor and integrity of the American academic tenure system, the competitive nature of top US research universities (as compared with the avowedly anti-competitive higher educational systems of some Continental European countries), and the competitive peer-reviewed model for the awarding of most federal research contracts.
- The combination of extended opportunity, workforce relevance, and cost-effectiveness provided by the American community college, with some 40 percent of first-time postsecondary students entering at the level of the two-year community college.
- The enormous supplementation of governmental (tax) revenues with tuition fees and philanthropy in the public as well as the private sector, which has the effect of greatly magnifying the resource base of US higher education. Tuition fees in the public sector range from 20 to 45 percent of instructional costs. Philanthropic support of both private and public colleges and universities in the United States

added in 2007 some $29.75 billion to college and university coffers for operations and additions to endowments, which in 2007 totaled some $149 billion (Council for Aid to Education, 2008; NACUBO, 2007.)
- The cost-effective preservation of access and opportunity – in spite of high tuition fees in all sectors – by financial assistance from federal, state, institutional, and other private sources, and including grants (mainly means-tested), loans (federally guaranteed and including both means-tested subsidized and unsubsidized), and education tax credits, totaling in 2007–08 some $143.4 billion (College Board, 2008, Table 1, p. 5.)
- The decentralization of public higher education in America to the 50 states, further decentralized to public higher education systems and quasi-autonomous public governing boards, all of which furthers institutional autonomy, competition, and experimentation (particularly in comparison to prevailing international models of ministry-run universities and faculty commonly bound by civil service status.)
- The quality, responsiveness and vibrancy made possible in US higher education by a robust private sector that includes the most prestigious colleges and universities (generally featuring very large endowments and selective admissions), as well as colleges with minimal selectivity and minimal endowments but which nonetheless feature good teaching, attention to students, and programs that are exceptionally flexible and responsive to the prevailing job markets. This tuition- and philanthropy-dependent private sector constitutes nearly 70 percent of the four-year institutions and approximately 22 percent of US higher educational enrollment.

In short, examining American higher education in an international comparative context in an increasingly globalized world is reinforcing. We seem to be doing some things right. And many of the features listed above – for example, portable course credits for degrees, public sector tuition fees, public sector governing boards, public institutional corporatization, sector diversification, faculty evaluation of teaching effectiveness, aggressive fund-raising, competitive research support – are spreading throughout the world. Given the incessant complaining about American higher education, especially from politicians, this external admiration and emulation should be of some comfort (even if it is unlikely to dampen our domestic criticism or restore our damaged budgets.)

This is not to say that we cannot learn from higher educational policies and experiences from elsewhere, especially the rapidly changing higher educational scene in the European Union, where significant reforms are taking place in, for example, research assessment, performance-based budgets, and the management of student indebtedness. But overall, our system (or non-system) works well – and especially so when considered in an international comparative context – in balancing the very strong and oftentimes diverging pulls from:

- students: to provide good teaching, appropriate curricula, and affordability;
- employers: to provide graduates with useable skills and work habits;
- faculty: to preserve academic freedom and faculty preeminence in the determination of what is to be taught and learned;
- politicians and taxpayers, who want value for their money (and do not altogether trust either faculty or the college administrators to provide the same);
- leaders – presidents, chancellors, deans, and others – who are charged with orchestrating these diverging pulls, defending the academy, and coping with the ever-present (and in 2009 profoundly worsening) financial austerity.

HIGHER EDUCATIONAL LEADERSHIP IN AN INCREASINGLY GLOBALIZED WORLD

The last point can serve as segue to our final consideration: what does our increasingly globalized world have to say to leaders of American higher education? As a former state college president, state system chancellor, and scholar of international comparative higher education finance and governance, I would answer my question in two parts.

If one of the consequences of globalization is an exacerbation of what has been a general decline in most states of public revenues – greatly accelerated and made totally real (if there was ever any question) by the current (2008–09) American-led but worldwide recession – then the first priority for college and university leaders must be leading through this increasing financial austerity. This calls upon leaders first to communicate forcefully – to trustees as well as to political and civic leaders – the vital and increasing importance of higher education both to meet the global economic challenges and to uphold the social values of widened higher educational participation and access, but also simultaneously to manage the situation of fiscal austerity by cutting low-priority programs and their staffs and improving the institution by academically thoughtful reallocation. This means, in part, having the courage not simply to profess that educational quality just might deteriorate if things keep on this way, but to admit, where it is true, that quality already has deteriorated and in fact is worsening in spite of all efforts to manage cost-effectively (and being prepared to back up the assertion and carry out any threatened cuts.)

At the same time, the increasingly globalized world calls for much more than managing through fiscal austerity and talking up the new globalized world. Presidents, chancellors, trustees, deans, and faculty who would be scholar-leaders must:

- stress second and even third language facility through real changes (if not yet made) in admission and graduation requirements as well as support for language departments and faculty;
- reward faculty and staff who reach out to students and scholars from abroad: to admit them, to integrate them into the life of the campus and the community, and to use their presence to strengthen and alter the learning experience of all students;
- recognize that international students need care and support that costs money, and that international students cannot be viewed simply as out-of-state tuition dollars or as a metric of quality or academic sophistication;
- provide financial and staff support to study abroad programs that are more than exotic junkets, but are given academic credit based on high learning expectations;
- support real curricular and departmental reorganization and restructuring that leads to new levels of international and global scholarship and learning;
- resist the seduction of being feted by a foreign university and putting one's signature to an institutional agreement, and recognize, rather, that real scholarly collaboration comes only from faculty, just as real academic value from international students comes from their academic and social interaction with the faculty and with the native students. The internationalization of the campus needs leaders' academic and financial support – but it happens with and through the entire campus.

It is a new and vastly more globalized world, and most American students, both undergraduate and graduate, are far behind their student counterparts in most of the countries in the world in understanding this new global reality. Leaders of American higher education are in a position to change this. And they must succeed.

REFERENCES

Cloete, Nico, Michael Cross, Johan Muller and Surykumarie Pillay (2000), "Culture, Identity, and the Role of Higher Education in Building Democracy in South Africa," in M. Cross, N. Cloete, E. Beckham, A. Harper, J. Indiresan and C. Musil (eds), *Diversity and Unity*, Johannesburg: Centre for Higher Education Transformation and The Ford Foundation.

College Board (2008), *Trends in Student Aid 2008*, New York: The College Board.

Council for Aid to Education (2008), Press Release 2/20/08, "Contributions to Colleges and Universities up by 6.3% to $29.75 Billion." Retrieved 2/10/09 from http://www.cae.org/content/news.asp.

Daniel, John, Asha Kanwar and Stamenka Ulvalic-Trumbic (2006), "A Tectonic Shift in Global Higher Education?", *Change*, 38 (4), July/August, 16–23.

Held, D., A. McGrew, D. Goldblatt and J. Perraton (1999), *Global Transformations: Politics, Economics, and Culture*, Stanford: Stanford University Press.

Marginson, Simon (2006), quoted in "How Do You Define Globalization?", Center for Higher Education Policy Analysis [University of Southern California], *The Navigator*, 6:1, Fall, 6.

Marginson, Simon (2007), "Revisiting the Definitions of Internationalization and Globalization," in Enders, Jürgen and Frans van Vught (eds), *Towards a Cartography of Higher Education Policy Change: A festschrift in Honour of Guy Neave*, Enschede, the Netherlands: Center for Higher Education Policy Studies.

National Association for College and University Business Officers (2007), *2007 NACUBO Endowment Study*, Washington, DC.

National Center for Education Statistics, Digest of Education Statistics, Table 26. Retrieved 2/10/09 from http://nces.gov/programs/digest/d07/.

National Center for Education Statistics, Projections of Education Statistics to 2017, Figure C, Actual and middle alternative projected numbers for total enrollment in degree-granting institutions: Selected years, 1992–2017. Retrieved 2/10/09 from http://nces.ed.gov/programs/projections/projections2017/sec2b.asp/.

Salmi, Jamil (2000), "Higher Education at a Turning Point," unpublished paper, nd [2000], Washington, DC: The World Bank.

Schofer, Evan and John W. Meyer (2005), "The Worldwide Expansion of Higher Education in the Twentieth Century," *American Sociological Review*, 70, December, 898–920.

Shanghai Jiao Tong (2008), "Academic Ranking of World Universities," retrieved 2/11/09 at: http://www.arwu.org/.

Sirat, Morshidi (2006), quoted in "How Do You Define Globalization?", Center for Higher Education Policy Analysis [University of Southern California], *The Navigator*, 6:1, Fall, 6.

Times Higher Education Supplement (2008), "World University Rankings" retrieved 2/11/09 at: http://www.timeshighereducation.co.uk/.

2. The realities of mass higher education in a globalized world
Philip G. Altbach

Mass higher education has become the global norm in the 21st century. In 2009, enrolments in postsecondary education are 125 million, up from 100 million less than a decade earlier. And expansion, now mainly in the developing world, continues even in the midst of economic crisis. China now has the world's largest higher education system, enrolling more than 27 million students. India is in the number 3 position, with 14 million students. But China serves around 20 percent of the age group and India 10 percent – there is much room for expansion. In much of sub-Saharan Africa, 5 percent or fewer of the age group are in postsecondary education. Virtually all of the industrialized and many middle-income countries have built mass higher education systems, enrolling more than a quarter of the age cohort. Most are moving toward enrolling 40 percent or more, and a few now enroll half (Organisation for Economic Co-operation and Development, 2008.)

We refer to "massification" as the process by which academic systems enroll large numbers – and higher proportions of the relevant age group – of students in a range of differentiated academic institutions. Even countries that until recently have had small and elitist academic systems are facing pressures for expansion. There is no country that is immune from the pressure for massification.

In most parts of the world, higher education was limited in size and scope until the 1960s. Sociologist Martin Trow divided the world's academic systems into three categories – elite (under 15 percent of the relevant age group participating in postsecondary education), mass (between 20 percent and 30 percent), and universal (above 30 percent) – arguing that higher education was inevitably moving toward universal access (Trow, 2006.) He argued that the traditional university structure in most countries could accommodate up to 15 percent of the age group, but that beyond that number structural changes would be needed. Trow proved to be both too optimistic and too pessimistic. The countries at the upper end of the scale, such as the United States and Canada, stopped expanding and currently enroll slightly more than half of the age group. Countries that Trow identified as moving toward mass higher education at the end of the 1960s have dramatically expanded – most of Western Europe now enrolls more than 30 percent of the age cohort – and some are close to half. Most dramatically, a few Latin American countries, such Asian nations as South Korea, Taiwan, and the Philippines, and some countries in Central and Eastern Europe are expanding rapidly and are close to universal access.

The 1990s saw the emergence of mass and universal access in many parts of the world. All of the larger Western European nations – Germany, the United Kingdom, France, and Italy – have expanded significantly, and all now enroll 30 percent or more of the age cohort. The Asian middle-income countries that had been experiencing rapid economic growth were hit by economic problems in the late 1990s. In general, economic cycles have not significantly affected expansion either in this part of the world or elsewhere – demand for access continues almost regardless. Expansion has been steady in most of the developing world – including China and India – and Latin America has seen dramatic growth. Only in sub-Saharan Africa, beset by a severe long-term economic and political crisis, did growth slow significantly in some places. Despite regional variations, at the end of the century, expansion of higher education is a worldwide trend.

While confirming global expansion and the creation of mass systems of higher education, it is important not to overgeneralize these trends. Some academic systems have already reached a level of maturity or are subject to social or economic conditions that will stymie expansion. Japan, for example, already has a high level of participation in higher education and is experiencing a drop in the university-age population, and it suffered through a long economic downturn during the 1990s. Experts predict that total student numbers will decline modestly – nontraditional age students may compensate for some of the declines in numbers of traditional age students – and some less prestigious private colleges and universities will fail as a result of an enrollment slump. By way of comparison, the United States, which also has a high rate of participation, is currently experiencing expansion due to short-term demographic growth in the 18- to 22-year-old population. In almost every country, however, nontraditional age students continue to increase their rates of participation. Older people who may have been unable to obtain a degree when they were young or who see the need to upgrade their skills are demanding access to higher education, and most countries have moved to accommodate them.

The mass higher education systems emerging worldwide have an inherent logic that will characterize key elements of academe in the coming decades. Traditional patterns of organization and governance will, of course, continue to exist – universities are highly conservative institutions and change comes slowly. But the logic of mass higher education will affect all countries and academic systems.

The American higher education system serves as a kind of model for the rest of the world in an era of mass higher education, given that the United States was the first country to experience mass access to higher education – beginning in the 1920s and dramatically expanding in the 1950s. The patterns and structures that evolved in the United States have provided models for other countries to examine – and in some cases emulate – as they confronted expansion (Altbach, 1998a.) Most other academic systems were elitist until the middle of the 20th century or even thereafter and thus did not need to cope with large numbers of students. As they grew, these systems were forced to adapt to new realities, which often proved to be a difficult task. Italy, for example, still relies on a traditional academic organizational structure that does not function well with larger enrollments. Britain restructured its academic system in the 1980s to deal with larger student numbers. In developing countries, the elite models imposed by colonial rulers have remained basically unreformed and no longer work well. Many of the world's academic systems are groping for new models that will operate effectively in the context of mass higher education.

Twenty-first-century globalization has had a significant impact on mass higher education – and at the same time massification has influenced the globalized academic environment. The dramatic expansion in the numbers of students studying outside the borders of the home countries is one manifestation of this impact. Some 2.5 million students were studying abroad in 2009; that number is likely to increase to 8 million by 2025 (DeWit et al., 2008.) International study has many causes, but one of them is the lack of capacity in home countries – an impact of massification. Other international initiatives, including the rapid growth of branch campuses, twinning programs, joint degree arrangements, and franchising of academic programs, among others, have been put into place in large part to increase capacity in countries that need more opportunities for access.

There is also a significant global flow of academic talent, again in large part to meet the demands for qualified professors in countries that lack enough teaching staff. While much of this flow has been from developing countries to industrialized nations, there is also a significant flow among developing countries. There is also a realization that students need to have global skills to effectively participate in the global economy and in a job market made ever more competitive by mass higher education (Stearns, 2009.) Thus, there is a direct and symbiotic relationship between globalization and the realities of mass higher education.

This chapter discusses some of the central realities of the massification of higher education worldwide. The following topics are central to the phenomenon of mass higher education in the 21st century:

- the challenge of funding;
- new sectors of higher education, including private higher education, for-profit higher education, and new vocational institutions;
- distance learning as a means of coping with demand;
- the differentiation and complexity of academic institutions;
- the "managerialization" of academic institutions and the creation of the "administrative estate";
- the nature of the academic profession;
- the diversity of students and student culture.

THE CHALLENGE OF FUNDING

Higher education is expensive. The cost of providing instruction, libraries and laboratories, and the other accoutrements of higher education has grown dramatically ("Financing Higher Education," 1998.) Libraries and laboratories in particular now require major investments of resources. The new communications technologies as well as keeping abreast of the dramatic growth in knowledge are also costly.

Significant changes in attitude on the funding of higher education have evolved over the past three decades. Earlier, in most countries a consensus existed that higher education was a "public good" that contributed significantly to society by imparting knowledge and skills to those who were educated at universities and other postsecondary institutions. Since higher education was considered a public good, it was agreed that society should bear a large part of the cost. In the 1980s, attitudes began to change. Beginning with the World Bank and extending to many governments, higher education began to be viewed as mainly a "private good," benefiting the individual more than society as a whole (World Bank, 1994.) The logic of this change in thinking places more of the burden for financing higher education on the "users" – students and their families. In many countries, policies require students to pay a growing proportion of the cost of postsecondary education.

Many countries have experienced a significant change in attitudes with regard to public spending. The 1980s saw a gradual breakdown of the consensus built up following World War II on the role of the state in funding not only higher education but public services in general, and an accompanying policy of high taxes to pay for these state services. The administrations of Margaret Thatcher in Britain and Ronald Reagan in the United States had a major impact in this area. Even in Sweden, the Social Democrats lost their majority for a time, and the welfare state was to some extent weakened. The collapse of the Soviet Union and of state socialism in Eastern Europe further strengthened conservative thinking. Finally, the impact of world economic trends and competitiveness placed pressure on many governments to trim public spending (Kuttner, 1997.) In the wake of the 1992 Maastricht Treaty and the advent of euro-based economic policies in the European Union, public spending growth has been limited and in some countries cut. Australia and New Zealand have also been at the forefront of this trend. Many analysts have identified these policies with globalization and the neo-liberal policies stressed by the World Bank and other international agencies and have linked them to the continuing funding problems faced by academic systems everywhere (Stiglitz, 2002.)

Thus, at the same time that higher education is faced with significant expansion in the number of students, the traditional source of funding in most countries, government, is less willing to invest in postsecondary education, placing significant pressure on systems of higher education. Expansion cannot be halted, because public demand is immense and many European countries guarantee access to those who pass secondary school examinations. Higher education institutions and systems have had to accommodate more students with fewer financial resources.

There have been a variety of responses to this situation. In much of Western Europe, including the United Kingdom, expansion has continued or has even accelerated because government policy has remained committed to increased access. In Germany, France, and Italy, higher education remains essentially free while at the same time government funding has not increased to match enrollment growth. The result has been overcrowding at the universities and deterioration in the conditions of study. In Germany, student discontent resulted in the largest demonstrations since the 1960s. After major political turmoil, fees were introduced in England and Wales for the first time as a way to provide funding to handle increased enrollments and reduced government allocations while increasing access and attempting to maintain quality. Fees were introduced by a newly elected Labour government in 1998 and have been increased since then. Indeed, Labour legislated "top-up" fees, giving academic institutions for the first time the power to set their own fee levels. In other parts of the world, such as in Latin America, Central and Eastern Europe, and parts of Asia, private initiative has been encouraged as a way of serving increased demand for postsecondary education, and private higher education is increasing its share of total enrollments.

NEW SECTORS OF HIGHER EDUCATION

As higher education expands, traditional institutions such as universities grow. In addition, new types of institutions are inevitably added in order to serve larger numbers, and also to provide more diverse education and training for a more disparate clientele. The university remains at the core of an expanded higher education system. Other forms of postsecondary education provide both expanded access and diversity. Because of the financial pressures discussed earlier as well as private institutions' ability to respond more rapidly to new demands, private higher education has quickly expanded.

Nonprofit private universities and colleges now constitute a significant part of the postsecondary systems of many countries. Such schools are beginning to emerge in countries where the private sector has not previously been active (for example, Malaysia, Hungary) (Geiger, 1986; Altbach, 1999.) Private sectors can be quite diverse in terms of quality, orientation, and focus, as well as sponsorship and financial aspects. Religious institutions are a significant part of the private higher education sector in many countries. In Latin America, where the Roman Catholic Church established many of the oldest and most prestigious universities, religiously sponsored higher education is especially influential.

These nonprofit institutions have been overshadowed – at least in terms of numbers – by newer, more entrepreneurial private universities and by specialized institutions, many of which are of questionable quality (Altbach, 1998b.) A similar phenomenon exists in Central and Eastern Europe, where there has been a proliferation of private institutions established to serve specific segments of an expanding market for higher education. Many of the newer private institutions have scarce resources, and most focus on fields of high demand, such as management studies, computer science, and information technology. Private institutions may also offer instruction in fields that are inexpensive to teach, such as some arts and social science subjects that require no laboratory facilities or other costly equipment. The newer private institutions are often entrepreneurial – they take advantage of "market niches," advertise their "products," and operate much as private businesses.

The private higher education sector enrolls a majority of students in many countries. It has traditionally enrolled 80 percent of the student population in Japan, South Korea, Taiwan, and the Philippines. More than half the students in Indonesia now attend private institutions. Similarly, the private sector now enrolls more than half the students in Mexico, Argentina, Brazil, and several other Latin American countries, and is a growing sector in Central and Eastern Europe. In the United

States, private enrollments have remained steady at around 20 percent of the total for a half-century or more, and Western Europe has not seen dramatic growth. Clearly, private higher education is the fastest growing segment of postsecondary education, and it has provided the capacity to serve growing demand.

In the past several decades, there has been a dramatic growth of the for-profit sector. In the United States, the University of Phoenix, which has the ability to offer degrees and is accredited by one of the regional accrediting agencies, has pioneered the degree granting activity in the for-profit sector (Breneman et al., 2006.) This institution, with branches in a dozen states, is now the largest private university in the United States. It offers vocationally tailored degrees in such fields as management studies by using information technology and part-time faculty. In many other countries, new for-profit schools have been established, mainly in high-demand fields.

While the traditional university remains the central institution in postsecondary education worldwide, the university represents a small part of the total postsecondary enterprise. Higher education is becoming increasingly vocational in focus, and the institutional mix of higher education reflects this interest. In the United States, the community college sector has grown in size and importance. These two-year institutions, which are mainly vocational in focus, now enroll 25 percent of American students (Cohen and Brawer, 1996.) Similar accommodation to vocational interests can be seen in other countries. Examples of such vocationally oriented non-degree schools in Europe are the *Fachhochschulen* in Germany and the HBO institutions in the Netherlands. Much of the growth in higher education in Europe and in some other countries is taking place in the non-university sector.

A recent emphasis on the role of the research university in the knowledge economy has highlighted these key institutions (Salmi, 2009; Altbach and Balán, 2007.) Research universities, which stand at the top of any nation's higher education system, are the central institutions for basic and applied research. They are the main points of interaction with the world scientific system and with universities in other countries. Research universities also educate the next generation of academics. For these and other reasons, they are keys to an effective academic system. At the same time, they are expensive to establish and maintain.

DISTANCE HIGHER EDUCATION

Mass higher education has stimulated an interest in distance education. The advent of new technologies has permitted distance education to develop in new and unexpected ways. In fact, the revolution in distance education is still in its early stages. Distance education is not, of course, a new idea. Correspondence courses and other methods of delivering education without bringing students together have long been in existence. The University of South Africa, for example, has for more than a half-century mainly offered academic degrees through correspondence. Similarly, the pioneering contemporary distance education effort, the British Open University, started in the 1960s, before the advent of the new technologies. It began its educational programs with a combination of written course materials, television, and direct meetings with course tutors in small group settings. While the Open University is somewhat less expensive than traditional higher education, it is not dramatically cheaper. Now, with more reliance on purely distance methods, costs have been reduced (Mason, 1998.) Increasingly, distance education providers rely on the Internet for all instruction and evaluation – with the concept becoming almost synonymous with the use of Internet based technology.

The past two decades have seen the development in many countries of distance higher education that makes use of the new technologies. By 2000, eight of the ten largest distance higher education providers were in developing or middle-income countries, with the largest, Adadolu University in Turkey, serving 578,000 students, and China's TV University following with 530,000 (Task Force on Higher Education and Society, 2000, p. 31.) In Japan, the University of the Air uses a combination of methods of delivering instruction, including television. Everyman's University in Israel has also built up a clientele for its services. The most dramatic expansion of distance higher education has been in several developing countries. Thailand has two large distance education institutions offering degree programs throughout the country and enrolling more than a half-million students.

Distance higher education is still in the process of development (Van Dusen, 1997.) Few studies have been done on the effectiveness of the instruction provided through distance education. The financial conditions are also not clear, although the limited existing data show that costs are lower but not dramatically so. The mix of computer-mediated instruction, direct contact with an instructor (perhaps through videoconferencing, web-based communication, or e-mail), and reading material constitutes a powerful combination of instructional techniques that are in the process of being molded into an effective tool for learning.

Many questions remain concerning the true costs, the appropriate use of technologies, and issues related to monitoring. Many have rushed to use distance education as a "quick fix" to provide access, hoping that the technologies will catch up with the demand. Too little attention has been paid to effectiveness and quality (Robins and Webster, 2002.)

Distance education is ideally suited to the international delivery of educational initiatives. It is easy to send educational programs across borders, and there are already many Internet-based educational offerings. Questions of control and of cultural and other biases that may be part of cross-border education have yet to be answered. There is much to be learned about how teaching and learning works in a cross-cultural context.

Already, millions of students are participating in this sector worldwide, the large majority of them in developing countries. Distance higher education allows students to be admitted without the construction of expensive campuses and libraries or the hiring of teachers to put in individual classrooms. While distance programs may not result in dramatic savings in direct instructional costs, they do eliminate construction and other infrastructure expenditures.

Distance higher education is an integral part of a mass higher education system (Brown and Duguid, 1996.) It can serve students in remote locations, permits rapid expansion, and is flexible in permitting rapid changes in curriculum. However, it remains unclear if the best-quality education can be delivered in remote locations without providing students access to libraries or to direct contact with instructors. Theoretically, at least, distance higher education at its best could provide a quality education. Whether the kind of programs now offered in countries such as Thailand and India can truly achieve excellence remains an open question.

THE DIVERSITY AND COMPLEXITY OF ACADEMIC INSTITUTIONS AND SYSTEMS

Not only are new institutional types and ways of delivering instruction part of mass higher education, existing universities also are changing. In most cases, institutions are growing in size and in the diversity of programs offered to students. Clark Kerr's description of the multiversity in the United States is relevant internationally (Kerr, 1995.) While universities retain their basic core functions and governance structure, departments, faculties, and schools grow in size and number. Whole new institutes or other academic units may be added. The very mission of the university may also expand. The traditional dedication to teaching and research may extend to direct involvement with industry and other institutions in society and service to many constituencies. In most cases, growth takes place by accretion – by adding on new functions and responsibilities and increasing the size of existing units without changing the basic structure of the institution.

This pattern of institutional growth has been both a strength and a weakness. It has permitted universities to expand to meet society's needs and to maintain their centrality in the higher education system. At the same time, it has made universities more difficult to manage and has severely damaged traditional patterns of governance. The size and complexity of the modern university has increased bureaucracy, alienated both faculty and students, and undermined the ideal of participation and shared governance. The tradition of control by the professors, enshrined in the medieval University of Paris and protected through the centuries, may be facing its most serious threat in the current period. It is worth keeping in mind that the ideal of shared governance and a strong element of faculty control originated in the German Humboldtian ideal in the 19th century and was adapted later in the American university model in the early years of the 20th century (Ben-David and Zloczower, 1962.) As universities have grown larger, it has been very difficult to maintain traditional forms of governance. Institutions have necessarily become more bureaucratic, and direct faculty control or even significant faculty participation has declined.

In this respect, Western Europe is moving closer to the United States in terms of basic institutional control. The Netherlands is a leading example of this trend in governance reform. In the United States, the traditional power of the faculty has been eroded by administrative control due in part to the logic of expanding institutions and in part to demands for accountability, although professorial power remains stronger in the research universities than in other institutions (Hirsch and Weber, 2001.)

Not only has governance changed as the result of institutional expansion, the work of the university has also expanded, and new offices, departments, schools, and other structures have emerged to take on these new functions. In the United States, the proliferation of organized research units (ORUs), often called centers or institutes, reflects the expanded research role of the leading universities. These ORUs often have a good deal of autonomy, especially when they are funded by external agencies. Links with industry are considered a central part of the contemporary mission of many universities, and administrative offices have been established to facilitate university–industry relationships. Public service has grown in importance as well, with offices being established to administer this area. As student numbers have grown, universities have often added staff to deal with students. In all cases, the increase has meant more administration and control.

As the curriculum has expanded, new departments and institutes have been created. Interdisciplinary teaching and research have also grown in importance, and academic units have been established to foster interdisciplinary work. Entire new fields have emerged in the past several decades.

Computer science and informatics, for example, did not exist several decades ago. Now, these fields are among the most important in academe. Management studies has gained in importance, as have fields such as international trade. New discoveries in the biomedical sciences have led to new departments, institutes, and centers.

THE RISE OF THE ADMINISTRATIVE ESTATE

Administrative power was pioneered in US universities, which have traditionally had a strong executive function in higher education. College and university presidents are appointed by the board of trustees rather than elected by the faculty, and senior administrators, such as vice presidents and deans, are in turn appointed by the president, generally with the advice of relevant faculty. Senior administrators control the budget, academic planning mechanisms, and the other levers of institutional power. Institutional patterns vary, with the most prestigious universities having a greater degree of professorial power and autonomy than those lower in the academic hierarchy (Youn and Murphy, 1997.)

As their functions expand and diversify, universities add administrators to deal with them. In the United States, the fastest growing sector in higher education is academic administration. While the number of faculty members has remained fairly steady, administrators have increased in number (Shattock, 2003; 2009.) The new functions are usually too complex for faculty members to handle on a part-time and nonexpert basis. They require full-time attention and specialized expertise in accountancy, law, management, health services, statistics, and the many other concerns of the contemporary university.

The American model is one approach to handling the administrative functions of the institution. In Germany and some other European nations, universities have a dual administrative structure, with an elected rector presiding over the academic functions of the university and a government-appointed administrator (the chancellor), who has responsibility for the purely administrative aspects of the institution. The chancellor is a civil servant and not an academic, and he or she typically stays in the position for an extended period while the academic rector serves for a two- or three-year term. As the administrative structure and budget of the university grew, the power of the chancellor increased. At the same time, the German *Länder* (states) and governments in some other countries devolved some of their budgetary and other controls to the academic institutions, giving them more autonomy. Academic institutions have become more complex but in some ways more autonomous.

THE ACADEMIC PROFESSION

As noted, the academic profession has lost some of its power and autonomy within the university. Academic work, for a growing number within the profession, is changing. Indeed, the academic profession itself is changing to meet the new realities. New types of academics are taking their places in the universities and colleges – clinical professors, research professors, part-time and adjunct academic staff, and others are all part of the mass system. The professorial ideal of the autonomy to teach without much control from external authority is less often achieved. In many countries, workloads have increased and class size has grown.

Academic work is to some extent becoming more specialized. Growing numbers of teachers are hired only to teach and not to engage in research or contribute to the growth of scholarship. The elite professors who are employed by research-oriented universities and produce the large proportion of published scholarship and who obtain most of the research grants are a decreasing minority within the academic profession. In the United States, it is estimated that fewer than one-fifth of the professoriate is in this "research cadre" (Haas, 1996.) The rest of the American professoriate is, for the most part, engaged mainly in teaching rather than in research and service. While the professoriate in most European countries, as well as Japan and South Korea, expresses a high degree of interest in research, a relatively small portion of the profession is actually producing published scholarship (Enders, 2001.)

There are significant structural changes taking place in the academic profession. In many countries, the proportion of full-time academics is declining as part-time teachers grow in number. This is true in the United States, where it is estimated that more than 30 percent of teaching is now done by part-time faculty. The number of full-time but nonpermanent faculty members has increased. These teachers often carry a higher teaching load than permanent staff members and cannot obtain a regular professorial position at the university. In Latin America, part-time faculty are the norm, although some countries have tried to increase the number of full-time professors because they recognize that part-time faculty have little loyalty or commitment to the institution at which they are teaching. Other parts of the world are moving toward the Latin American case without anticipating the inevitable result.

These changes in the nature of the academic labor force will have significant implications (Altbach, 2003.) Fewer well-qualified young people will be attracted to academe once they realize that they cannot look forward to a full-time career. Average salaries will drop as the profession increasingly consists of part-time and temporary junior staff. Research orientation and productivity will decline as fewer professors are focused on research. There will be less institutional loyalty and commitment, and the university will have fewer professors to participate in governance.

Mass higher education has reduced both the power and the autonomy of the professoriate. The "traditional" professor is no longer the standard for academic appointments. There are now alternative academic career paths, most of which are not as favorable to the professoriate as in the past. The terms and conditions of academic work are being changed to reflect the realities of mass higher education. These changes are perhaps inevitable, but they also create problems for the future of the university. Will the most qualified individuals be attracted to academic careers under the new circumstances? Will the universities be able to produce the research that increasingly complex societies and economies require? Will a sufficient portion of the professoriate be committed to the ethos and governance of the university? These and other questions are of considerable importance as the logic of mass higher education affects the professoriate.

STUDENTS

Of course, students are at the heart of the mass university. The growing numbers of students completing secondary education, demands for social mobility, the needs of industrial and postindustrial societies, and the emphasis on obtaining diplomas and degrees have all contributed to the demand for higher education. In many countries, including some developing countries, a university degree is a requirement for a middle-class occupation. Student numbers have risen dramatically from the 1960s to the 1980s, when some countries saw a reduction in growth. For most developing countries, expansion did not stop – it continues unabated. Even in the United States, Germany, and much of the rest of Europe, where there is little or no rise in the university-age population, a combination of increasing graduation rates from secondary education and demand from nontraditional age groups has kept up the pressure on universities to expand access. In only a few countries, such as Japan, has demand for higher education stagnated – and even Japan would experience growth if access was opened to nontraditional age groups.

The composition of the student population has changed with the advent of mass higher education. In the industrialized countries, higher education has been dominated by the middle classes for a century or more, and as the middle class has expanded, the universities have grown. Access for the working class is now widespread. In developing countries, higher education is increasingly available to the middle classes and even to working-class young people. In many countries, nontraditional students, those who are older or who may lack standard secondary education credentials, are gaining access to higher education. The proportion of women students has dramatically increased: in the United States and most European countries, women comprise at least half the student population, although there are major variations by field of study. This increasingly diverse student population means a breakdown in a common student culture.

Students are also more varied in terms of their academic abilities and interests, and this too has had an impact on the university. In differentiated academic systems, students are selected into different types of institutions according to their interests and abilities. New types of institutions have been created for students who may not be suited for traditional academic study. For example, in the United States, the two-year vocationally oriented community colleges require only graduation from secondary school for entry. They are "open door" institutions.

Students are less carefully selected, contributing in part to the large numbers who drop out of postsecondary education or take a longer time to complete their academic degrees. This "wastage" has financial and other implications but is part of the reality of mass higher education. Academic systems that traditionally had a laissez-faire approach to study and degree completion are tightening up requirements and instituting accountability measures for students. Students who do not make satisfactory academic progress are given deadlines and then terminated. Many countries are moving toward an American-style course-credit system because it provides regular assessment of students and a way of monitoring academic progress.

Students are increasingly looking at postsecondary education as a means to improve employment opportunities, enhance income, and stimulate social mobility. They are less interested in the intrinsic values of higher education. Students see themselves as consumers of educational products. This change has significant implications for student attitudes, the relationship between students and academic institutions, and the way the university and other postsecondary institutions relate to students.

CONCLUSION

Mass higher education has brought with it significant changes in how academic institutions relate to society. When higher education served an elite, universities were small and the budget for postsecondary education was relatively modest. A general consensus existed concerning the role of the university in society, and considerable autonomy was granted to universities. Higher education is now central to all societies. Universities provide the essential training for virtually all occupations necessary for technologically based societies and for the business and government sectors as well. Universities provide new knowledge through research. Higher education is a matter of major concern for large segments of the population because the sons and daughters attend postsecondary institutions. Further, higher education is now expensive, both in terms of the government budget and increasingly the direct costs to individual students and their families. For many countries, higher education comprises a significant part of the state budget, which makes governments more concerned about the performance and policies of postsecondary education (Neave and van Vught, 1994.) As higher education has moved from periphery to center, it has naturally received more attention from society. This has resulted in more accountability.

In many countries, mass higher education has been forced on the universities. In much of Europe, access is guaranteed to students who complete their secondary school examinations; growing numbers passed these examinations and chose to enter the universities. Governments in general did not, however, provide the funding needed to provide a quality education to these students; as a result, the conditions of study have deteriorated. In many developing countries, the rise of a middle class and a growing economy increased the demand for access, and higher education was forced to accept growing numbers of students, again often without adequate funding. In the United States, where expansion took place first, a combination of increased public funding, an active private sector, and the growth of a highly differentiated academic system with institutions of varying quality and purposes, led to the development of a reasonably effective mass higher education system.

REFERENCES

Altbach, P. (1998a), "The American Academic Model in Comparative Perspective," in P. Altbach, *Comparative Higher Education: Knowledge, the University and Development*, Norwood, NJ: Ablex, pp. 55–73.
Altbach, P. (1998b), "The Anatomy of Private Higher Education," *International Higher Education*, 12, 9–10.
Altbach, P. (ed.) (1999), *Private Prometheus: Private Higher Education and Development*, Westport, CT.: Greenwood.
Altbach, P. (ed.) (2003), *The Decline of the Guru: The Academic Profession in Developing and Middle-income Countries*, New York: Palgrave.
Altbach, P. and J. Balán (eds) (2007), *World Class Worldwide: Transforming Research Universities in Asia and Latin America*, Baltimore, MD: Johns Hopkins University Press.

Ben-David, J. and A. Zloczower (1962), "Universities and Academic Systems in Modern Societies," *European Journal of Sociology*, 31 (3), 45–84.
Breneman, David, Brian Pusser and Sarah Turner (eds) (2006), *Earning from Learning: The Rise of For-Profit Universities*, Albany, NY: SUNY Press.
Brown, J. S. and P. Duguid (1996), 'Universities in the Digital Age,' *Change*, July–August, 11–19.
Cohen, A. and F. Brawer (1996), *The American Community College*, San Francisco: Jossey-Bass.
DeWit, Hans et al. (eds) (2008), *The Dynamics of International Student Circulation in a Global Context*, Rotterdam, the Netherlands: Sense Publishers.
Enders, J. (ed.) (2001), *Academic Staff in Europe: Changing Contexts and Conditions*, Westport, CT: Greenwood.
"Financing Higher Education: Innovation and Changes," (1998), *European Journal of Education*, 33, 5–130.
Geiger, R.L. (1986), *Private Sectors in Higher Education: Structure, Function and Change in Eight Countries*, Ann Arbor: University of Michigan Press.
Haas, J.E. (1996), "The American Academic Profession," in P. Altbach (ed.) *The International Academic Profession: Portraits from Fourteen Countries*, Princeton, NJ: Carnegie Foundation for the Advancement of Teaching, pp. 343–90.
Hirsch, W.Z. and L.E. Weber (2001), *Governance in Higher Education: the University in a State of Flux*, London: Economica.
Kerr, C. (1995), *The Uses of the University*, Cambridge: Harvard University Press.
Kuttner, R. (1997), *Everything for Sale: The Virtues and Limits of Markets*, New York: Knopf.
Mason, R. (1998), *Globalising Education: Trends and Applications*, London: Routledge.
Neave, G. and F. van Vught (eds) (1994), *Government and Higher Education Relationships Across Three Continents: The Winds of Change*, Oxford, UK: Pergamon.
Organisation for Economic Co-operation and Development (2008), *Higher Education to 2030, Vol. 1: Demography*, Paris: OECD.
Robins, K.R. and F. Webster, (eds) (2002), *The Virtual University?: Knowledge, Markets, and Management*, Oxford, UK: Oxford University Press.
Salmi, Jamil (2009), *The Challenge of Establishing World-Class Universities*, Washington, DC: The World Bank.
Shattock, Michael (2003), *Managing Successful Universities*, Buckingham, UK: Open University Press.
Shattock, Michael (ed.) (2009), *Entrepreneurialism in Universities and the Knowledge Economy: Diversification and Organizational Change in European Higher Education*, Maidenhead, UK: Open University Press.
Stearns, Peter (2009), *Educating Global Citizens in Colleges and Universities: Challenges and Opportunities*, New York: Routledge.
Stiglitz, J. (2002), *Globalization and its Discontents*, New York: Norton.
Task Force on Higher Education and Society (2000), *Higher Education in Developing Countries: Peril and Promise*, Washington, DC: The World Bank.
Trow, M. (2006), "Reflections on the Transition from Elite to Mass to Universal Access: Forms and Phases of Higher Education in Modern Societies since World War II," in James Forest and Philip Altbach (eds), *International Handbook of Higher Education*, Dordrecht, the Netherlands: Springer, pp. 243–81.

Van Dusen, G.C. (1997), *The Virtual University: Technology and Reform in Higher Education*, Washington, DC: Graduate School of Education, George Washington University.

World Bank (1994), *Higher Education: The Lessons of Experience*, Washington, DC: The World Bank.

Youn, T. and P. Murphy (eds) (1997), *Organizational Studies in Higher Education*, New York: Garland.

3. Higher education crossing borders: programs and providers on the move

Jane Knight

Internationalization is one of the major forces having a profound effect on higher education in the beginning decade of the 21st century. Internationalization is a multifaceted process aimed at integrating an international dimension into the purpose, goals, functions, and delivery of higher education. A key element of the internationalization process in universities is academic mobility/cross-border education. The fact that "universe" is fundamental to the concept of universities demonstrates the presence of the international dimension since their establishment as institutions of higher education and research. Furthermore, the mobility of students, scholars and knowledge has been a central feature of higher education for centuries. But, it is only during the last two decades that there has been an explosion of interest in education programs, universities and new commercial providers moving across national borders and education hubs have emerged as part of the new knowledge economy landscape.

Table 3.1 looks at the evolution of terms related to the international dimension of higher education over the past 60 years. It shows that even though the term "internationalization" has been used for years in political science and governmental relations, its popularity in the education sector has really only soared since the early 1980s. Prior to this time, "international education" and "international cooperation" were the favored terms, and they still are in some countries. In the 1990s the discussion centered on differentiating the term "international education" from "comparative education," "global education" and "multi-cultural education." Today, the emphasis is on cross-border, transnational and borderless education with education hubs, cities and gateways as the latest developments.

Table 3.1 Evolution of international education terminology

Terms popular since the mid 1990s	Terms used since the early 1980s	Terms used since the 1950s
Generic terms		
globalization	internationalization	international education
borderless education	multi-cultural education	international development cooperation
cross-border education	intercultural education	
transnational education	global education	comparative education
virtual education	distance education	correspondence education
educational hubs, cities, gateways	offshore or overseas education	
internationalization 'abroad'		
internationalization 'at home'		
Specific elements		
education providers	international students	foreign students
corporate universities	study abroad	student exchange
liberalization of educational services	institution agreements	development projects
networks	partnership projects	cultural agreements
virtual universities	area studies	language study
branch campus	double/joint degrees	
twinning and franchise programs		
Global Education Index (GEI)		

Source: Knight 2005, updated 2008.

INCREASED DEMAND FOR HIGHER EDUCATION AND THE CROSS-BORDER RESPONSE

In most countries, especially those in transition, the demand for post-secondary education, including professionally related courses, is increasing. This is due to changing demographics, a greater number of secondary school graduates, the movement to lifelong learning, and most importantly, the growth of the knowledge economy and the need for skilled workers. While demand for higher education is growing, the capacity of the public sector to satisfy this need is challenged. As a result, alternative ways to provide education are emerging. These include new developments in cross-border education activities, more private and commercial education/training providers, a greater emphasis on distance education and the development of education hubs (Knight, 2008.)

The Global Student Mobility 2025 Report (Bohm et al., 2002) predicts that the demand for international education will increase from 1.8 million international students in 2000 to 7.2 million in 2025. The Ministry of Industry and Trade in Singapore reports that education is a 2.2 trillion dollar business (MTI, 2004.) These are staggering figures and help to explain and forecast the growth in worldwide academic mobility. It is highly questionable whether this demand can be met solely through student mobility, and thus the numbers and types of education providers and programs being delivered across borders will need to grow.

A fascinating but very complex world of cross-border education is emerging. The last few years have been a hotbed of innovation and new developments. For instance, Phoenix University has become the largest private university in the United States (owned and operated by the Apollo Group) and is now present or delivering courses in Mexico, Canada, Chile, Puerto Rico and the Netherlands. Another Apollo company, Western International University, offers courses in India and China. The Netherlands Business School (Universitiet Nijenrode) has recently opened a branch campus in Nigeria, and Harvard is active in the Dubai Health Care City in the United Arab Emirates. Furthermore, Jinan University will be the first Chinese university to open a branch campus outside China, with Thailand as the projected location. Laureate Education (formerly Sylvan Learning Systems) has purchased all or part of private higher education institutions in Chile, Mexico, Panama and Costa Rica and owns universities in Malaysia, China, Australia, Germany, Peru, Ecuador, Brazil, Honduras, Spain, Switzerland, and France. Dubai is home to two new developments – the "Knowledge Village" and "International Education City." Both are economic free zones and have attracted universities from India, Australia, Canada, Ireland, Iran, Pakistan, Russia, the United States and the United Kingdom. They are offering courses through franchising agreements and branch campuses and are co-located with private research, development and training companies. Columbia University has been active in Jordan since 2005 and is planning to open a branch campus. Qatar has developed an Education City and has invited (and paid for) foreign universities to establish undergraduate and graduate level programs. To date, Virginia Commonwealth University, Weill Cornell Medical College, Texas A&M University, Carnegie Mellon University, Georgetown University School of Foreign Service, and Northwestern University are operational there. New York University in

Abu Dhabi will begin operations in 2010 and will consist of a liberal arts college, graduate programs, and a center for advanced research and scholarship, all of which will be fully integrated with NYU in New York.

But setting up these branch campuses is not without its challenges and failures. Johns Hopkins' Bio-Medical Research Facility and the University of New South Wales have both pulled their operations out of Singapore's Global Schoolhouse initiative, and after three years of offering programs George Mason University has closed its full degree granting campus in the United Arab Emirates without producing a single graduate. These are only a few examples of hundreds of new initiatives that have developed in the last ten years (Verbik and Merkley, 2006.) They involve higher education providers (including institutions and companies) delivering their programs to students in their home countries and in third countries through twinning, franchising, branch campuses, and joint/double degree programs and in new second generation cross-border developments such as education cities, hubs and gateways. We have now entered a new era of cross-border education driven by the knowledge society, ICTs, and the market economy.

The purpose of this chapter is to delve into some of the trends, issues, challenges, and implications of these new developments in order to better understand cross-border education itself. The primary focus here is on the movement of education programs and providers across borders, not the mobility of students. The emphasis is on higher education; however, many of the issues and challenges apply to other levels. It is important to recognize that cross-border education raises many different issues depending on whether one is a receiving (host) country or a sending (source) country; this chapter addresses both perspectives and thus is not limited to North American initiatives or issues.

THE TERMINOLOGY OF INTERNATIONAL EDUCATION

It is important to be clear about terminology used in this discussion. As indicated in Table 3.1, the growing interest in the delivery of higher education has spawned an increase in the number of terms used to describe the new developments. The following provides a description of relevant terms.

Globalization is described as a process that is increasing the flow of people, culture, ideas, values, knowledge, technology, and economy across borders, resulting in a more interconnected and interdependent world. Globalization is multifaceted and not limited to economic forms as is too often assumed. The impact of globalization is neither neutral nor uniform as it affects each country in a different way. It can have positive and/or negative consequences, according to a nation's individual history, traditions, culture, priorities and resources. Education is one of the sectors impacted by globalization and the growth in cross-border education is seen as one of the direct results of globalization (Knight, 2006a.)

Internationalization of higher education is also a process, albeit a different process than globalization. Internationalization of higher education is described as "the process of integrating an international, intercultural, and global dimension into the purpose, functions (teaching, research, service) and the delivery of higher education" (Knight, 2004.) The concept of "nation," in terms of people, cultures, systems, is central to this term, thus distinguishing it from globalization, which has the "world" as its focus.

Internationalization strategies refer to campus-based activities and cross-border initiatives and can include:

- international development projects;
- institutional agreements and networks;
- the international/intercultural dimension of the teaching/learning process, curriculum, and research;
- campus-based extracurricular clubs and activities;
- mobility of academics through exchange, field work, sabbaticals and consultancy work;
- recruitment of international students;
- student exchange programs and semesters abroad;
- joint/double degree programs;
- twinning partnerships, branch campuses.

Cross-border education refers to the movement of people, knowledge, programs, providers, ideas, curricula, projects, research and services across national or regional jurisdictional borders. Cross-border education is a subset of internationalization and can be part of development cooperation projects, academic exchange programs and commercial initiatives. Cross-border is a term that is often used interchangeably with other terms such as transnational (Davis et al., 2000), offshore, and borderless (CVCP, 2000) education. While there are some conceptual differences among these terms, they usually refer to similar types of activities – franchise, branch campus, virtual university, double/joint degree.

Trade in education services is a term used by both the trade and education sectors, but primarily the former. It focuses on those cross-border education initiatives that are commercial in nature and are usually intended to be for-profit in nature, though this is not always the case. This term coincides with the advent of the General Agreement on Trade in Services (GATS), which includes the education sector as a tradable service.

Education provider is now used as a more common and inclusive term, encompassing both traditional higher education institutions and for-profit organizations and companies. Traditional higher education institutions are no longer the only international deliverers of academic courses and programs. International conglomerates, media and information technology companies, and new partnerships of private and public bodies are increasingly engaged in the provision of education both domestically and internationally. Therefore, this chapter uses the term "providers" to mean all types of entities that are offering education programs and services abroad.

CROSS-BORDER EDUCATION: A FRAMEWORK AND TYPOLOGIES

Cross-border education refers to the movement of people, programs, providers, knowledge, ideas, projects, values, curriculum, policy, and services across national boundaries. Table 3.2 provides a framework for understanding the nature of cross-border education and illustrates two significant trends. The first trend is the vertical shift downward from student mobility to program and provider mobility. It is important to note that the number of students seeking education in foreign countries in still increasing; however, more attention is currently being given to the cross-border delivery of foreign academic courses and programs. The second shift is from left to right, signifying substantial change in orientation from development cooperation to competitive commerce, or in other words, from aid to trade.

A more detailed explanation of the framework provides further insight into some of the complexities and new challenges characterizing cross-border education. One of the first questions to ask is: What are the defining factors/principles for an analytical framework of cross-border education? Many come to mind: What elements of education move? How does the movement occur? Why does education move? Where is this movement happening? Who is funding it? Who is awarding the qualification? Who is regulating it? Given the changing nature of the rationales driving cross-border education, the worldwide scope of delivery, and the new modes of provision, the notions of "why, how, and where" can be eliminated as the defining factors. Rather, the crucial category is "what" moves across borders. Four categories are suggested: people, programs, providers, and projects/services.

Table 3.2 Framework for cross-border education types of mobility

Category	Forms and conditions of mobility		
	Development cooperation →	Educational linkages →	Commercial trade →
People Students Professors/scholars Researchers/ Experts/consultants	↓	Semester/year abroad Full degrees Field/research work Internships Sabbaticals Consulting	
Programs Course Program Sub-degree or degree Postgraduate	↓	Twinning Franchised Articulated/validated Joint/double award Online/distance	
Providers Institutions Organizations Companies	↓	Branch campus Virtual university Merger/acquisition Independent institutions	
Projects Academic projects Services	↓	Research Curriculum Capacity building Educational services	

Source: Knight (2005).

People The first category covers the movement of people, whether they are students or professors/scholars/experts. Students are mobile in a number of ways. They can take whole degrees in another country, participate in a study abroad exchange program, undertake field work or an internship, register for a semester/year abroad program, and so on. The funding for such cross-border education can be through exchange agreements, scholarships from government, public or private sources, or self-funding. Professors/scholars and experts can be involved in teaching and research activities, technical assistance and consulting assignments, sabbaticals, seminars, and other professional activities. These types of initiatives can be self- or institution-funded, be based on exchange agreements, involve contracts and fee for service, or be supported by public and private funding.

Programs The program, not the student, moves in this category. The delivery of the program is often done through a partnership arrangement between international/foreign and domestic providers or can be an independent initiative by a foreign provider. The programs can be delivered by distance, face-to-face, or mixed mode. Franchising, twinning, and new forms of articulation and validation arrangements are the most common. In some cases, the program and qualification awarded is provided by the source country institution/provider, but the teaching and support is done in part or totally by a local institution/provider. In other cases, the foreign provider takes complete responsibility for delivering the academic program but may have a local business partner investing in the operation. Distance delivery of a program involves yet another set of circumstances.

Providers The key factor in this category is that the institution/provider moves to have physical or virtual presence in the receiving/host country. The student does not move to the provider; rather, the provider moves to serve the student. The movement of a provider can involve a more substantial range of programs and academic/administrative support services – for example, by establishing a satellite campus or even a full institution. In other scenarios, the provider moves by purchasing/merging with a local institution. Virtual universities are yet another example of the provider moving across borders through distance delivery of selected programs. The providers can include private and public, for-profit or non-profit, educational institutions, organizations, and companies. Recognized bona fide institutions/providers and non-recognized rogue providers are both included in this category.

Projects/services A wide range of education-related projects and services needs to be considered when analyzing cross-border education. Such activities include a diversity of initiatives such as joint curriculum development, research, benchmarking, technical assistance, e-learning platforms, professional development, and other capacity-building initiatives, especially in the area of information technology. The projects and services could be undertaken as part of development aid projects, academic linkages, or commercial contracts.

THE GROWTH OF CROSS-BORDER PROVIDERS

The increase in worldwide demand for higher education has resulted in a diversity of providers delivering education across borders. The providers are classified into two categories: (1) the traditional higher education institutions (HEIs), who are normally oriented to teaching, research and service/commitment to society, and (2) the new or alternative providers, who primarily focus on teaching and the delivery of education services.

Traditional higher education institutions include public non-profit, private non-profit and private for-profit institutions. Many countries have a mixed system of publicly and privately funded HEIs. There is a definite blurring of the boundary between public and private institutions as public universities are now finding it necessary to seek private financing and are charging a tuition or service fee. On the other hand, in many countries private institutions are eligible for public funds and engage in social non-profit activities.

One important factor is whether the HEI is part of a home national education system and recognized by a national bona fide licensing/accrediting body. In cross-border education recognition/registration is critical to ensuring the legitimacy of the institution and the qualifications provided. The majority of traditional universities are bona fide institutions that comply with domestic and foreign regulations (where they exist.) But, there is also an increase in rogue or low-quality providers who are not recognized by bona fide accreditation/licensing bodies in either the sending or receiving countries. "Rogue providers" are often accredited by self-accrediting groups or by agencies that sell accreditation (accreditation mills.) In addition, there is a worrisome increase in the number of "degree mills" operating around the world (Garrett, 2005.) These are often no more than web-based companies selling certificates based on "life experiences" and they do not deliver any education programs at all.

New or alternative providers are diverse in nature, but are typically described as companies or organizations that provide education programs and/or services for profit purposes. They are more oriented to delivering education and training programs than undertaking research and scholarly activities. These new providers include media companies such as Pearson (UK) and Thomson (Canada); multinational companies such as De Vry (US), Informatics (Singapore), and Aptech (India); corporate universities such as those run by Motorola and Toyota; and networks of universities, professional associations and organizations. Together they make for a fascinating array of entities involved in the new arena of cross-border education. These new types of cross-border providers can be bricks and mortar institutions or virtual universities and can complement or compete, collaborate or simply co-exist with domestic higher education providers (and other cross-border providers.) They can be located as single entities in a country or co-located in new educational hubs and cities.

The number of new actors involved in the promotion, provision, and now regulation of cross-border education is increasing exponentially.

Whether one is supportive or critical of the change, the reality is that the education sector in many countries is becoming a competitive and dynamic marketplace for both local and foreign providers.

TOWARDS A TYPOLOGY FOR PROGRAM AND PROVIDER MOBILITY

Cross-border program mobility is defined as "the movement of individual education/training courses and programs across national borders through face-to-face, distance, or a combination of these modes. Credits toward a qualification can be awarded by the sending foreign country provider or by an affiliated domestic partner or jointly" (Knight, 2005.) Table 3.3 provides a description of the six major forms of program mobility.

Table 3.3   Typology of cross-border program mobility

Category	Description
Franchise	An arrangement whereby a provider in source country A authorizes a provider in another country B to deliver its course/program/service in country B or other countries. The qualification is awarded by provider in country A.
Twinning	A situation whereby a provider in source country A collaborates with a provider located in country B to develop an articulation system allowing students to take course credits in country B and/or source country A. Only one qualification is awarded by provider in source country A.
Double/joint degree	An arrangement whereby providers in different countries collaborate to offer a program for which a student receives a qualification from each provider or a joint award from the collaborating providers.
Articulation	Various types of articulation arrangements between providers in different countries permit students to gain credit for courses/ programs offered/delivered by collaborating providers.
Validation	Validation arrangements between providers in different countries allow provider B in receiving country to award the qualification of provider A in source country.
Virtual/ distance	Arrangements where providers deliver courses/programs to students in different countries through distance and online modes. May include some face-to-face support for students through domestic study or support centers.

Source: Knight (2005).

It is clear that a key factor in program mobility is who awards the course credits or ultimate credential for the program. As the movement of programs proliferates, there will undoubtedly be further changes to national, regional, and even international regulatory frameworks. The question of "who grants the credits/awards?" will be augmented by "who recognizes the provider?" and whether the program has been accredited or quality assured by a bona fide body. Of critical importance is whether the qualification is recognized for employment or further study in the receiving country and in other countries as well. The perceived legitimacy, recognition, and ultimate mobility of the qualification are fundamental issues yet to be resolved.

Given that several modes for program mobility involve partnerships, a crucial question is: who owns the intellectual property rights to course design and materials? What are the legal and moral roles and responsibilities of the participating partners in terms of academic, staffing, recruitment, evaluation, financial, and administrative matters? While the movement of programs across borders has been taking place for many years, it is clear that the new types of providers, partnerships, awards, and delivery modes are challenging national and international policies and regulatory frameworks and that there are more questions than answers at present.

Cross-border provider mobility is described in this typology as "the physical or virtual movement of an education provider across a national border to establish a presence to provide education/training programs and/or services to students and other clients" (Knight, 2005.) The difference between program and provider mobility is one of scope and volume in terms of programs/services offered and the local presence (and investment) by the foreign provider. Credits and qualifications are awarded by the foreign provider (through foreign, local, or self-accreditation methods), by an affiliated domestic partner, or jointly. Table 3.4 provides a description of the six major forms of provider mobility.

The virtual and physical movement of providers to other countries raises many of the same registration, quality assurance, and recognition issues of program mobility. But it also involves extra considerations, especially if a network or local/foreign partnerships are involved. Setting up a physical presence requires paying attention to national regulations regarding status of the entity, total or joint ownership with local bodies, tax laws, for-profit or non-profit status, repatriation of earned income, boards of directors, staffing, granting of qualifications, selection of academic programs and courses, and so on. Trade rules often impact provider mobility and so, for some countries, it means that strict regulations are being developed to closely monitor and, in some cases, restrict new providers coming into the country. In other instances, incentives are being offered to

Table 3.4 Typology of cross-border provider mobility

Category	Description	Examples
Branch campus	Provider in country A establishes a satellite campus in country B to deliver courses and programs to students in country B (may also include country A students taking a semester/courses abroad.) The qualification awarded is from provider in country A.	Monash University from Australia has established branch campuses in Malaysia and South Africa. University of Indianapolis has a branch campus in Athens.
Independent Institution	Foreign provider A (a traditional university, a commercial company or alliance/network) establishes in country B a stand-alone HEI to offer courses/programs and awards.	The German University in Cairo, Phoenix Universities in Canada, and Puerto Rico (Apollo Group)
Acquisition/ merger	Foreign provider A purchases a part of or 100% of local HEI in country B.	Laureate Education (formerly Sylvan Learning Systems) has merged with and/or purchased local HEIs in Chile, Mexico, and other LA countries.
Study center/ teaching site	Foreign provider A establishes study centers in country B to support students taking their courses/programs. Study centers can be independent or in collaboration with local providers in country B.	Texas A&M has a "university center" in Mexico City. Troy University (USA) has an MBA teaching site in Bangkok.
Affiliation/ networks	Different types of "public and private," "traditional and new" providers from various countries collaborate through innovative types of partnerships to establish networks/institutions to deliver courses and programs in local and foreign countries through distance or face-to-face modes.	Partnership between the Caparo Group and Carnegie Mellon University to establish campus in India. Netherlands Business School branch campus in Nigeria in partnership with African Leadership Forum (NGO)
Virtual university	Provider that delivers credit courses and degree programs to students in different countries through distance education modes and that generally does not have face-to-face support services for students	International Virtual University, Hibernia College, Arab Open University

Source: Knight (2005).

attract high-quality institutions/providers to set up a teaching site or full campus. This is especially true when knowledge parks, technology zones, or "education hubs" are being developed to attract foreign companies and education/training providers (Knight, 2006a.)

RATIONALES AND IMPACTS OF CROSS-BORDER HIGHER EDUCATION

An examination of the rationales and impacts related to the increase in cross-border education requires a 360-degree view of the issues. Such an overview involves giving serious consideration to the diverse and often contradictory perspectives and expectations that different groups of stakeholders may have in both receiving and sending countries. This is not a straightforward or linear task of analysis. Rather, the viewpoints differ drastically according to whether the perspective is that of a student, a provider, a governmental or nongovernmental body, and whether the perspective is that of the exporting or importing country. In short, the analysis of rationales and impacts can be complicated.

Rationales at the National/country Level

Perhaps the best place to start is to look at the more macro-level rationales that are driving internationalization in general and determine which are appropriately applied to cross-border education. Traditionally, the rationales for internationalization have been presented in four groups: social/cultural, political, academic, and economic (Knight and de Wit, 1997.) In the past several years, much has been written about changes in rationales both within and between this classification of rationales (Altbach and Knight, 2007; De Wit, 2002.) These generic categories remain a useful way to analyze rationales; however, globalization has contributed to the blurring of the boundaries. It has therefore been necessary and useful to identify cross-cutting meta-rationales at both the country and the institutional/provider level. The rationales for internationalization at the national/system level (Knight, 2004) are several:

Human resources development/brain power/skilled labour The knowledge economy, demographic shifts, mobility of the labor force and increased trade in services are factors driving nations to place more importance on developing and recruiting human capital or brain power through international education initiatives. In general, there is a positive stance toward what is being called brain train, where international students and researchers are increasingly interested in taking a degree in country A, followed by a second degree or perhaps internship in country B, leading to employment in country C and probably D, finally returning to their home country after 8 to 12 years of international study and work experience. However, this phenomenon affects small and large, developed and developing countries in different ways as it is often the larger and more developed countries that capture brain gain, while smaller, less developed nations at the bottom of the brain chain experience more brain drain. Therefore, for some countries an increased brain drain is a genuine risk attached to student mobility, especially when international student recruitment policies are linked to aggressive immigration policies. Smaller countries, on the receiving end, see cross-border education as an effective means to lessen the chances of their tertiary education graduates staying abroad after finishing their studies or, in the case of education hubs, recruiting students from the region and retaining them as skilled labor.

Strategic alliances The international mobility of students, academics, and programs, as well as collaborative research and education initiatives, are also seen as productive ways to develop closer geo-political ties and economic relationships among countries. Over the past ten years, there has been a definite shift from alliances for cultural purposes to those for economic purposes. The development of strategic alliances is attractive to both sending and receiving countries and providers and is rapidly expanding within larger frameworks of regional harmonization of higher education systems and economies.

Income generation/commercial trade For sending countries there is a strong motivation to use cross-border education as a means of generating income from fee-based education programs and services. More emphasis is now being placed on economic and income-generating opportunities. New franchise arrangements, foreign or satellite campuses, on-line delivery, and the increased recruitment of fee-paying students are examples of a more commercial approach to internationalization. The fact that education is now one of the 12 service sectors in the General Agreement on Trade in Services is positive proof that importing and exporting education programs and services is a potentially lucrative trade area.

Nation building/capacity building While some countries are interested in exporting education to generate income, other countries are interested in importing education programs and institutions for nation-building purposes – especially for the knowledge economy. The fact that the increased demand for education cannot always be met by domestic capacity makes importing foreign programs and providers an attractive option. It is a way to increase access to education and to augment/improve national capacity.

Socio-cultural development There are mixed views and sometimes conflicting opinions related to socio-cultural rationales. On the one hand, there is the belief that national identity and indigenous customs can be maintained by having students stay in the home country while studying for a foreign qualification. A contrasting view questions how relevant and culturally appropriate course content and teaching/learning processes are when imported from other countries. A third opinion emphasizes the advantages to students who live and study in a country and culture different than their own. Such an experience opens their eyes and increases their international understanding and cross-cultural skills while at the same time they learn how their own country relates to the rest of the world. These kinds of experiences and insights are difficult to replicate in virtual or cross-border provision.

A report from the OECD's Centre for Education Research and Innovation is entitled *Internationalisation and Trade in Higher Education: Opportunities and Challenges* (OECD, 2004.) It provides case studies on the cross-border mobility of students, programs, and providers in North America, Europe, and the Asia-Pacific region. Four rationales for cross-border education are presented and analyzed: mutual understanding, skilled immigration, revenue generation, and capacity building. This is another helpful approach to examining rationales of cross-border education, especially those of the sending or exporting countries.

Rationales at the Level of Students and Providers/institutions

As already mentioned, it is important to examine the rationales and anticipated impacts from the viewpoint of students enrolled in cross-border courses/programs and from that of the institutions/providers involved in delivering the education. Table 3.5 presents some differing perspectives on several key factors.

HIGHER EDUCATION HUBS AND CITIES

Countries, propeled by the need to establish a firm footing in the knowledge economy, are racing to create second generation cross-border education strategies – regional education hubs, economic free zones, education

Table 3.5 *Different perspectives on rationales and impacts of program and provider mobility*

Rationales and Impacts	Enrolled students in home[a] country	Institution/provider in source[b] country	Institution/provider in home country
Increased access/ supply in home country	Ability to gain foreign qualification without leaving home. Can continue to meet family and work commitments	Attracted to unmet need for higher education and training	Competition, collaboration or co-existence with foreign providers
Cost/income	Less expensive to take program at home without travel or accommodation costs. Tuition fees from quality foreign providers may be too high for majority of students	Strong imperative to generate a profit for cross-border operations. Fees could be high for receiving country	Varied rationales and impacts depending on whether institution/provider is competing or cooperating with foreign providers
Selection of courses/ programs	Increased access to courses/programs in high demand by labour market	Tendency to offer high-demand courses which require little infrastructure or investment	Need to offer broad selection of courses which may not have high enrolments and/or have major lab or equipment requirements
Language/ cultural and safety aspects	Can have access to courses in foreign and/or indigenous language. Remain in familiar cultural and linguistic environment. Post-9/11 students have stronger concerns about safety and security	Language of instruction and relevance of curriculum to host[b] country important issues. If foreign language used, additional academic and linguistic support may be needed	

Table 3.5 (continued)

Rationales and Impacts	Enrolled students in home[a] country	Institution/provider in source[b] country	Institution/provider in home country
Quality	Can be exposed to higher or lower quality course provision	Depending on delivery mode, quality may be at risk. Assurance of relevant and high-quality courses may require significant investment	Presence of foreign providers may be a catalyst for innovation and improvement of quality in courses, management and governance
Recognition of qualification	Foreign qualification has to be recognized for academic and employment purposes	May be difficult for academic award and for institution to be recognized in foreign country	Recognized home providers have an advantage and are attractive to foreign providers for award-granting powers
Reputation and profile	Due to massive marketing campaigns, international profile is often mistakenly equated with quality of provider/program	Profile and visibility are key factors for high enrollments and strategic alliances	Home (domestic) providers are challenged to distinguish between those providers with high/low profile and high/low quality

Notes:
[a] Home country = sending country.
[b] Source or host country = receiving country.

Source: Knight (2007).

cities, knowledge villages, gateways, and hot spots. While these initiatives include familiar cross-border strategies such as branch campuses and franchise programs, they are of another magnitude as they try to co-locate foreign universities with private companies, research and development enterprises, and science and technology parks to collectively support and develop new knowledge industries. The branch universities in education hubs play a pivotal role in developing a skilled work force by attracting and educating local and regional students (Mok, 2008.)

It is revealing to read newspaper headlines in Hong Kong, Dubai,

Bahrain, Singapore, Botswana and Seoul to name a few, announcing major new investments in establishing regional education hubs or education cities. Higher education is a key economic and political actor critical to countries wanting a leadership position in the new knowledge economy and a geo-political footprint in the marked trend towards regionalization. It is a new era when one sees higher education as an anchor for positioning a country's economic and technological competitiveness in its region and beyond. The diversity of rationales, partnerships, strategies, financing, and policy frameworks for establishing regional education hubs demonstrates that each country adopts an approach consistent with its national/regional context. But, the common factor among all is the need to prepare and maintain a skilled work force for engaging in the knowledge economy and service sector.

There is no lack of new terms to describe an education hub. Each country, in fact each sponsor, chooses different concepts to brand its initiative. Current terms include education hot spot, gateway, hub, cluster, free economic zone, global schoolhouse, world city, knowledge village, international academic city, university town, and the list goes on. An analysis of the terms reveals that, except for "higher education free economic zone," the terms are more oriented to carving out a marketing niche than indicating a particular economic or academic approach. In fact, the diverse use of terms can lead to major confusion. For instance, "education city" is a preferred term but is used in starkly different ways. Bahrain Education City refers to a complex of buildings, recreation and commercial facilities, laboratories and residential areas (BEDB, 2008), while Hong Kong Education City is an internet-based portal for teachers, students, parents and the community. A term that has not been used for obvious reasons is "education marketplace" – but it might be the most accurate description for many of the hub models.

Two regions of the world, the Middle East (United Arab Emirates, Qatar and Bahrain) and Asia (Singapore, Hong Kong, Malaysia and South Korea), are actively involved with the business of establishing these second generation cross-border initiatives, albeit in different ways. Worth noting is that all are relatively small countries trying to develop a niche in the knowledge economy. The establishment of international education cities and regional education hubs is new territory for the higher education sector. That being said, it is important to recognize that it is not always the higher education sector that is sponsoring these new education initiatives. Economic development boards, tourism authorities, science and technology parks, and multinational investment companies see higher education institutions/providers as key players and partners in these new initiatives. In many cases, branch campuses of foreign institutions are seen as tenants in huge multifaceted complexes just like any other commercial enterprise. Universities, in partnership with the private sector, are seen to play a pivotal role in the preparation of future knowledge workers and the production of new knowledge.

The hub model is an approach being used by other sectors as well. In fact, it may be justified to say that hubs (transportation, innovation, education, health, finance, trade, fashion, and so on) are the current flavour of the month, making the question of sustainability very relevant. Even though the success and sustainability of these new developments are yet to be determined, it is important to analyze the motivating factors and the implications, especially in relation to the quality of the education and the recognition of the qualifications.

Diversity of Rationales and Expectations for Education Hubs

The first question to ask is what is driving these new second generation cross-border schemes and who benefits? The immediate answer is that it depends on the national agenda and the sponsoring entity as the rationales and intended outcomes are many and diverse. A government-led initiative, such as in Hong Kong, uses a different policy framework and set of rationales than a Free Economic Zone Authority in Korea. And an international investment company in the United Arab Emirates has different intentions and expectations than a social/cultural/educational not-for-profit organization such as the Qatar Foundation.

Nevertheless, a common driver for all initiatives is the need to prepare a skilled job-ready workforce to be competitive in the knowledge economy. This appears to be the number one priority and is particularly true for nations with limited natural resources or a weak manufacturing sector such as Singapore. In terms of education benefits, broader course offering and access to foreign expertise in pedagogy and research are often cited, but usually less so than economic and human capital motives. The traditional internationalization benefits such as increased international knowledge and intercultural skills for faculty and students, and enhanced quality, are seldom stated – Hong Kong being an exception. Overall, economic, immigration, and employment reasons are cited more often than social, cultural and education ones. This is a sign of the times and a trend worthy of closer scrutiny (Knight, 2006a.)

Table 3.6 presents the rationales and expectations of education hubs/cities for three different stakeholder groups – students, foreign institutions/providers and the host government or sponsor. It is revealing to see the areas of overlap and divergence. The major point of convergence is an increase in skilled labor and further opportunities for employment.

Table 3.6 *Rationales and expectations of different stakeholder groups*

Stakeholder group	Rationales and expectations
Student (local and international)	Access to higher and further education opportunities Foreign academic credential Specialized program not offered domestically Employment and career path International outlook
Foreign institutions and providers	Status-building and increased competitiveness Income generation New research partnerships with private and public bodies Recruit faculty and students for home campus Contribute to capacity building efforts in host country
Sponsor and host government	Prepare and recruit skilled work force Support knowledge-based industries Attract foreign direct investment Establish geo-political status and soft power in region Modernize domestic higher education sector

Source: Knight (2009).

The push and pull of attracting world class institutions to a regional hub or free zone is a struggle that many countries are facing. Economic incentives, high-level diplomatic negotiations between national leaders, or conversely back door arrangements, all characterize the deal making involved in attracting foreign institutions and providers. Brand recognition and world rankings are current trends (sometimes called an obsession) both motivating and influencing the development of new hubs and education cities. In fact, having one or two prestigious institutions from the US or UK as an anchor, or so-called "big name," is becoming a prerequisite. Attracting a foreign university as a "prize collectable" is a new and more prevalent phenomenon that one could not have imagined just two decades ago.

World-class universities are still in the eye of the beholder in spite of all the attention being given to rankings. The presence of national, regional, international and discipline/profession-specific rankings allows universities of all types to be deemed "prestigious" by some self-appointed ranking body whether it be a magazine, newspaper, consumer guide, university, or private company. While certain ranking systems are more respected than others, criticisms of methodology, allegations of language and discipline biases, and the self-interest of sponsors put the validity and reliability of rankings at risk. Yet, in spite of these criticisms and the acknowledged bias of the ranking game, efforts to recruit world-class institutions by the owners/promoters of education hubs continue to accelerate.

EMERGING ISSUES AND CHALLENGES

Brain Drain/Gain

The increase in cross-border movement of scholars, experts and teachers/ professors is due in part to the increasing competitiveness for human capital in the knowledge economy. Not only is there a trend for higher education personnel to move from country to country, they are also attracted to the corporate sector where benefits can be more attractive than in the education sector. The higher education sector is affected by this mobility both positively and negatively, depending on whether a country is experiencing a net brain drain or gain. There are implications for education policies but also for immigration, science and technology, trade, employment and foreign relations. There are also direct links between foreign student recruitment/mobility and the immigration needs for skilled labor of the recruiting country or region, as illustrated with education hubs. Thus, the complex and increasingly inter-related dynamics between national policies for international education, migration policies and nation building/human capacity building efforts are areas worthy of serious investigation.

The General Agreement on Trade in Services (GATS) and Higher Education

GATS has been a wake-up call for higher education leaders around the world. Higher education has traditionally been seen as a public good and social commitment. But with the advent of new international trade agreements, higher education has also become a tradable commodity or more precisely, in terms of GATS, an internationally tradable service. GATS is often seen as the catalyst for the increased growth in commercial higher education between countries. Many educators would argue that GATS is responsible for these new developments. But, others would contend that the opposite is true by pointing out that increased for-profit education at national and international levels has actually led to education becoming a multi-billion dollar business and thus a profitable sector to be covered in trade agreements (Knight, 2006a.) Academic mobility (students, programs, providers) is regarded by many as a huge commercial business and is expected to increase exponentially as the demand for higher and continuing education escalates (Larsen et al., 2004.) GATS has been seen by many as presenting new opportunities and benefits, and by others as introducing new risks. Thus, while international academic mobility is not new, the presence of international trade law to regulate it is new and is causing controversial debates within the higher education community.

Student Access

Demographic changes, lifelong learning, changing human resource needs created by the knowledge economy, as well as growing numbers of graduates from secondary level education are increasing the unmet demand for post-secondary education and training. Does cross-border education help countries satisfy this growing demand for further education? Many would answer "yes" and that increased access for students is a driving motivation for all forms of cross-border education. But there remains the issue regarding the equity of access and whether it will be available only to those who can afford it or have the necessary linguistic skills – usually English. No precise data exist on the rate of participation of students in cross-border programs or provider mobility at the national or international level. Only a few countries such as Australia, Hong Kong, the United Kingdom, Singapore, and Malaysia collect reliable data on enrollments in cross-border education programs. This is an area requiring further national and international attention, as without solid data it is challenging to develop appropriate policy and regulatory frameworks.

Quality Assurance of Cross-border Education

It must be noted that, in the last decade, increased importance has been given to quality assurance at the institutional and national levels. New regional quality networks have also been established. The primary task of these groups has been quality recognition and assurance of domestic higher education provision by public and private higher education institutions. However, the increase in cross-border education by institutions and new private commercial providers has introduced a new challenge (and gap) in the field of quality assurance. Historically, national quality assurance agencies have generally not focused their efforts on assessing the quality of imported and exported programs, with some notable exceptions. The question now facing the sector is how to deal with the increase in cross-border education by traditional higher education institutions

(HEIs) and the new private commercial providers who are not normally part of nationally based quality assurance schemes (Knight, 2006b.)

It is probable that sectors in addition to education will be interested in developing international quality standards and procedures for cross-border education. This is especially true for education hubs which are owned and managed by investment companies or economic boards. ISO standards and other industry-based mechanisms such as the Baldridge Awards are examples of quality systems that might be applied or modeled for cross-border education. The education sector has mixed views on the appropriateness of quality standards being established for education by those outside the sector. At the same time, there are divergent opinions on the desirability and value of any international standards for quality assurance as this might jeopardize the sovereignty of national level systems or contribute to standardization – not necessarily the improvement of quality standards.

It is also important to acknowledge that a great deal of cross-border mobility of students, teachers and programs occurs through non-profit initiatives such as academic partnerships and development cooperation. Therefore, commercial trade of education services is not the only factor driving the urgency of addressing international quality recognition and assurance. It is important to clarify that GATS and any other bilateral trade agreements do not claim to be establishing rules for quality assurance and recognition of education but they are important catalysts for more urgent attention being given to the issues at hand (Neilson, 2004.)

New Developments in Accreditation

The increased awareness of the need for quality assurance and/or accreditation has led to several new developments in accreditation, some of which are helping the task of domestic and international recognition of qualifications, and some of which are only serving to hinder and complicate matters. First, it is important to acknowledge the efforts of many countries to establish criteria and procedures for quality assurance recognition systems and the approval of bona fide accreditors. At the same time, it is necessary to recognize the increase in self-appointed and rather self-serving accreditors, as well as accreditation mills that simply sell "bogus" accreditation labels.

Market forces are making the profile and reputation of an institution/provider and its courses more and more important. Major investments are being made in marketing and branding campaigns in order to get name recognition and to increase enrollments. The possession of some type of accreditation is part of the campaign and assures prospective students that the programs/awards are of high standing. The desire for accreditation status is leading to a commercialization of quality assurance/accreditation as programs and providers strive to gain as many "accreditation" stars as possible in order to increase competitiveness and perceived international legitimacy. The challenge is how to distinguish between bona fide and rogue accreditors, especially when neither the cross-border provider nor the accreditor are nationally based or recognized as part of a national higher education system.

At the same time, there are networks of institutions and new organizations that are self-appointed and engage in accreditation of their members. These are positive developments when seen through the lens of trying to improve the quality of the academic offer. However, there is concern that they are not totally objective in their assessments and may be more interested in generating income than improving quality. While this can apply to both cross-border and domestic provision, it is particularly worrisome for cross-border provision as attention to national policy objectives and cultural orientation is often neglected.

Another development that is worrisome is the growth in accreditation mills. These organizations are not recognized or legitimate bodies and they more or less "sell" accreditation status without any independent assessment. They are similar to degree mills that sell certificates and degrees with little or no course work. Different education stakeholders, especially the students, employers and the public, need to be aware of these accreditation (and degree) mills which are often no more than a web address and are therefore out of the jurisdiction of national regulatory systems (UNESCO/OECD, 2005.)

Recognition of Qualifications

Increased academic mobility raises the issue of credential recognition to a more prominent place in international education policy. The credibility of higher education programs and qualifications is extremely important for students, their employers, the public at large and, of course, the academic community itself. It is critical that the qualifications awarded by cross-border providers are legitimate and will be recognized for employment or further studies both at home and abroad.

Relevance of Curriculum

Canned courses and homogenized or irrelevant curriculum are a continuing concern for cross-border education initiatives. An ongoing challenge for branch campuses and franchise programs has been the adaptation of curriculum to the host country's cultural and jurisdictional conditions while retaining a rigorous equivalency to the program of the "home" institution granting the qualification. The intention to attract students from across the region and beyond introduces the question of how to adapt curriculum and teaching methods to a group of students with such widely diverse cultural, linguistic and education backgrounds.

Faculty Qualifications and Support

Put simply, who is going to be teaching in the branch campus or franchise programs? This depends on the conditions established by the awarding institution and by the receiving country authority. There is a large grey zone in policies related to terms of employment, support services, cultural preparation, and required qualifications for instructors in these international programs. In some situations, foreign staff is required to teach all programs; in other situations, foreign oversight of local or third country teachers is acceptable. However, using instructors with no history or commitment to the "home" institution raises another set of issues. The graying of academics, a phenomenon in many of the countries active in providing cross-border education, may be an unexpected blessing if they can be persuaded to undertake a teaching contract in the branch campus. But the challenges involved in teaching students from systems with a very different set of expectations and values about higher education should not be underestimated. Increased attention needs to be given to the whole area of providing qualified and committed faculty to deliver courses in the branch campus setting and to the conditions under which these faculty are hired.

CONCLUDING REMARKS

The purpose of this chapter has been to explore the scope and practice of delivering education across national borders. There is ample evidence that demand for higher education in the next 20 years will outstrip the capacity of some countries to meet the domestic need. In fact, demand has already exceeded supply in many parts of the world. Students moving to other countries to pursue their studies will continue to be an important part of the international dimension of the higher education landscape. But student mobility will not be able to satisfy the enormous appetite for higher education from densely populated countries wanting to build human capacity to fully participate in the knowledge society. This is leading to the growing importance of cross-border education programs and providers.

A scan of trends, issues, and new developments in program and provider mobility shows a diversity of new types of education providers, new delivery modes, and innovative forms of public/private and local/foreign partnerships and new types of education hubs. New courses and programs are being designed and delivered in response to local conditions and global challenges, and new qualifications/awards are being conferred. The growth in the volume, scope, and dimensions of cross-border education has the potential to provide increased access and to promote the innovation and responsiveness of higher education, but this turmoil also brings new challenges and unexpected consequences. There are the realities that (1) unrecognized and rogue cross-border providers are active; (2) much of the latest cross-border education provision is being driven by commercial interests and gain; and (3) mechanisms to recognize qualifications and ensure quality of the academic course/program are still not in place in many countries. These conditions present major challenges to the education sector. It is important to acknowledge the huge potential of cross-border education but not at the expense of academic quality and the integrity of qualifications.

Words like diversity, innovation, complexity, opportunities, and challenges have been used repeatedly in this chapter to describe the development and evolution of cross-border education. Internationalization in the broadest sense means the process of integrating an international, intercultural, and global dimension into the purposes of higher education; into the primary functions of teaching, research, and service/outreach; and into the delivery of education at home and abroad. Academic cooperation, educational exchanges/linkages, and commercial provision are all part of internationalization and facilitate the mobility of students, programs, providers, and projects across borders. The education sector is not alone in looking for ways to guide, monitor, and regulate the movement of education programs and providers. It needs to work in close cooperation with other sectors and to play a pivotal role in ensuring that cross-border education reflects and helps to meet the individual country's educational goals, culture, priorities, and policies.

NOTE

* This chapter is adapted from J. Knight (2005), "Cross-border education: an analytical framework for program and provider mobility" in J. Smart and W. Tierney (eds), *Higher Education: Handbook of Theory and Practice* (Vol. 21, pp. 345–96), Dordrecht, Netherlands: Springer, and J. Knight (2008), "Cross-border Education: Programs and Providers on the Move" in *Higher Education in Turmoil: The Changing World of Internationalization* (pp. 96–122), Rotterdam, Netherlands: Sense Publishers.

REFERENCES

Altbach, P.G. and J. Knight (2007), "The Internationalization of Higher Education: Motivations and Realities," *Journal of Studies in International Education*, 11 (3–4), 290–305.
BEDB (2008), *Education and Training*, Bahrain Economic Development Board, www.bharainedb.com/education.aspx.
Bohm A., D. Davis, D. Meares and D. Pearce (2002), *The Global Student Mobility 2025 Report: Forecasts of the Global Demand for International Education*, Canberra, Australia: IDP.
CVCP (2000), *The Business of Borderless Education: UK Perspectives*, London: Committee of Vice-Chancellors and Principals.
De Wit, H. (2002), *Internationalization of Higher Education in the United States of America and Europe: A Historical, Comparative, and Conceptual Analysis*, Westport, CT: Greenwood Press.
Garrett, R. (2005), "*Fraudulent, sub-standard, ambiguous: The alternative borderless higher education*," Briefing Note 24, London: Observatory on Borderless Higher Education.
Knight, J. (2004), "Internationalization Remodelled: Rationales, Strategies and Approaches," in *Journal for Studies in International Education*, 8 (1), 5–31.
Knight, J. (2005), "Cross-border education: An analytical framework for program and provider mobility," in J. Smart and W. Tierney (eds), *Higher Education: Handbook of Theory and Practice*, Vol. 21, Dordrecht, the Netherlands: Springer, pp. 345–96.
Knight, J. (2006a), *Higher Education Crossing Borders: A Guide to the Implications of GATS for Cross-border Education*, Paris: Commonwealth of Learning and UNESCO.
Knight, J. (2006b), "Cross-border Higher Education: Issues and Implications for Quality Assurance and Accreditation," in *Higher Education in the World 2007–Accreditation for Quality Assurance: What is at Stake?*, Barcelona: Global University Network for Innovation.
Knight, J. (2007), "Cross-border Tertiary Education: An Introduction," in *Cross-border Tertiary Education: A Way Towards Capacity Development*, Paris: OECD, World Bank and NUFFIC, pp. 21–46.
Knight, J. (2008), *Higher Education in Turmoil: The Changing World of Internationalization*, Rotterdam, Netherlands: Sense Publishers.
Knight, J. (2009), "Quality Dilemmas with Regional Education Hubs and Cities," in S. Kaur, M. Sirat and B. Tierney (eds), *Addressing Critical Issues on Quality Assurance and University Rankings in Higher Education in the Asia Pacific*, Pulau Pinang, Malaysia: Penerbit Universiti Sains Malaysia.
Knight, J. and H. de Wit (eds) (1997), *Internationalization of Higher Education in Asia Pacific Countries*, Amsterdam: European Association for Education (EAIE) in cooperation with IDP Australia and the Program on Institutional Management in Higher Education (IMHE) of the Organisation for Economic Co-operation and Development (OECD).
Larsen, K., K. Momii and S. Vincent-Lancrin (2004), *Cross-border Higher Education: An Analysis of Current Trends, Policy Strategies, and Future Scenarios*, London: Observatory on Borderless Higher Education.
Mok, K.H. (2008), "Singapore's Global Education Hub Ambitions: University

Governance Change and Transnational Higher Education," *International Journal of Education Management*, 22 (6), 527–46.
MTI (2004), *Growing our Economy*, Ministry of Trade and Industry, Singapore Government, http://app.mti.gov.sg/data/pages/507/doc/DSE_recommend.pdf.
Neilson, J. (2004), "Trade agreements and recognition" in OECD, *Quality and Recognition in Higher Education: The Cross-border Challenge*, Paris: Organisation for Economic Co-operation and Development (OECD.)
OECD (Organisation for Economic Co-operation and Development) (2004), *Internationalisation and Trade in Higher Education: Opportunities and Challenges*, Paris: Centre for Education Research and Innovation, OECD.
UNESCO/OECD (2005), *Guidelines for Quality Provision in Cross-border Higher Education*, Paris: UNESCO and OECD.
Verbik, L. and C. Merkley (2006), *The International Branch Campus: Models and Trends*, London: Observatory on Borderless Higher Education.

4. International research collaborations
Elizabeth D. Capaldi

All research collaborations are complicated. There are issues of credit given to each investigator, intellectual property, financing, animal and human subjects, facilities, equipment and staff. These issues apply for all collaborations, including those within the United States. When borders are crossed even more complexities emerge. Yet international research collaborations are increasing and will likely continue to do so. We discuss here reasons to forecast an increase in international research collaborations and then review the complexities so that those who become involved have open eyes and the benefit of the experience of others.

REASONS FOR INCREASING INTERNATIONAL RESEARCH COLLABORATIONS

Problems Require an International Approach

The problems facing the planet that science can help solve often demand an international approach. Global warming, diseases that know no borders, cyber security, terrorism: all of these (and many more) are problems that we have to work on together. Funding for this type of research comes from governments, foundations and global corporations. For example, Arizona State University is getting some funding from the government of Ireland, the Rothschild Institute, USAID and the US Institute for Justice for a project to study how to resolve social conflict, a problem of worldwide importance and relevance. University collaborations jointly supported by the National Science Foundation and USAID work on such key initiatives as hunger and disease eradication, ecosystem assessment and science-based entrepreneurship in support of some of the poorest people on the planet. Today, development challenges often have a distinctly global context, including managing catastrophic natural disasters and mitigating the impacts of widespread health epidemics such as AIDS – all challenges that require the collective efforts of the world's science community.

Some Research Requires International Collaboration

Astronomy requires the telescope be placed in the right place on the globe, so astronomers cannot always work in their own country and must collaborate with the country where the telescope is placed. Some countries in Europe, such as Sweden, and other places have better recordkeeping and demographers may travel there or use their data bases to understand genetic processes. And of course in studies of geography, the environment, anthropology, and ecology scientists study phenomena that in whole or in part exist in a particular part of the world, so it makes sense to have dedicated facilities and local collaboration. Finally, some countries are more accepting of some types of research (for example, stem cell) than we are or have looser regulations, allowing some research to be done there that would not be approved in the United States.

High-budget research facilities are frequently made possible only by combining the resources of more than one nation. Today's science requires some such high budget facilities, and of these many have been built with the idea that they will be shared worldwide. Some 8000 scientists comprising about half the world's particle physicists and representing some 580 universities and 85 nationalities have gone to Lucerne to work with LAC Collider. More than ever before, we understand there are big scientific problems requiring big facilities that we must share.

The IceCube Neutrino Observatory – the world's first high-energy neutrino observatory – offers a powerful example of an international, interagency research platform. Neutrinos are hard-to-detect astronomical messengers that carry information from cosmological events. The Atacama Large Millimeter Array, currently under construction near San Pedro de Atacama, Chile, will be the world's most sensitive high resolution, millimeter wavelength telescope. The array will make it possible to search for planets around hundreds of nearby stars and will provide a testing ground for theories of star birth, galaxy formation, and the evolution of the universe. ALMA has been made possible via an international partnership drawn from North America, Europe, and East Asia, in cooperation with the Republic of Chile.

Increasing Worldwide Research Competency

Research competency is increasing around the globe, which also leads to increased opportunities for international research collaboration. Other parts of the world are intentionally ramping up their R&D as a quite specific development strategy. There is the well-publicized effort of the Chinese government in developing world-class universities. The Chinese are also providing substantial grants to universities perceived to have the greatest potential to make contributions to the economy. For example, Sanya and Shijiazhuang each received quite substantial research grants equal to about $225 million in the first round of projects. Other countries also have plans to grow their higher education system and expand their research capacity. Singapore is an interesting example. Singapore is investing tremendous accumulated reserves in ways they hope will secure their future as they have to increasingly compete with other nearby nations in Asia. So ten years ago Singapore set out to create the "Boston of the East" through developing world-class higher education. The Biopolis in Singapore is an extraordinary and impressive investment in R&D. Similarly the European Union through various initiatives such as the Lisbon accord is making significant investments in R&D to enhance its competitive position with a goal of reaching 3 percent of GDP within the European Union by 2010.

According to a report from the National Academies Press (2008), in 2003 37 percent of the papers in *Science*, 55 percent of the papers in the *Journal of Biological Chemistry* and 71 percent of the papers in the *Journal of the American Physical Society* were contributed by scientists outside the United States. According to the Organisation for Economic Co-operation and Development (OECD), the United States ranks 22nd in the fraction of gross domestic product contributed to non-defense research.

Worldwide, countries see R&D as the secret to their competitiveness. In addition to the economic driver for research there is growing interest in international rankings of universities, and one obvious way to build up rankings is to invest in research. The primary factor affecting the relative position in the US in rankings by investment in research is that others have invested more and thus improved their position. That is, the United States has not declined in absolute investment, just its relative position. The National Science Board's *Digest of Key Science and Engineering Indicators* for 2008 shows that the United States has led all nations in R&D expenditures for the past two decades, with a steady increase over time. The United States now ranks second among G7 countries in the share of gross domestic product devoted to R&D. This expansion of research capacity across the planet opens up the potential for more and more cross-border collaborative research, expanding the world's potential.

The Role of International Corporations

As corporations become more international or multinational they play an important role in the internationalization of research. The major corporations are global and they fund and participate in research on a worldwide basis. Corporations go where they find the capacity they need. China is good in speech recognition for companies who need that capacity. Japan excels in big equipment. Availability of a programming workforce facilitated Microsoft's locating in India. As more research is designed to increase economic competitiveness, corporate funding is becoming more important, and this corporate funding is an international business. In short, research is a competitive business and now it is a global competition.

POLICIES IN PROMOTION OF INTERNATIONAL COLLABORATIVE RESEARCH

The Role of Government

Science started in Europe and was international from the beginning. Copernicus, Galileo, Newton and Darwin were international figures. The universal quest for knowledge and the stature attributed to scientific communities worldwide have placed scientific and technological collaboration in the forefront of international relations. As worldwide relationships change, lives of individual researchers change. The US core principles for scientific collaboration have changed little since the great scientist and statesman Benjamin Franklin took up his position in 1776 as minister plenipotentiary in Paris. Our country has long believed, as put by NSF Director Arden Bennet, that "science collaboration and science diplomacy are essential ingredients for America's future progress and future prestige."

The United States is not alone in recognizing the inherent value in maintaining open channels of international scientific and technological exchange. Throughout the period of the late 18th and early 19th centuries war and national strife did not foreclose international scientific activity. Naval commanders afforded safe passage to the great explorers. British scientists lectured in Paris throughout the French revolution. Our forefathers recognized the important role played by science and technology in the growth of the nation and that command of these disciplines would define our position on the global stage. Dr. Vannever Bush highlighted the importance of international science to the US in his 1945 report that led to the establishment of the National Science Foundation. At about the same time the United Nations established UNESCO (United Nations Educational, Scientific and Cultural Organization) to contribute to peace and security by promoting international collaborations in education, science, and culture. Within the United Nations there is now a range of technical agencies (World Health Organization, World Meteorological Organization and so on.)

Today in nearly every major multilateral policy forum (G8, OECD, NATO, APEC, OAS) there are cooperative scientific communities. There are also many governmental bilateral cooperative agreements on science and technology. The first step toward these was in 1961 when President John F. Kennedy established the US/Japan Cooperative Science Program. The initial agreement, administered by the National Science Foundation, was followed by others and by 1975 the United States had signed 28 agreements, 14 of which are administered by the National Science Foundation.

Prior to the signing of the US/Japan agreement the scientific community saw little value in formalizing cooperative research arrangements and using diplomatic channels. A perceived primacy of US science has suggested to many that global doors would always be open. Moreover the process of establishing formal agreements was considered unpredictable and reactionary by a community generally recognized as systematic and discovery oriented. Moreover scientists tended to value their role as specialists, seeing no inherent value in joining forces under the umbrella of a general cooperative international science agreement. Finally, consistent with the tension between serving the common good and securing competitive gains, scientists and nonscientists alike expressed concern about loss of technological advantage.

Yet these agreements yielded results few would have predicted – providing valuable exchange of scientific expertise during the Cold War, securing avenues of information exchange with the People's Republic of China, prompting new investment in technological development in emerging countries, opening dialogue on intellectual property protection in otherwise closed economies, ensuring the prospect of science-based decision making in critical areas related to health. (The dialogue on intellectual property continues, and the lack of resolution has prevented some universities from working with overseas universities.)

The rapid flow of information across national borders might suggest less need for defined mechanisms of science and technology collaboration. However, in many cases governments in other countries are necessarily involved. Governments play an important role in funding. In many countries the government is much more intrusive in the development of universities and their research capacity than in the United States. The desire to respond to national needs often pushes governments to centralize key decisions about the size and direction of the higher education system. In some countries governments will determine which research collaborations are possible. Of primary importance is to at least ensure that planned research collaborations are not illegal or otherwise opposed by the government of the partner country.

Necessity of Faculty Leadership

Often universities are asked to sign collaborative agreements with international entities or corporations for research collaborations. These agreements are often empty of content and merely for show, in which case they are arguably harmless. However, these often involve system heads, presidents, mayors, and community leaders who then might have expectations. And the university's policies need to be observed carefully. Often universities cannot accept gifts offered at these events. Universities at the level of administration are not really the ones who can make the decision on these commitments. The leadership must be at the academic level. So commitments in the agreements need to be examined closely for what is being committed in terms of academic involvement, financial involvement and faculty involvement. If no faculty at the local campus have the desire and the ability to participate in the planned activity, the activity will not be successful. Faculty-led initiatives are more likely to succeed as without faculty involvement and expertise nothing can be done. Higher administrators can bless an agreement, but department chairs and deans are the key administrators. They know where there are complementary relationships. They know the quality of the research institution abroad. If the faculty are not interested in a collaborative venture, or if there is no money to support it, or if it takes away from their core activities on campus, or if it lessens the time graduate students get to spend on their degrees, the ventures are not going to work.

Legal and Regulatory Issues

Legal questions are often ignored, but obviously laws in other countries are not the same as in the US. And these laws affect what research can be done and how it can be done. We are not friendly to stem cell research, while Europe is. The genetic engineering that led to the biotech industry in Silicon Valley is not generally supported in Europe, but was in the US. Some counties have very different, or worse very little, legal structure. Always ask, what is the legal structure of the country where the work is to be done or the collaborator is located? Is there an operating judicial system? Are they independent or will they always favor their own citizens? What are the laws governing what you precisely wish to do? In Mexico for example, ASU ultimately established an independent corporation so researchers could deposit money in a local bank and rent a car.

The United States also has laws affecting the operation of researchers in other countries. Export administration regulations (EAR) are concerned with dual-use items that are designed for commercial use but have the potential for military application. The Commerce Control List lists items according to the type of item (whether the item could have defense uses), the reason for the export control (some items are limited only in certain ways) and the destination country (for some countries nothing can be brought, for others the rules are not so strict.) Penalties for violating these regulations, if criminal, range from $50K to $1 million, or five times the value of the export, whichever is greater, per violation, plus ten years' imprisonment. In the case of civil offenses, exporting privileges are revoked, with fines of $10K to $120K for violation. An example is a faculty member at Texas Tech who received two years in prison for making fraudulent claims and unauthorized exports of plague bacteria. Another example is ITT being fined $100 million for exporting night vision materials without a license.

The International Traffic in Arms Regulations controls defense articles, services and technologies specifically designed, developed or modified for military applications. An example at Arizona State University is a faculty member who had a subcontract containing export controls with a small business innovative research (SBIR) company under contract with the United States Air Force for developing plasma technology. Plasma technology is controlled by International Traffic in Arms Regulations (ITAR) and technical data would be considered an export to foreign nationals in the US or abroad. This faculty member employed graduate students from Iran and the People's Republic of China on the project and he went to China with his laptop that contained technical data related to the project. A federal jury convicted him of illegally exporting military technical information, and he could be sentenced to up to 160 years in prison and ordered to pay up to $1.5 million in fines.

The Office of Foreign Assets Control (OFAC) administers and enforces economic and trade sanctions that have been imposed against specific countries. No business of any kind can be conducted with persons or entities on this list. The combination of these rules and regulations can be quite complex. While fundamental research is excluded (meaning basic and applied research the results of which are published and shared broadly within the scientific community), the definition of terms can be subtle. As a hypothetical example, a grant with the NSF might involve placing low-technology GPS equipment along a fault line in the Middle East. An American and an international collaborating institution provide the research support, the training, the software programs to run the equipment and the equipment itself. One of the countries involved is on the embargoed countries list. The collaborating researchers visit the site every few months to check the equipment. The software program has been shipped for several years to institutions of higher education, not-for-profits and foreign governments and is available on a restricted website. The restricted website is used to ensure that commercial entities do not access and use the equipment for commercial gain. This project requires a license from the State Department for the equipment and a technical assistance agreement for training of the foreign nationals. The fundamental research exemption would not apply because of limitation on access to the software.

As can be seen, these questions are not ones in which faculty members will be expert. The regulations are lengthy, complex and difficult to interpret and they apply to more than sponsored research. The university shares in responsibility for violation of these regulations, thus it is incumbent on the institution to provide appropriate training and advice.

The regulatory environment also matters. US biomedical device companies are conducting more development work and initial clinical testing in their own R&D facilities abroad in response to the strict regulatory requirements and high risks of legal liability in the US. In addition, some other countries require companies to do research there to access their markets or in order to have an intellectual property agreement.

Cultural Considerations

Cultural differences affect every aspect of research, from the problems studied, to the approaches used, to issues of researcher interaction. When I was Vice Chancellor of SUNY I received a call from the Minister of Propaganda in China, who said, "Your Chancellor is working on a partnership with us," which was true. And he said, "Well the Dalai Lama is scheduled to speak at the University at Buffalo and we are not in favor of that." So I explained we have something called academic freedom in the United States. Obviously we cannot give in on that, but just as obviously when in China one needs to be sensitive to the differences. On a more individual level, a colleague of mine collaborates in Italy and she tells me the custom there is for the men in a research group to be first author of a resulting publication, regardless of contribution. This is obviously not how we do things in this country.

International Research and Economic Development

One reason governments and corporations support research is the expectation of innovation and the resulting economic development. Different countries accomplish this relationship differently. The early development of the biotechnology industry was characterized by a number of new firms, many of which were academic spin-offs, usually with academics working in conjunction with professional managers backed by venture capital. The norms in American universities that allowed academics to get involved in commercialization played a key role in this process (Hatakenaka, 2008.)

American universities, particularly the land grant and other state universities, have a tradition to serve the practical needs of the community. State governments now expect economic development as a result of investment in their universities. Moreover US government research funding in the post-war period was huge and also "mission oriented," coming mostly from key agencies with applied interests such as defense, health and energy. The role played by the Defense Advanced Research Project Agency (DARPA) in funding application oriented basic research is legendary, so much so that the American National Academy of Sciences recommended the creation of a "DARPA-like" agency in energy (NAS, 2005.)

Taiwan was more directive in creating a public research institution called the Electronic Research Service Organization (ERSO.) ERSO orchestrated the first major technology transfer agreement with RCA in the 1970s and subsequently developed an integrated circuits fabrication technology and established a spin-off company which diffused technological know-how. Taiwan also benefited from the large number of Taiwanese who went to the United States to study and remained to work. The information from these Taiwanese back to their government about Silicon Valley led to the Taiwanese version – a science park in Hsinchu, where ERSO was relocated.

In China, universities actually own spin-off companies (Eun et al. 2006.) Three of the most successful personal computer companies, Lenovo, Founder and Tongfang, were enterprises created by the Chinese Academy of Sciences, Beijing University and Tsinghua University, respectively. Some 40 university enterprises are already listed in stock markets in China and Hong Kong. Universities in China have had affiliated production units used for training students since the 1960s. Beginning in the 1980s the same vehicle has been used to commercialize university knowledge. In China the government does not provide much funding for research, thus universities have strong incentives to generate their own income.

In China there is obviously not the same culture of individual ownership and free enterprise as in the United States. Not only are purses "knocked off," but scientific ideas can be as well. Intellectual property is one of the thorniest issues in research collaborations within the United States, particularly between universities and corporations. There are similar complexities working with Chinese universities and in other international collaborations. For basic research this may not be particularly worrisome as little that is useful may be directly produced. But there is always the potential of a commercializable result and one must either feel comfortable with lack of control over this or try for agreements up front. MIT met with leaders of the European Union Framework Program and could not reach agreement with that program because of intellectual property issues. The National Science Foundation could perhaps have a role in establishing a common international agreement. Also wider acceptance of WTO and other international regimes related to intellectual property could help.

The United States is interested in ensuring science leads to economic development as shown by the Bayh-Dole Act, which gave universities that receive federal funding the obligation of developing the commercial implications of that research. However, other countries are even more interested in applied research and quick results. The long-term basic research that the United States invests in and that our own students do is not that well supported across the globe. The federal government funds more than 60 percent of universities' research base and the vast majority of federal money is for basic research, seeding the next generation of discoveries. Seventy-five percent of research in United States universities is defined as basic, as compared to only 4 percent in high-technology industries. Universities in several other countries are much more heavily funded by industry on a proportional basis. In China and Russia, for example, 30 percent of research is supported by industry.

Multinational corporations invest in research and do so globally. Thus they are a player and an important partner in international and other research collaborations. The Chinese government has been applying pressure for multinational corporations to invest in R&D as the price for access to the huge Chinese market, and competition among multinational corporations to win government approval has driven up R&D. Multinational corporations have a real need to localize their products and much of the research they fund in other countries is for this purpose.

Corporations also fund huge research projects. Recently BP funded a $500 million project on biofuels involving Berkeley, and Lawrence Livermore laboratory in Illinois. Large corporate endeavors are often large multidisciplinary projects to tackle a specific problem. There are also many R&D projects funded by corporations in the hope of innovating and producing new products. One does not need to go overseas to participate in these types of projects.

According to Dalton et al. (1999), there were over 700 foreign R&D centers in the United States as of 1997, heavily concentrated in certain areas, such as Silicon Valley and greater Los Angeles, Detroit, Princeton,

Research Triangle Park and Boston. The most frequently cited reasons for investing are to assist parent companies in meeting US customer needs, to keep abreast of technological developments in the United States, to employ US scientists and engineers, and to cooperate with other US R&D laboratories. There are also large numbers of US R&D facilities abroad, so US companies can adapt their products to local markets and take advantage of local expertise and workers. United States researchers can then collaborate internationally while staying at home. When I worked on the bioinformatics center of excellence in New York, we partnered with foreign companies who had R&D centers in New York. We had a partnership with Amersham, and one with Pharmacia. They wanted to be up to date on drug development and personalized medicine, the topic of our center of excellence.

These types of partnerships can involve many different types of investigators at many different types of institutions, while the really large projects are limited to the mega research universities, those with over $400 million in annual federal research expenditures. In the United States there are 150 institutions that have over $40 million in federal funding (see the reports of The Center for Measuring University Performance; *The Top American Universities: 2008 Annual Report*, by Capaldi et al., is the most recent report (http://mup.asu.edu/research2008.pdf.)) Of these, 41 have between $100 and $200 million in federal research expenditures, 27 have between $200 and $400 million, and 15 have over $400 million in annual federal research expenditures. These latter are mega research universities who can play in the major projects. But there are 659 institutions in the United States who have at least some federal funding for research, and each of these is available to partner with other institutions in some way.

Indeed all of us need to partner. We cannot do all of everything, so there is a lot of opportunity for all institutions to participate if we do not consider just mega projects. Indeed, to produce the economic development we have promised as a result of investing in research, we all need to participate. The mega and other top universities can do basic research and tackle large multidisciplinary problems as well as smaller projects. But, to bridge the "Valley of Death" between basic research and marketable new innovative products, we also need applied work and product development, the latter often in partnership with corporations. This is a role the polytechnic university sector plays in Finland and that can be played by institutions in the United States if we make intentional connections. The technology sector in The State University of New York can play that role, as well as Arizona State University's polytechnic campus and other similar institutions.

THE ADVANTAGE HELD BY THE UNITED STATES

An important difference between the United States and other countries is the close tie between education and research in our universities, a huge strength. Many countries that are involved in research do not have the same kind of graduate education that we do, with ties to research or the post-doctoral system. Most importantly, our undergraduate education, unlike that around the world, is broad and in most institutions of higher education is tied to faculty who are also expected to do scholarship. In other countries the undergraduate major is started earlier, and most educational effort is expended in science and engineering, often in a much more technically focused way than our curriculum. In the United States, we also require humanities, arts and the social sciences, and expect leadership, service, and communication skills as a result of an undergraduate education. In the rest of the world, undergraduate education is more narrow and often quite technical. But what is called for now, most agree, is people who can be creative, who can be interdisciplinary, who can work with others, and who can lead.

Hill (2007) suggests that we are moving to a "post-scientific" society in which wealth generation and leadership will be based more on creativity, the social sciences, the arts and new business processes. He suggests the United States can continue to lead, by focusing on these areas and letting other countries do the nuts and bolts of science and engineering that underpin the more global processes that will be necessary. Other locations have the benefit of a low-cost workforce. We have the benefit of an educational system that can focus on integration of knowledge and building new systems. It is an interesting thought. And finally, the United States also still maintains a lead in quality and impact, producing an amazing 63 percent of the world's most highly cited papers, housing 75 percent of the world's top 20 universities and employing 70 percent of the world's Nobel prize winners (Galama and Hosek, 2008.)

NOTE

* I am deeply grateful to the other session panelists, Molly Broad, Claude Canizares and Mark Yudof, whose comments contributed greatly to this chapter, as well as to Anthony Rock, Vice President for Global Engagement at Arizona State University, and Winfred M. Phillips, Vice President for Research at the University of Florida.

REFERENCES

Bush, V. (1945), *Science: The Endless Frontier: A Report to the President by Vannevar Bush, Director of the Office of Scientific Research and Development*, July, Washington, DC: United States Government Printing Office.

Dalton, D.H., M.G. Serapio and P.G. Yoshida (1999), *Globalizing Industrial Research and Development*, Washington, DC: US Department of Commerce, Technology Administration, Office of Technology Policy.

Eun, J., K. Lee and G. Wu (2006), "Explaining University-run enterprises in China: A theoretical framework for university–industry relations in developing countries and its application to China," *Research Policy*, 35, 1329–46.

Galama, T. and J. Hosek (2008), "U.S. Science is holding its own: Despite cries of alarm, we remain the global leader in innovation," *Pittsburgh Post-Gazette*, July 9.

Hatakenaka, S. (2008), "The role of higher education in high tech industry development: What can international experience tell us?," working paper for presentation at the ABCDE Conference, June.

Hill, C.T. (2007), "Global Innovation: The post-scientific society," *Issues in Science and Technology*, Fall, 78–88.

National Academies Press (2008), revisions to *Rising Above the Gathering Storm: Energizing and Employing America for a Brighter Economic Future*, July, http://www.nap.edu/html/11463/11463_revisions.pdf.

National Academy of Sciences (2005), *Rising Above the Gathering Storm: Energizing and Employing America for a Brighter Economic Future*, Washington, DC: National Academies.

5. Offering domestic degrees outside the United States: one university's experiences over the past decade
Mark S. Kamlet

INTRODUCTION

One of the notable, and even transformative, directions that Carnegie Mellon University has pursued over the past decade has been its various activities related to globalization. As provost of the institution during this period, I have had an excellent seat to observe what has happened in terms of this internationalization and I have been able to participate in parts of it. To put this in some context, Carnegie Mellon, as recently as the early 1970s, was in many ways a regional university – if one very well regarded, especially in technology and the arts. Most of its students came from the immediate tri-state area. Our ambitions at that time in terms of extending our footprint internationally were limited. Instead the institution focused on enhancing its research capabilities and increasing its reputation nationally. While the number of international students coming to Carnegie Mellon slowly but steadily increased, our focus was very much on the world coming to us and not the other way around. As recently as a decade ago, if an alumnus lived outside the United States, we did not send him or her a copy of the *Carnegie Mellon Magazine*, ostensibly to save postage but also because our international connections and presence were not seen as important defining parts of the University.

That has changed in ways that I will describe. While roots of the change can be traced back further, the pace of change certainly accelerated in the last decade. We now have over twenty Carnegie Mellon degree programs in locations outside Pittsburgh, with over a dozen degree programs outside the United States. (Indeed, we have a number of Carnegie Mellon degree programs where the students enrolled may come from and live in many different countries, making it impossible for me to answer the question I am sometimes asked: "In how many countries does Carnegie Mellon offer degrees?")

Perhaps a fitting symbol of the whole range of our efforts to globalize occurred in February 2009, when we held a full board of trustees meeting in Qatar at our campus in Education City. We have a large board, some 60 members, and we probably had the largest attendance at that board meeting of any I can recall. I think it fair to say that a decade previously it could not have been imagined by the board or the senior administration of the university that before the end of the decade the Carnegie Mellon board would be holding its meeting in Doha, Qatar, at a Gulf campus where we have over 150 full-time faculty and staff, enrolling approximately 100 students each year and about to graduate our second class.

There are many reasons we have chosen to pursue offering these degree programs outside our main campus. However, one of the reasons was not any desire to abandon or make less important our Pittsburgh presence. In fact, we had hoped that becoming part of a global network would actually be a very positive thing for the vibrancy of our Pittsburgh campus and for bringing research grants, students, and even international company research labs from abroad to Carnegie Mellon Pittsburgh. I think our experience over the past decade has borne this out.

In view of Carnegie Mellon's various efforts in offering degrees outside the United States, I was asked by the conference organized by the TIAA-CREF Institute to write about some of the "nuts and bolts" issues that we have encountered and that may be of relevance to other universities pursuing their own paths of globalization, including our ways of having partnered with the various entities one works with in these endeavors – for example, governments, foreign universities, companies, foundations, NGOs, individual philanthropists, and other domestic universities.

I am happy to do so, but I do so humbly. While I view Carnegie Mellon's global thrust over the past decade as having a very positive impact on the university, we are still very much on a learning curve. There have been many issues that we have encountered and wrestled with, sometimes finding what we consider very good ways to proceed and, in other cases, still trying to find the right approach and balance. On all the matters I will be discussing, we are perpetually trying to learn from our experiences. It is also the case that our basic framework and path is one that may not be seen as applicable or even appealing to other universities, which may take other paths to their own globalization efforts. (Indeed, selfishly perhaps, part of me hopes that our experience internationally cannot be duplicated easily and/or that the rationales that are compelling for us may, for good reasons for our peers, be not as compelling to them.)

Nonetheless, it is hard for me to imagine that if other universities do pursue such activities, there will not be some relevance for them from our particular experiences. Admittedly, the devil is often in the details, and it is in these details that some of the mutual learning is most valuable. Here are some topics that come immediately to my mind:

- the fascinating topic of Oracle software currency conversion issues;
- twenty key points to keep in mind when it comes to tax equalization compensation for faculty and staff outside the United States;
- options for structuring promotion and reappointment and other career ladder issues for faculty who are not on the main campus during the majority of their time;
- internal financial relationships among the colleges and departments and between them and the central administration within Carnegie Mellon;
- federal government oversight of overhead with regard to research conducted outside the country;
- how to keep different departments in Pittsburgh from killing one another in their desired expansions into South Korea in overlapping areas;
- how to set up a private foundation in Japan, and how to avoid being viewed as a taxable entity in India.

And those are just a small subset of the types of things we have encountered, and indeed seemingly encounter every day. (One thing that certainly pops into mind as I write this paragraph is the thought that surely there should be some mechanism or forum by which we can all share our experiences. Each of us inventing or reinventing the wheel on many of these logistics is doubtless not a very appealing way to proceed.)

I will focus most of the discussion in this chapter on the situations in which Carnegie Mellon provides education that leads to a Carnegie Mellon degree and in which all or at least most of the student's time is spent outside of Pittsburgh. The current listing of such programs is provided in Figure 5.1.

In fact, we have many other training and related efforts that do not lead to formal degrees and that occur outside the United States. Let me briefly mention two of them. Carnegie Mellon is home to a US Department of Defense federally funded research and development center called the Software Engineering Institute (SEI.) For 20 years, SEI has been designated by the US Department of Defense, and now by the Department of Homeland Security, as its primarily academically-based computer emergency response partner. This is done largely through the Carnegie Mellon's Computer Emergency Research Team (CERT.) CERT partners with and monitors for the DoD their internet security and works with them on real-time cyber security situations. Over time, an international

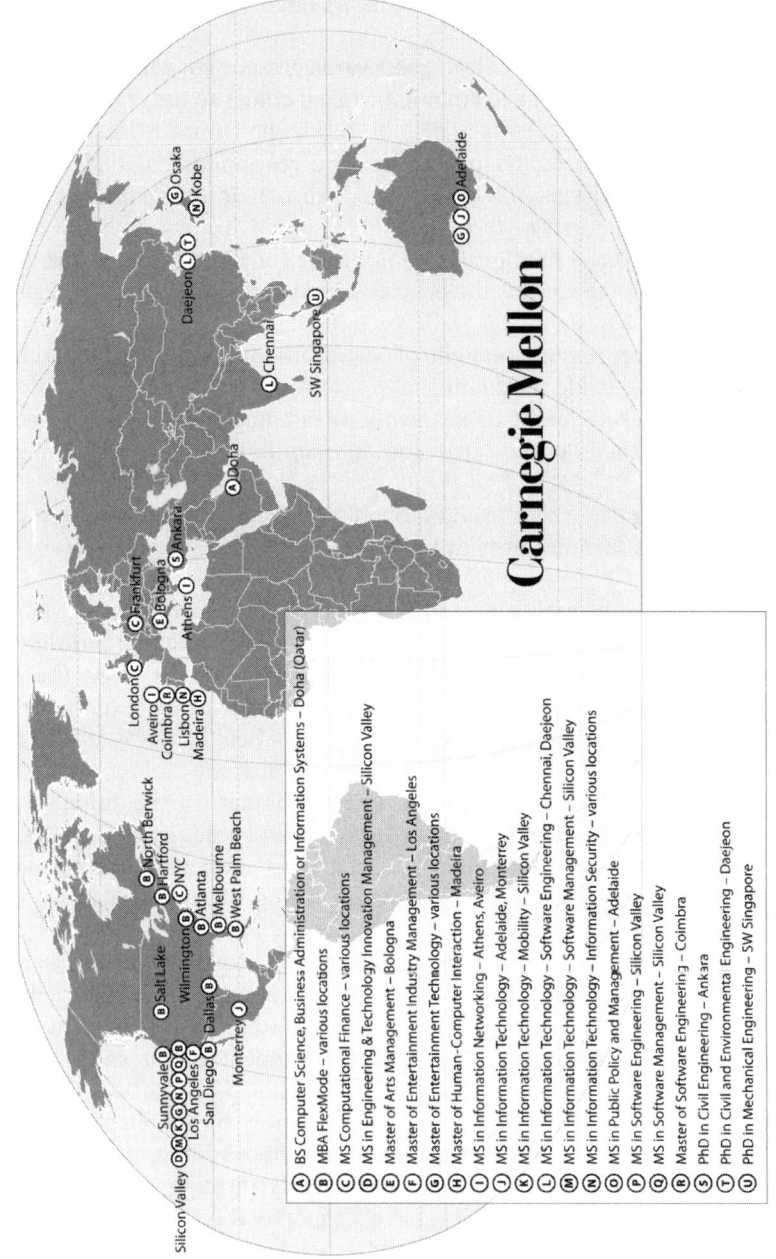

Figure 5.1 *Educating global citizens: degree programs outside of Pittsburgh, 2000–present*

network of CERTs has come into being, with the Carnegie Mellon CERT serving throughout as the so-called "coordinating" CERT, linking these country and region specific CERTS together. Figure 5.2 is a map of the over 100 international CERTs that we coordinate.

Another feature of the SEI is that it invented and oversees the so-called Capability Maturity Model (CMM – now technically the Capability Maturity Model Integrated, or CMMi), which is a method endorsed by the Department of Defense for assessing the sophistication and quality of an organization in doing software development. CMMi assesses an organization on a 1 to 5 scale, 5 being the best. An organization must be assessed at CMMi Level 3 to do subcontract work in software development for the Department of Defense. We do not have the capacity to do the evaluations ourselves of the many companies and organizations seeking to be rated. Instead, we oversee and train a network of trainers who are certified by Carnegie Mellon to do CMM assessments. These activities are not inconsequential in terms of the global footprint and reputation of Carnegie Mellon internationally. Firms throughout the world compete for Level 5 capability on the CMMi, with the majority of Level 5 organizations being in India. In my earliest trips to India as provost I was struck by the extent to which Carnegie Mellon was probably better known in India, due to CMM, than it is in certain regions of the United States. Figure 5.3 indicates the number of licensed partners we have internationally who do CMMi certification.

Having noted the existence of the CERT and CMM related efforts, I will not describe them in greater detail, although they clearly are part of globalization activities by the university. And, there are many other globally related topics that due to space and time constraints I will not discuss except to briefly mention them now. One is what Carnegie Mellon has sought to do over the past decade in preparing domestic students at our Pittsburgh campus, especially undergraduates, for lives and careers in which their global knowledge and competence will be a paramount consideration. Thus, I will not be talking about "study abroad" or other mechanisms to encourage all undergraduates to have an important and substantive international engagement during their years at the University, nor programs such as that run by our business school where MBA students can spend a "mini" (one half semester) outside the United States.

Another topic I will omit is the experience we seek to offer international students when they come to our Pittsburgh campus to study. This is a particularly important topic for us. The most recent data I have seen, dating back two years, indicate that among undergraduates Carnegie Mellon has a greater percentage of international students than any top research university in the United States (trailed by just a small amount by MIT and

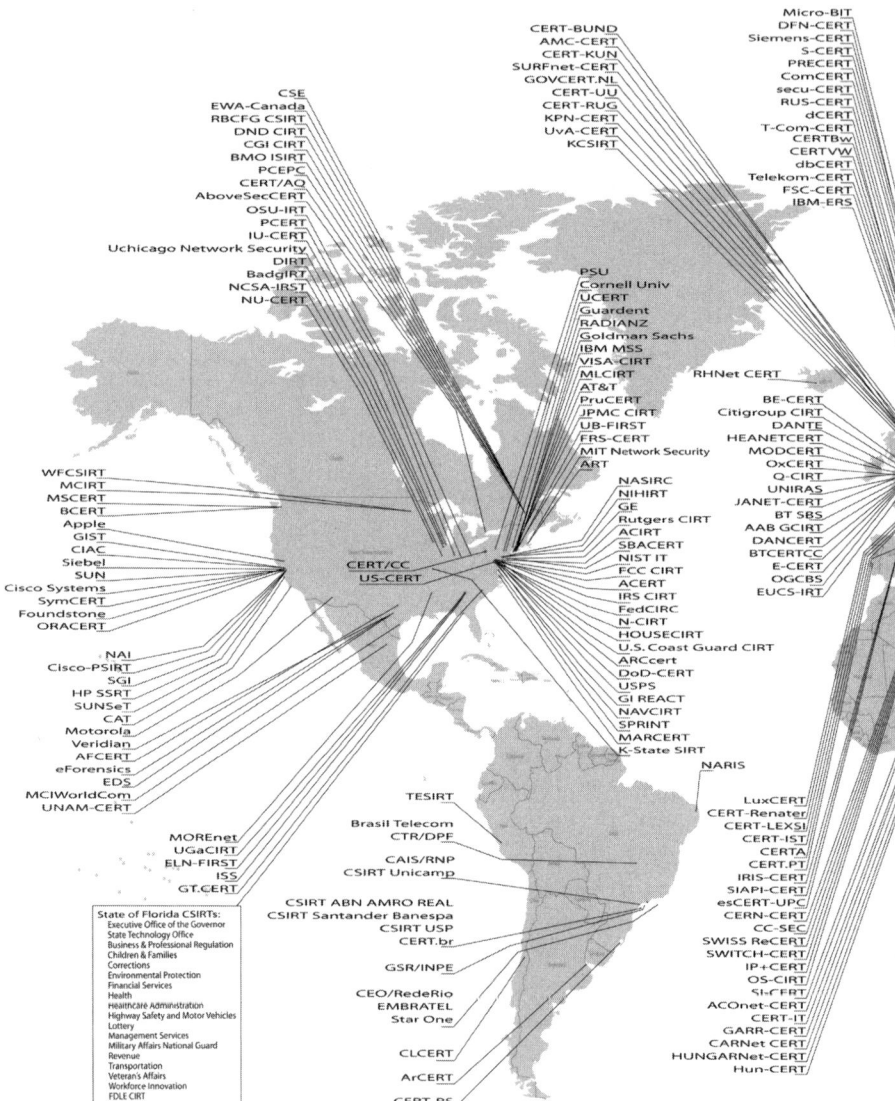

Figure 5.2 CERT locations

Offering domestic degrees outside the US 89

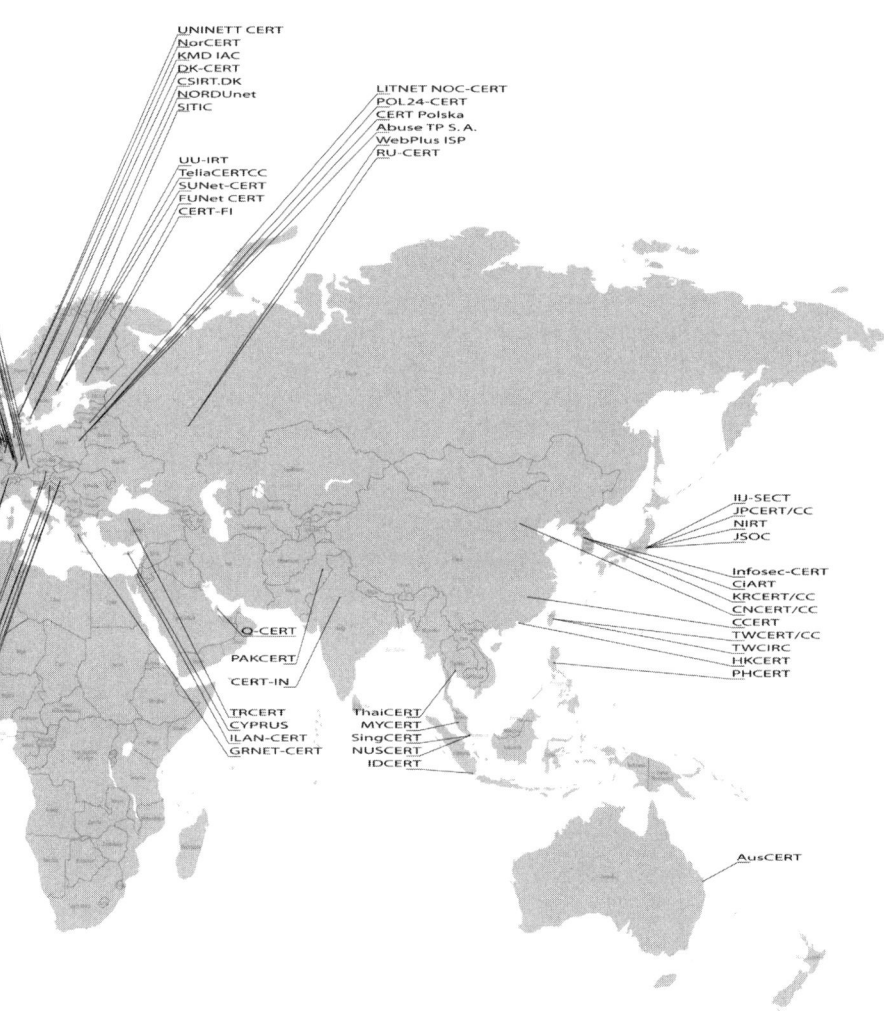

90   *Higher education in a global society*

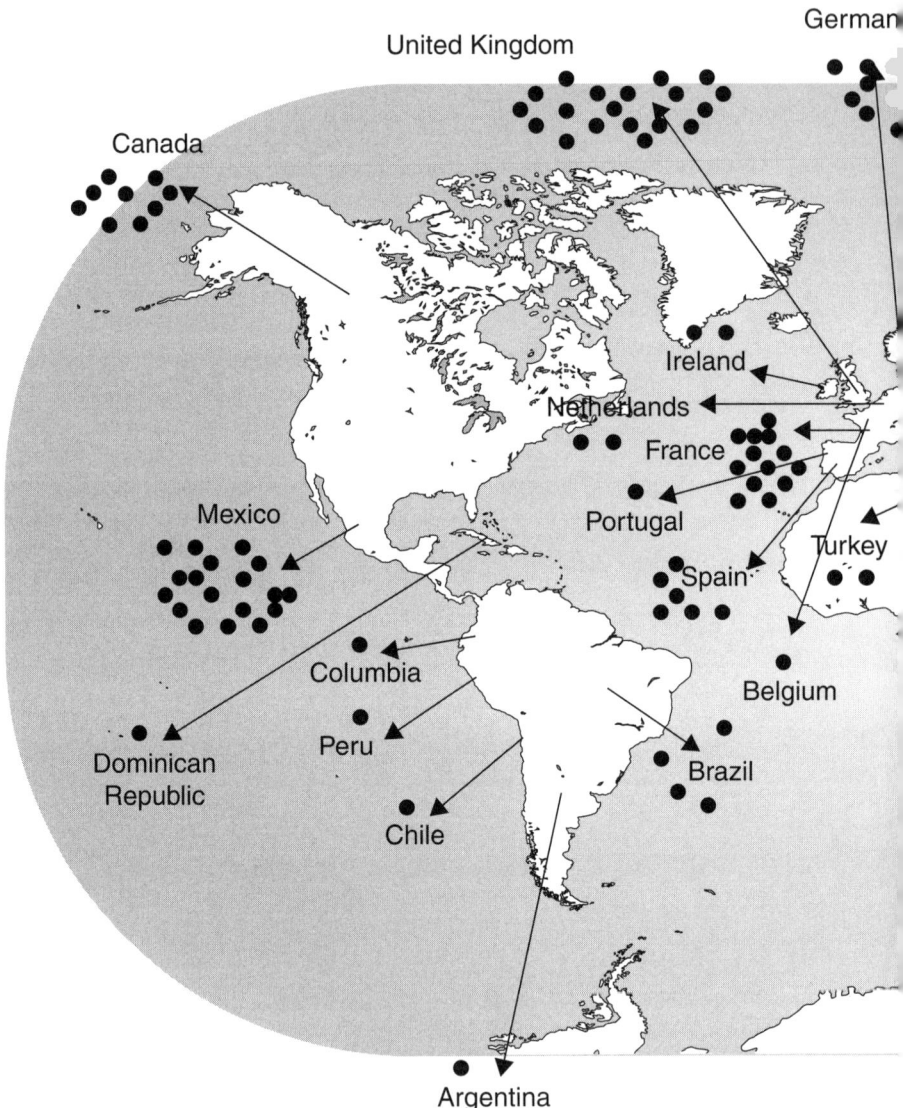

Figure 5.3   Software Engineering Institute (SEI) – current partner affiliations

Offering domestic degrees outside the US

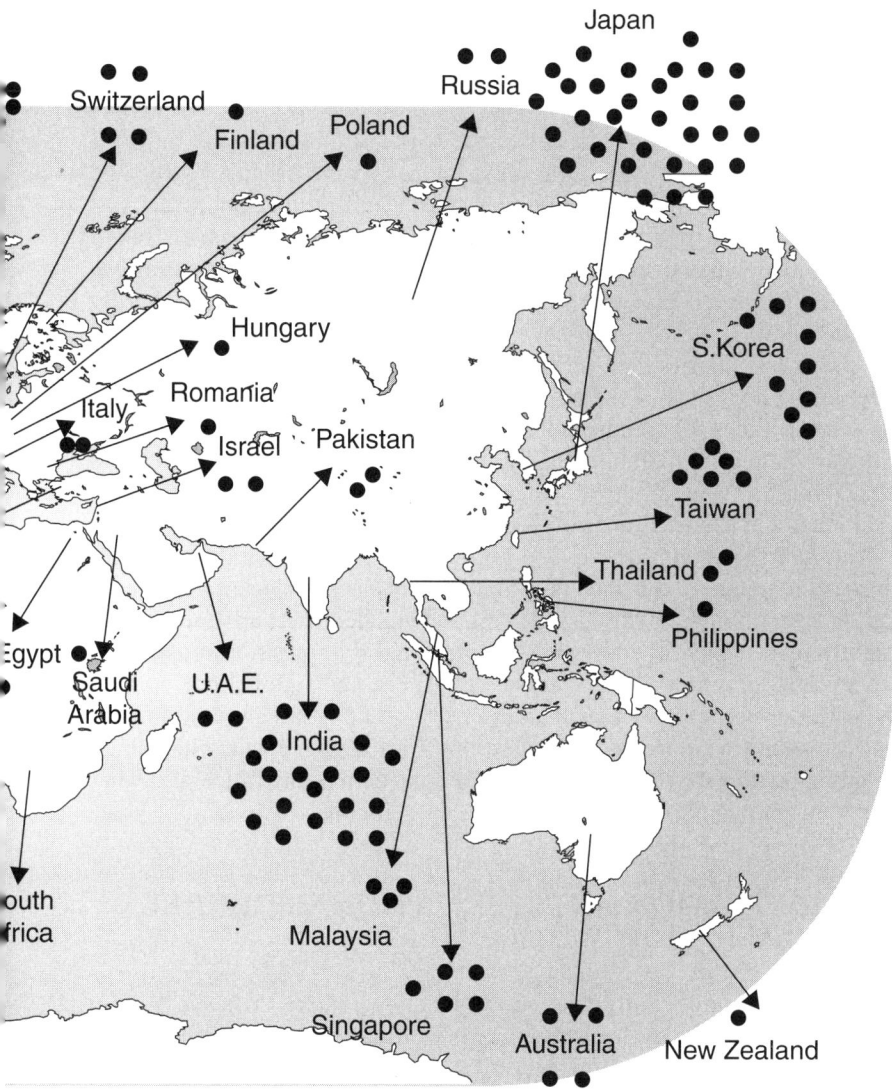

Columbia.) And, the percentage of undergraduates who are from outside the United States is itself very much smaller than is true for most of our masters and Ph.D. programs, where the percentages are in many cases well over 50 percent.

I will not be discussing a series of networks of universities in different regions that Carnegie Mellon has played a lead role in organizing, the two most prominent being in India and in Latin and South America. I will not be discussing the rapid growth there has been over the past decade in the extent to which our faculty work with faculty who are at institutions outside the United States (in regard to which, of course, we are hardly unique.) I will not be discussing the international activities of several for-profit subsidiaries that the university has established that are engaged internationally. (One of these organizations, iCarnegie Inc., for instance, provides content for training software engineers at over a dozen separate software colleges in China.) Lastly, I will not be discussing the various research centers and areas of expertise that have arisen in the last dozen years that address what are now seen to be fundamentally global issues.

The fact that there are now so many of these activities that are very important aspects of the university and that are clearly relevant for globalization, even though not discussed in more detail here, perhaps underscores the extent to which it is less and less meaningful a question to ask "Are we a global university?" or "Do we seek to become a global university?" As with our peers, there is such an extensive set of global connections and activities that the more relevant questions are concerned with which parts of globalization are right to focus on for a particular institution and what has been learned about best practices in pursuing these activities.

THE EVOLUTION OF INTERNATIONAL DEGREE PROGRAMS: HOW WE GOT HERE

As indicated above, Figure 5.1 shows locations where Carnegie Mellon provides education that leads to a Carnegie Mellon degree where all or at least most of the student's time is spent outside of Pittsburgh. How did our engagements in these programs come to be? I think our global strategy and directions cannot be answered without some sense of history. There are a number of traits of Carnegie Mellon that have played an important role in the globalization efforts of the past decade that did not originally stem from any specifically globalization interests per se. One of them is that for financial reasons the institution has by necessity had to be very entrepreneurial (or, as has sometimes been said, has had to be fairly scrappy.) From the 1970s, we started to climb in national and international rankings thanks in large part to our research accomplishments, and we found ourselves competing for faculty and students with institutions with far greater wealth and larger endowments than we had. Alas, the central administration could not always provide the resources the academic units needed.

One response of departments to this dilemma was the evolution of professional masters programs. This stems in part from the intra-university fiscal structure at the university. At Carnegie Mellon, the central administration gets all undergraduate tuition and (basically) all overhead from externally sponsored research. Neither is returned to academic units in a formulaic manner.

In contrast, academic units keep about 80 percent of money that comes in for tuition for graduate students. When faced with fiscal needs for which the central administration cannot help, academic units over time became very active in establishing professional masters programs to supplement their resource base, and central has encouraged this entrepreneurship. Usually when I say this, the first thing the listener thinks is that this is somewhat crass and he or she wonders how quality standards are not compromised in the interest of finances. In fact, while there is a clear financial incentive to running such programs, we have found that this very feature tends as well to place a very high priority on having the quality of such programs to be very high. One reason for this is that adult professionals are not going to be willing to take time out of their careers and pay tuitions that are in the vicinity of $40,000 per year if these programs do not deliver very large tangible benefits through the skills and training developed to the careers and to the earning capacity of the students in these programs. Because of this, these programs have generally been in the very top tier in terms of national rankings and overall academic reputation.

Over time, over 30 such professional masters degrees have come into being and are offered on our Pittsburgh campus. They include programs in entertainment technology, computational biology, computational finance, human–computer interaction, software engineering, information systems management, information technology, information networking, information security, biotechnology management, public management, arts management, medical management, health care policy and management, entertainment industry management, communication planning and information design, professional writing, and logic and computation. And this does not count the many master of fine arts programs or traditional professional masters programs like master of business administration or master in public policy and management.

Some of these programs are offered by multiple parts of the campus. For instance, the masters in computational finance is offered by the Tepper School of Business, the Statistics Department, the Mathematics

Department, the School of Computer Science, and the Heinz College, thereby spanning five separate colleges. These consortia of departments and colleges negotiate their own financial arrangements among themselves, subject to the central administration getting its approximately 20 percent of tuition.

I do not know of any top research university that has this range of professional masters programs or ones that span such a range of academic units, many of which would not normally be thought to be homes for professional programs. The budgets of many academic departments at Carnegie Mellon are very much affected, at least on the margin, by their professional masters programs. These departments include Mathematical Sciences, Biology, English, Design, Philosophy, Architecture, Human–Computer Interaction, Machine Learning, Language Technologies, Robotics, Electrical and Computer Engineering, the Tepper Business School, and the Heinz College. One can note that most of these programs focus very much on our strengths in computer science, information technology, and management fields.

These programs have in many cases been developed and been offered for ten or more years in Pittsburgh. They are well institutionalized. They have been thoroughly developed curricularly and logistically by the faculties of the Carnegie Mellon departments in Pittsburgh. They have been market and industry tested. They have their own academic administrative personnel structure. It is these programs, already developed and of high demand, that constitute many of our international degree programs. When we go to offer these programs outside the United States, without diminishing the many important cultural challenges (and opportunities) that occur in different locales, we know we have a product that "works," a curriculum that is strong, and one that has displayed a proven track record.

A second distinctive feature of Carnegie Mellon that predates globalization but that is of great relevance for our subsequent ability to proceed as we have during the past decade is our tradition of experimentation at educational technology and pedagogical methods. I believe virtually every type of way of delivering a program to students, at a distance and otherwise, and seemingly every combination of ways, has been tried at one time or another. For us, one size does not fit all, and many different approaches and combinations have been used.

I have occasionally made a joking observation about Carnegie Mellon's vaunted tradition of interdisciplinarity: that when one has seen one excellent example of a department or center pursuing interdisciplinary research, one has seen exactly one excellent example. Every model is different. What works, keeps the peace, and allows for a sustainable interdisciplinary equilibrium in one setting on our campus may be exactly wrong in some other department or center.

So, too, for our experience in technology-enhanced education and at delivering courses outside Pittsburgh. But we have been persistent, inventive and exploratory. I remember hearing in the 1980s that someone in computer science was teaching a class in Mexico from Pittsburgh. (It was in software engineering.) I wondered how this could be. I wandered by what was basically a makeshift recording studio in one of our buildings. There were two cameras. One followed the instructor. The other recorded the material on what was basically an overhead projector. There was a "producer" who edited the two cameras on the fly. The signal was then beamed to a satellite from a huge dish antenna on the top of the building. This in turn was beamed to a satellite dish receiver at the Instituto Tecnológico y de Estudios Superiores de Monterrey. There a group of students and an instructor from Monterrey Tech gathered to listen and watch (on very low definition digital images) the lecture. If any student had a question, he or she wrote it on a piece of paper and handed it to their faculty member on site in Mexico. He went to the one terminal located there and sent an electronic message to the producer in the control room in Pittsburgh. That person printed the message and walked over, tapped the professor on the shoulder, and handed him the question.

That was, of course, a long time ago but over the years and across different settings this tradition of "let's try such and such and see if it works" has continued. There is almost always a heavy emphasis on there being a Carnegie Mellon faculty member in front of the students for some periods of time. But this may be augmented by curricular materials and content that are delivered over the net in real time by faculty in Pittsburgh. Or, sometimes these same faculty deliver the content in real time from the distant location, but broadcast it back to students in Pittsburgh. Lecture materials and the like are sometimes provided asynchronously, and we have been using perhaps a half dozen different formats over the years. Sometimes a key senior professor works on the curriculum for a given class, but digital versions of the lecture are then used as the basis for presentation of the materials to distant learners, with various other teaching assistants or other faculty there on site to interact with the students. (And, in these cases, we have even utilized various compensation arrangements for the faculty member who designed and first delivered the material when it is then used as the basis for class segments led by other faculty.) Other times the students work at a distance but come together in Pittsburgh or elsewhere for a week once or twice a semester.

We have had some curricula where, rather than having students take traditional classes, the entire program of study is operationalized through a series of group project courses, with "learning by doing" being the primary approach and with faculty serving as coaches but not lecture deliverers.

We also have been very involved with what we call "cognitive tutors," who present course material through an active-learning, computer-mediated method based on substantial use of artificial intelligence techniques to customize material in real time for different students. This has been manifested in such efforts as the Open Learning Initiative as well as spin-off efforts such as Carnegie Learning.

THE ANATOMY OF THE ESTABLISHMENT OF DEGREE PROGRAMS ABROAD: THE M.S. IN COMPUTATIONAL FINANCE AS A CASE STUDY

Both of these traditions – the development of professional masters programs and the use of different and creative ways of content delivery – turned out to be important capabilities when we began to experiment with international delivery of degrees, although in some cases we sort of walked into those activities backwards, not even knowing that was our intent. A good example is our master of science program in computational finance. This program emerged organically on the Pittsburgh campus, as previously mentioned. It was offered for years in Pittsburgh and was very successful.

It then dawned on the units involved that there could well be a large demand for offering the program to working professionals on Wall Street, as well as full-time students, and that this might be pursued on Wall Street without harming the number of students coming to Pittsburgh for the program. So, we tried it out. We rented a nice facility with good classrooms that presented what at that time was good compressed video. We began to experiment on the margin with different ways to best deliver content. Generally, we would fly faculty to New York on a regular basis; sometimes the actual lecture would be broadcast from Pittsburgh and at other times delivered there. We had various teaching assistant arrangement to duplicate "office hours." Faculty members also held office hours over the web, and teaching assistants were available face to face. It went very well and the program thrived.

Then some of the banks that were paying tuition for their employees who were enrolled in the program suggested it would be even better for them if the program could be delivered in London. So, with a guarantee by the banks involved for the tuition for a preset number of students, with the obligation being on them to identify employees who met our entrance requirements to apply to the program, and with relatively easy exit options should the program not prove sustainable, we decided we would try it. It seemed almost just an incremental step to begin offering the degrees in

London. Then we began also doing so in Frankfurt and one year even in Bangalore. All of a sudden, we were offering Carnegie Mellon degrees internationally. And, we continued to experiment with different arrangements for the length of time to locate a faculty member abroad, how to deal with time differences, how to deal with different internet bandwidths, and so on.

The reader will note that in this particular case we did not join forces with a particular partner university. That has in fact typically been our pattern, although I will mention some exceptions below. In part, this has largely been because our focus has been on already existing Carnegie Mellon degrees. Also, many universities abroad charge relatively low tuitions compared to ours, made up for by subsidies from their governments. That is a hard arrangement to make work for us. Also, if there are local universities with strengths in the areas in which we would like to offer our degrees, it is hard to avoid having this be seen as a form of competition and a shift in tuition revenues from the potential partner university to us. On those terms, it is not always the path of least resistance to attempt to partner with an existing university. In short, we have had to find situations where there was some sponsor that would be willing to pay the types of tuition fees needed to justify our offering the degree, and it generally had to be in an area or domain that, while bringing high "value added" to the students, was not available in that market. That has meant typically we have opened our own operations in the areas we have offered degrees.

THE NEED FOR CENTRAL ADMINISTRATIVE CAPACITY

Perhaps in part because we have often set out on our own, without embedding our educational offerings within a partner university, we have typically had to deal with a whole host of complex institutional interactions. In the case of the masters in computational finance program in New York, this included, for instance, meeting various requirements set forth by New York State's Department of Education. Mutually agreeable terms were eventually arranged, but it did require time and effort on both parties' part.

More generally, this has been a common theme for us in providing degrees outside Pittsburgh, be it in the United States or internationally. There are inevitably relatively complex legal, tax, human resource, and regulatory environments that one must come to terms with successfully. Over time we have evolved groups within the central administration coming from legal, finance, human resources, and the provost's office that have now garnered a wealth of experience and expertise on these matters. The issues involved are often far from simple. And there are definite economies of scale and economies of scope in the development of this expertise. The types of expertise are, moreover, not the types that a given academic department or college would typically have or be expected to have.

For instance, many of the programs have extensive memoranda of understanding which can take long and tough negotiations. These are followed by formal legal contractual terms, which again can be complex to negotiate. Thus, while the programs are "run" in terms of academic and curricular matters, the recruiting of students and the setting of financial aid by the relevant academic units within the colleges and departments of Carnegie Mellon requires a non-trivial infrastructure from central, and thus the units and central are quite interwoven in the context of any given effort. In this regard, an effort by a US university to offer, say, a single degree program outside the United States runs the risk that a surprisingly large administrative infrastructure is required and it cannot be amortized across multiple programs.

A second conclusion that one quickly comes to is that it is more expensive, sometimes significantly more expensive, to offer degrees outside Pittsburgh and especially outside the United States than to do so on the home campus. The administrative and transactions costs are not small. Nor are the financial incentives to have faculty and staff participate in these programs outside Pittsburgh and outside the United States inconsequential. We are often approached by potential partners abroad who would like us to offer a top quality Carnegie Mellon degree (which we are willing to do, assuming we have total control over necessary academic matters and assuming the quality standards on students can be met) but at a much reduced price compared to tuition in Pittsburgh – which we decidedly cannot do. One of the first steps in discussions is to make that clear to prospective partners.

OTHER PROFESSIONAL MASTERS PROGRAMS

One way or another, many of our international masters engagements have had a somewhat similar beginning to that of the masters in computational finance in the above case study, although each had distinctive arrangements in terms of the specifics of the partnerships involved and approaches to content delivery.

The best I can do, I believe, is to provide some examples. The dean of Carnegie Mellon's engineering college and I were traveling with the president and several others from Carnegie Mellon in Greece on a set of interactions with a particular university outside Athens. However, at the behest of a trustee, we made a side visit in Athens to a prominent Greek academic who had been at Columbia for many years but returned at the end of his academic career to Greece. He talked to us about the desire of a prominent Greek CEO to give back philanthropically to the region by bringing top-quality technical education into Greece. The particular area that was being explored mapped closely to a long-standing Pittsburgh masters program in information networking. He was in discussion with several other prestigious US universities but had run into some bureaucratic frustrations with those universities. We wished him luck, said those were great universities, but indicated that we were ranked highly, had a long-standing program in this area, and would be happy to talk further. We indicated that we would need a guarantee regarding financing because we were not in a position to subsidize this activity, and they in turn needed guarantees on quality and nature of the faculty and so forth. We could meet each other's terms. Long story short, nine months later we began enrolling our first class in Athens in our MSIN program there.

An interesting issue arose because in Greece the government will not fully accredit any degree not offered by a Greek university. That condition is part of the country's constitution. On the other hand, that did not prevent Carnegie Mellon from offering a degree based on our own standing (and accreditation.) There was, I think, a natural set of pro/con sentiments on the part of the government. On the one hand, there was understandable worry from some in the government and its regulatory system about a foreign university coming into the country. On the other hand, there was also an understandable sense within some parts of the government that if Greece wished to base part of its future on trying to be a knowledge and technology based economy, partnering with a top US university with world-class strength in the given technology area was perhaps exactly the way that country should proceed.

To solve this, the philanthropist and his company set up a foundation that in turn provided the needed not-for-profit structure into which we could embed a program that could be completely under our control in terms of curriculum, admission decisions, faculty, content, and so forth. We were provided the use of a very nice, state of the art physical facility for our teaching and research space needs. That framework has worked well now for seven years. There are about 25 students who come into the program every year. There are a couple of teaching track faculty jointly appointed at Carnegie Mellon and the foundation and a bevy of CM Pittsburgh faculty who go to Athens to teach for periods of time, sometimes broadcasting back to Pittsburgh from Athens or vice versa.

In South Africa, the partnership involved the South African federal government, which funded a group of black South African women from distressed regions to pursue a masters in software engineering. The first year of the program was offered in South Africa with digital materials from Pittsburgh and various teaching assistants and instructors on the ground. The second year was spent in Pittsburgh. The program worked well but presented some real issues involving time zones, distances, internet connectivity, and so on. Nonetheless, we felt it was a sustainable model. Unfortunately, the South African currency experienced a significant devaluation, and the government had to suspend the program after two cycles. (However, we have had some discussions more recently about reviving the program.)

In Australia, the sponsor was a combination of a South Australian government and the Australian federal government. The country and the state each felt that attracting international (as well as Australian) students to a top-notch, technically oriented set of masters programs would mesh well with their country's economic development strategy. As with Greece, the prevailing regulations prevented degrees being offered in Australia by other than an Australian university. In this case, working at the federal and state level, legislation was introduced and passed that allowed us to come into the country. Lovely facilities were made available. Adelaide is a fabulous city, and we began offering three masters programs in Adelaide.

If South Africa began to push the limits of time zones, Australia represented the ultimate testing of that problem. I used to joke that one reason why Adelaide was ideal for Carnegie Mellon was that if one asked where one would pop out if one went from the Pittsburgh campus straight through the center of the earth and back out the other side, it would be at our programs in Adelaide. As such and by necessity, our approach in Australia is to have a full-fledged set of faculty and Carnegie Mellon administrators who live and work for a semester (or more) at a time in Adelaide.

In Portugal, the sponsor was a combination of the national government, a set of Portuguese universities, and some private Portuguese corporations. The then newly elected prime minister of Portugal had campaigned on a pledge of putting in motion efforts to form meaningful bonds during his first year in office with at least two top-tier international universities to work with Portuguese universities to bring technological sophistication to the country to a greater degree than would otherwise be possible. I believe it was on day 364 that an MOU was signed between Carnegie Mellon and the Portuguese government, about a month after a similar agreement was reached with MIT. The Carnegie Mellon connection was in areas of electrical and computer engineering, human–computer interaction, technology and entrepreneurship. MIT's connection was in other engineering areas. It is also worth noting with regard to the Portugal programs that the fact we had a particular top senior faculty champion from Portugal was very important. Indeed, as a general statement, it has been our experience that having a particularly distinguished Carnegie Mellon faculty member from the country involved who is willing to serve as a champion of the effort is, if not a pure prerequisite, a very important positive factor in moving the programs forward.

In Japan, the driving force was the governor of the Hyogo prefecture in the capital city of Kobe. Hyogo wanted to establish a presence in cybersecurity and technology management that domestic universities were not well set up to achieve. The arrangements were similar to the above in terms of the government providing the facilities and ensuring support for a minimum level of student support.

In Silicon Valley, which most would not consider a foreign country from the perspective of Pittsburgh (although there has been some debate on this), we established a campus in 1999 at Moffet Field, right next to NASA's Ames Research Center. This was one of our first such domestic ventures outside Pittsburgh. There were many reasons for wishing to have a presence in Silicon Valley. As a top university in information technology, a presence in the Mecca of the IT industry had and continues to have many appeals. We have an extraordinary number of alumni in Silicon Valley. And, not only has Silicon Valley been at the heart of the IT industry but is also, more generally, one of the global centers for entrepreneurship. Again, having a presence there had and still has many appeals.

Ten years later, we are still there and, I am happy to say, our professional masters of education programs are doing pretty well, as are some budding research activities (ranging from mobility to robotics.) We have several hundred students in a variety of IT-related masters programs, with enrollments growing smartly. But, at the same time, I think it is fair to say that we have learned a lot from our experiences in setting up an operation in Silicon Valley.

For example, we did not have a sponsor or partner to assure fail-safe financial sustainability. Instead, the notion was that we would recruit and bring in the requisite number of students with the requisite tuition. It is fine to have that arrangement if you are successful, and it is also fine to have that arrangement if you also have an exit strategy that is not financially problematic. Alas, we did not have such a strategy with regard to the latter. We made an investment of approximately $10M in plant and equipment, and when enrollments ramped up slower than we had planned we were without the kinds of options we would have wished for.

The other prong of our strategy was a vibrant research partnership with NASA Ames. We received a $27M research contract with NASA Ames concurrent with opening our campus there. Through no fault of ours and no fault of NASA Ames, the higher politics of NASA priorities reduced that effectively to a small fraction of the original amount within the first two years of our operation. Nonetheless, first under the leadership of Dean James Morris (previously our dean of Computer Science) and now under the leadership of Dean Pradeep Khosla (our dean of Engineering), we seem to be pointed in a positive direction in Silicon Valley.

Before concluding this quick synopsis of our professional masters programs abroad, let me mention several other models we have pursued. In software engineering, we have arrangements with a top Korean university where we in essence offer a "dual degree." Faculty from that university teach some of the key courses in that curriculum, and CM faculty do as well. The students spend a semester on the Pittsburgh campus.

Still a different model is one we have pursued for seven years with the Singapore Management University's College of Information Systems. They offer an undergraduate degree in information systems. We teach none of their courses and we offer no Carnegie Mellon degree. But we have worked hard and very productively with them in setting up their curriculum, in helping recruit their faculty, and in pursuing some joint research projects with their faculty. In addition, the Singapore government and SMU sponsor a program where some of their students come to Pittsburgh, taking our own Pittsburgh information systems classes, and using them for credit to finish their SMU degree. In addition, if they are admitted and choose to, they can be enrolled in a joint bachelor's and masters program, finishing both the B.S. and M.S. in five years.

In all these programs, we put a very large emphasis on being "the real deal." We want to be good partners, and partners for the long run. Yet, it is not always the case that these programs last forever. The financial situation of our sponsors and partners can ebb and flow, and indeed the most recent global financial crisis is a case in point where we are working with some of our sponsors to make sure the programs can survive through these difficult times. Still, most have stood the test of time and hopefully will continue for years to come.

As I have indicated, we pay great attention to quality because at the end of the day that is the one critical characteristic that must be maintained. This takes many forms and is greatly facilitated by the fact that these programs have long-standing instantiations in Pittsburgh. We make sure the exams, homework assignments, and grading standards are the same as for the home campus. We often have blind admissions where the pool of students are evaluated for admission by a common committee regardless of whether they will be attending Pittsburgh or a program abroad. We are proud of the graduates of these programs and they are proving to be pursuing highly successful professional careers.

PH.D. PROGRAMS – ONE OF TWO "GREAT EXCEPTIONS"

The vast majority of our efforts offering degrees outside Pittsburgh are professional masters programs. I want to talk briefly about new efforts over the past few years with Ph.D. programs, and then I want to talk in somewhat more detail about our one undergraduate program.

In doing so, I would like to start by making a distinction that I feel is important. As I mentioned above, in the case of professional masters programs, the key metric of quality is career "value added," whereas for undergraduate and for Ph.D. programs the metric is the sheer academic excellence of the students and the sophistication of the curriculum.

For this reason, we have been reluctant to explore nearly as proactively the offering of Ph.D. programs or undergraduate programs outside the Pittsburgh campus. Yet, in the last few years, with Portugal and with Korea, to name two examples, we have moved into the Ph.D. arena, but very much in a tight partnership with top universities from those respective countries. In essence, there are some extraordinary Ph.D. students and some very excellent faculty in these countries with whom we would like to work. In the programs we have set up, the students spend about half their time doing core academic requirements in their home country and the other half taking requirements in Pittsburgh. We impose all the usual requirements of field exams and so forth, as does our international partner. When it comes time for the student to do their thesis, they have a committee that can be drawn from the two universities. Where they spend the majority of their time geographically in pursuing their thesis depends on who their primary advisor is and the source of funding. We are in the early stages of these efforts, but they seem promising.

UNDERGRADUATE PROGRAMS: THE EVEN GREATER EXCEPTION

The biggest challenge in offering degree programs outside our US home campus, by an order of magnitude, is in offering Carnegie Mellon undergraduate degrees. Here, too, the quality of the program is a function not only of professional value added, as it is for professional masters programs, but also of the absolute excellence of the academic standing of the students and the rigor of the curriculum. When we offer physicians a course in accounting, we want to offer a course that is most practically beneficial to them in their professional roles, whether as medical practitioners or hospital administrators. When we offer an undergraduate computer science degree, we want the courses that the students complete to be among the most demanding in the nation in the sheer academic level of achievement that is required.

In addition, there is another dimension that is daunting in considering offering an undergraduate degree outside the main campus. The enterprise of undergraduate education is more than an academic enterprise alone. One is fundamentally assuming the role of helping develop and mature young individuals at the age of 18 into adulthood.

Yet, if the challenges are the largest, the potential rewards and transformational impacts on the home campus are as well. That, at least, has been our experience in our effort, which is entering its sixth year, of a full undergraduate set of offerings in Education City in the country of Qatar. Our discussions with Qatar began seven years ago. Five years ago we opened our doors to a class of about forty students, almost all Arab Islamic students from the Gulf area, about half Qatari citizens. We offered full-fledged Carnegie Mellon degrees in computer science and business. In the years since, we have added an undergraduate degree in information systems.

There is no event in my decade as provost pertaining to the globalization activities of Carnegie Mellon University that was more unanticipated *ex ante* or as impactful on the University *ex post*. This impact has been very positive and gratifying on many dimensions. There is a tremendous amount that can be said about the unprecedented effort in Education City. But, here I just want to focus on a number of points.

Our partner in this effort is the Qatar Foundation, led by Sheika Mozah Bint Nassar Al-Misned. The Qatar Foundation has been a truly outstanding partner. They made it clear from the outset that we commit to sacrifice no iota of quality from our standards for Pittsburgh. The rigor of the curriculum, grading and so forth had to be identical to our programs in Pittsburgh. At our insistence but with their very keen assent, we have complete control on academic matters such as curriculum, faculty, courses, admissions, and so forth. We both agreed that there would be a metacurricular and extracurricular experience for the students as close as possible to what we have in Pittsburgh.

A fascinating aspect of our activities in Education City is that, in addition to the Qatar Foundation being our partner, we are partnered with some of the finest US universities who also are core members of Education

City: Cornell, Virginia Commonwealth, Georgetown, Texas A&M, and Northwestern.

One of the fascinating issues for all of us in terms of "partnership" arrangements is how we can all work together to make the whole of Education City greater than the sum of its parts. This notion has been termed the creation of a *multiversity*: developing synergies among the branch campuses in ways that can be done nowhere else in the world, leading to a truly distinct opportunity for higher education in the 21st century – where a student can take business or computer science from Carnegie Mellon and international relations from Georgetown, to name but one of many permutations.

All of the branch campuses, as well as the Qatar Foundation, recognized that before we focused on interactions among the campuses, the first and clearly predominant priority in the establishment of Education City had to be establishing the individual branch campuses and providing the assurance that the quality and rigor of the degree programs in Education City, as well as the academic performance of the students, are of the same high standard as at the home campuses. This has, in turn, required each of the campuses to retain full autonomy over each of their core academic prerogatives. These include degree requirements, course and faculty selection and presentation, decisions on admissions into the programs, and the like.

This has involved a tremendous effort by literally hundreds of individuals from each of the individual campuses and the Qatar Foundation leadership. I think it is the judgment of each of the campuses that this great and primary challenge is indeed being achieved, and in fact is being achieved more thoroughly and successfully than we might have felt possible in the short time that Education City has existed. Most of the branch campuses have now graduated students and, without putting words in the mouths of each dean, president, and chancellor, it seems clear that these graduates are viewed by each campus as clearly having academic accomplishment and achievement fully equal to graduates of the home campus. While it will of course require constant vigilance to ensure that this level of quality is always maintained, there is a strong sense of having now achieved "proof of concept" in this primary goal of Education City.

In addition to the academic learning in the classroom, as noted above, college is also about broad-based personal development and maturation, personal wellness and quality of student life. Collectively, these may be viewed as the second priority in the establishment of Education City. Much progress has now been made in each campus in these regards. Each branch campus devotes much attention to student affairs and student life. In addition, the Office of Faculty and Student Services in the Educational

Division of the Qatar Foundation complements these campus-specific efforts with Education City-wide activities and efforts in these areas.

The notion of the multiversity then becomes the third priority in the evolution of Education City, although certainly a priority that is highly complementary with the first two. As noted above, the notion of the multiversity is rooted in the synergies that can arise from the co-location of six world-class universities in a single site, and the potentials for each campus to be stronger from being able to draw from the other campuses, with Education City students being able to take advantage of the entire set of universities in Education City, something that can be done nowhere else in the world.

Space does not allow me to give full justice to the many cooperative efforts that are underway. These involve substantial cross-listing of courses, co-teaching of courses, mutual summer and K-12 programs, and much more. But, I am optimistic that there is much potential in our mutual pursuit of the international university of the future. I am optimistic that this enterprise represents an internationally significant effort to bring the Western and Arab Islamic worlds together, with great benefits for both.

BACK TO THE DETAILS

In these notes I have been trying to keep some if not much of the discussion at a "nuts and bolts" level. In this spirit, I would like to end by mentioning one additional practical issue we have often encountered. This is the challenge faced by the academic directors who are engaged in championing these international programs. No matter how entrepreneurial and administratively adept they may be, they are often surprised by the sheer managerial demands that are imposed upon them by the contractual obligations that they are suddenly having to manage.

Let me give two examples. We had an outstanding department head who had a great idea of a set of options for students who could spend each of four semesters at different locations, in the US and abroad. (Let us call them country A and country B.) This had many challenges but much appeal. At one point, we asked how the finances of moving the student from one country to another at the end of the semester would work. We were told that this had been fully budgeted. The response from those in central who know about some of the tax details indicated that, while that was fine, this is a taxable benefit to the student if you pay for the plane ticket. We cannot simply tell the students that they should be aware of this when they do their taxes. It must be withheld. Moreover, it is more complex in the sense that not only do we have to withhold income from the students, but the amount depends on the tax treaties between the US (country A) and country B. And, if the student is from country C, then it also depends on the tax treaties between countries C, A, and B. This all eventually got resolved, but not easily, and is indicative of the added dimensions of complexity that can be encountered when formal contracts impose managerial control restrictions that are not as common on the home campus.

As a second example, the director of another program had some faculty who were promised condos that were not ready in time. They were in alternative quarters – not terrible, but not what they had been promised. While it was only a matter of weeks, the director provided some side benefits that had some financial ramifications to those who were displaced. As an act of common sense this was wise. Had it been done on the Pittsburgh campus, the reaction would likely have been that this was against common procedures but under the circumstances it seemed a reasonable way to proceed. But given the contract that applied on this international program, since such action was not consistent with explicit standard procedures at the Pittsburgh campus and since there were no such procedures, the separate auditors of our contract would surely classify such expenditures as unallowable.

I think that any of the directors or key administrators involved in our degree programs outside the United States will say that the frequency of issues such as these – unintended inflexibility due to the specific wording of initial contractual terms, without itemizing explicitly potential exceptions – becomes one of the challenges in setting up and sustaining such programs. These types of things can be overcome and kept from being undue distractions. But, as complicated as administrative standard operating procedures may be on the home campus, and as complex as faculty handbooks and other policies can be on the home campus, there is a greater amount of time (and ultimately cost) on management issues of these sorts both in the international programs themselves and by the central administration back in Pittsburgh. This echoes back to one of the themes I began with: namely the added challenges facing legal, financial, human resource, and provost office staff in supplying the administrative infrastructure that can allow international programs to thrive. And, that in turn underscores another item mentioned early on, which is that establishing and running top quality programs outside the main campus, as rewarding as they can be on many levels, is more not less demanding on management and more not less expensive to do. Universities that enter into such arrangements not aware of these realities will probably encounter a period of painful adjustment as these truths become evident.

CONCLUSION

The various efforts towards globalization of Carnegie Mellon – including importantly the offering of Carnegie Mellon degree programs outside of Pittsburgh and outside of the United States – have been major priorities for the university over the past decade. The jury is surely still out on some aspects of how these programs will evolve and fare over time and their ultimate impact on the fabric of the university. Still, from my judgment, the rewards institutionally (and societally) have been greater than we would have guessed.

As the programs have grown and developed, they have garnered generally positive support from the home campus, including students, faculty, and trustees. We have become a broader and more "worldly" university, with many positive feedbacks between our efforts outside the United States and those within the home campus. We have broadened our network of connections to individuals, institutions, companies, governments, and other universities in parts of the world which will be areas of growth in terms of wealth, power, and influence over the coming decades. It will be fascinating to see if over the next decade there are synergies that come from these connections, perhaps in ways that we cannot but anticipate at present.

Other universities, as I have mentioned, will doubtless pursue their own paths in terms of whether and how they become involved in educational programs outside their main campus. Regardless, I hope that this chapter provides some food for thought in terms of one university's experiences to date, and that some aspects of our experiences are of relevance and help for others that may be following similar or related paths.

6. Creating successful study abroad experiences

M. Peter McPherson and Margaret Heisel

Study abroad growth among U.S. college and university students has surged in the last decade, increasing by a remarkable 150 percent. Scholars have always valued the combination of international travel and study, providing as it does the opportunity not only to gain a new perspective on an academic interest or learn a different approach to a discipline, but also to experience the energy and excitement that immersion in a radically different environment can supply. The increases we are seeing in study abroad recently, however, have also been fueled by changes that are fundamentally altering relations among countries – changes that are redefining what students need to know for careers and civic life in the 21st century. Technology, communications, access to travel, and, most importantly, the globalized economy have altered how students and educators see international study. The information revolution, the global economy and capital market, environmental concerns, and global health and safety have dramatically increased students' need for direct experience abroad.

For the future, it is clear that resources – both the opportunities and the problems associated with resources – will be shared across national borders. And with this shift comes a greatly increased need for cooperation and coordination and for international experience as a fundamental part of higher education. The business community as well as educators now recognize the need for international study as an element of higher education programs, not only for the exposure to a foreign culture, but also for the opportunity for experiential learning – the chance to engage directly and concretely with issues and problems in a global context.

It is not just universities in the U.S. that are enlarging their study abroad programs. Japanese, Korean, Canadian, and Australian universities all are beginning to plan semester abroad programs for their students. The European Union has initiated a very ambitious program called the Bologna Process in order to promote student mobility. While it is designed to harmonize higher education systems across the European Union in ways that will reflect evolving political and economic changes, its fundamental assumption is that it is essential for students, in preparing for economic and social life, to gain an education that transcends national boundaries. The goals set for the Bologna Process are ambitious and will take years to accomplish, but quite clearly the underlying premise of this effort is that students must have the capacity to move among national educational systems with ease and efficiency.

Students in other nations also often gain international experience by pursuing full degree programs abroad. In fact, U.S. higher education has benefited from and dominated this field for some time, receiving large numbers of talented international students into its degree programs, especially at the graduate level. This pattern, too, is now changing as Australia, the United Kingdom, Canada, and European nations, among others, are energetically competing to bring more of these international students to their educational institutions. In the future the exchange of students across borders is likely to be extremely varied in terms of origins and destinations, and competition for the highest achieving students will be international.

AMERICAN EDUCATION'S INTERNATIONAL IMPERATIVE

It is critical for America's future economic well-being and its social and political security that our students gain a global perspective. The Lincoln Commission, established by Congress in 2004 to recommend legislation to address this issue, stated the case forcefully: "What nations do not know exacts a heavy toll. The stakes involved in study abroad are that simple, that straightforward, and that important" (Commission on the Abraham Lincoln Study Abroad Fellowship Program, 2005, p.3.) The report of the Commission set a goal for American undergraduate study abroad participation at one million students by 2017 – a fivefold increase from the roughly 200,000 students who studied abroad in 2005–06.

While study abroad is growing as a part of global higher education, there is ferment and experimentation in the field as institutions struggle to understand and respond to the emerging changes in technology and international access and communication. As with all transforming events, it is hard for large and historic institutions to grasp the full consequences of social and economic change and adapt their structures. Thus, many different international academic programs are emerging.

These new programs also of course are conditioned by the heterogeneity of U.S. colleges and universities. As one of the core institutions of the American society, one which mirrors the values and outlook of the nation, our system of higher education has been highly successful in contributing to the economic and social development of the United States, and it has undergone many different changes over time. But it is not monolithic; it is made up of thousands of individual institutions with significantly different perspectives, curricula, goals, and structures.

So it is not surprising that we are witnessing many different responses to globalization within higher education. Some of these include international research partnerships, faculty and student exchanges, branch campuses, dual and joint degrees, and recruitment of international students for undergraduate and (most especially) graduate programs. But undergraduate study abroad occupies one of the most prominent places in this network of educational internationalization, and now is offered at most U.S. colleges and universities. And, within this growth, a very diverse pattern of offerings is emerging, shaped by the needs of all the various academic disciplines, by economic, environmental, social, and political challenges, and by the interests of participating students.

In this chapter, we will present a profile of students studying abroad, describe some of the most significant types of study abroad, and discuss some of the challenges and opportunities that lie ahead for this very important aspect of U.S. postsecondary education and for the students who will be entering colleges in the coming years.

STUDY ABROAD PARTICIPANT PROFILE

The number of students participating in study abroad has been rising at a steady and goodly pace. Last year, numbers increased by 8 percent, to a total of 241,791. Surveying the past decade, the numbers have gone from just less than 100,000 in 1996–97 to their present level of almost 250,000 – a remarkable 150 percent increase.

Most participants study abroad in either their junior or senior year. The majority are women (65 versus 35 percent) and roughly 80 percent are Caucasian. The majority of participants are social science, management/business, or humanities majors. The fastest growing area is business/management, reflecting the globalization of the economy during the last decade and clear recognition of the importance of international experience for students in this field.

Study Abroad in the Academic Major

It is likely that the proportion of business majors studying abroad will grow even more sharply in the coming decades. Already we are seeing some institutions, such as the University of Minnesota's Carlson School of Business, incorporate international study as a graduation requirement. Beginning with students entering in 2008, all undergraduate majors will be required to meet this new standard. Michigan State University's Broad College of Business has made global awareness and engagement an institutional priority, and is "working to define what it means to be a world grant university in the 21st century" (Michigan State University, 2009.) Leading private universities' business schools around the country also are rapidly building new and innovative international programs for their students. MIT's Sloan School of Business, the University of Pennsylvania's Wharton School, Harvard Business School, and many others have announced global initiatives to provide their students direct experience in the global economy. *The Wall Street Journal* (April 21, 2009) reported that "international experiential learning – where students are immersed in real-world experiences – is becoming mainstream." The *Journal* highlights nontraditional study abroad programs, such as the partnership between the University of South Carolina's Moore School of Business and the Chinese University of Hong Kong, in which students will have a chance to spend two years studying at each institution.

In addition, fields such as health science and engineering also are working rapidly to build new programs that will allow their students to gain "hands-on" contact with the discipline across national borders. Global health, for example, is one of the fields undergoing explosive growth and rising importance all across higher education. The University of North Carolina, the University of Washington, Duke University, Yale, the University of California and many others are rapidly building new programs that span the globe. They are employing multi-disciplinary expertise to study the engagement of medicine, economics, social systems, politics, and environmental science in health problems. Increasingly it is clear that solving health problems will require cooperative work across national borders. Another example is that of environmental science programs in which issues and problems are taken up in the local context, allowing students to directly confront the balance that must be struck between economic development and environmental preservation, viewed up close through observation and interviews with local scientists, officials and workers.

Likewise in engineering programs, international experience is beginning to be recognized as critical to 21st century problems. The Rensselaer Polytechnic Institute (RPI) is beginning collaborations with the Technical University of Denmark and the Nanyang Technological University of Singapore, with the expectation of expanding to many other institutions in Asia, Europe, South America, Australia, and Africa. RPI expects to welcome international students to enroll in the place of those who are studying abroad. Massachusetts Institute of Technology, Purdue, Georgia

Tech, and the University of Rhode Island all are promoting international experience in their engineering programs. The National Academy of Engineering has reported that

> U.S. engineers must become global engineers. The engineer of 2020 and beyond will need skills to be globally competitive over the length of her or his career. It is essential for the experience of engineering students as well as faculty members to include a global perspective and an appreciation of the societal implications in their work. (National Academy of Engineering, 2005)

Destinations and Duration

For many years, the region of the world receiving the highest numbers of U.S. study abroad participants has been European countries. The United Kingdom has traditionally been the destination of the greatest number of students, no doubt in part because of shared language and the relative ease of transferring academic credits from universities in this region to North American colleges and universities. France, Italy, Spain, and Australia also have been among the top destinations (Bhandari and Chow, 2008, Figure 9C.)

But in recent years, an increasing number of students are choosing other destinations. Asia, Africa, Latin America, and the Middle East all are growing annually, some by double digit proportions. Duration of study abroad also is in transition. In its earlier history, study abroad most frequently was a semester-long or year-long program. But over the past decade, that pattern has changed. Today only 5 percent of study abroad students spend a full calendar or academic year abroad. The greatest proportion (55 percent) spend between two and eight weeks abroad and 36 percent spend a semester abroad (Bhandari and Chow, 2008, Figure 9D.)

TYPES OF STUDY ABROAD EXPERIENCE

Faculty-led Programs

One of the most common types of programs is that of a U.S. college/university faculty member leading a program in which he/she teaches a course or multiple courses in a foreign location. These programs generally provide students access to unique resources available at that site. For example, a program in the economics of developing nations might take place in South Africa and allow participants to meet and speak with government and private sector leaders there, as well as community organizers, labor leaders, and others. With the theoretical coursework structure provided by the faculty member, these discussions and site visits at workplaces, government projects and other facilities offer students a completely different and vastly enriched opportunity to understand the challenges of these countries and the ideas being tested in addressing these challenges.

Exchange Programs

American colleges and universities also develop agreements with academic institutions in other countries allowing students to enroll in a partner institution, to experience the pedagogy, academic structure, and particular disciplinary perspective of coursework in another culture. These exchanges are usually quite cost effective and provide in-depth exposure to another country, promoting full integration into the local environment. Exchange programs also can promote ongoing relationships between the partner institutions, stimulating joint research projects and faculty exchange as well. Such exchanges also can contribute greatly to students' language skills. (A variant of this type of program is "direct enrollment," in which a student from a U.S. institution independently applies to and enrolls at a foreign university, taking coursework along with local students and fully integrating his/her academic and social life into that of the foreign site.)

Internship, Research, and Service Programs

These programs are designed to give students a significant work or research experience in a host country or culture, while also providing academic and social support. The programs generally immerse the student into a foreign workplace or social service agency where the participant not only is integrated into the local culture but also has the opportunity to gain practical knowledge related to an academic discipline in which he/she is interested. These experiences may or may not allow for academic credit. As an example, a student might be placed with a health care facility in Latin America, working with physicians, nurses, government health officials and agencies such as the United Nations in developing programs for local populations. In such cases, students gain a broad and nuanced understanding of local beliefs, practices, customs, and health care policies. At the same time, their language skills can be developed and their understanding of the local socioeconomic and political environment will grow immeasurably.

But beyond these major categories, there are a plethora of other types of programs and learning experiences in which students are engaging. We do not have reliable data surveying all the varying structures of study abroad programs, but anecdotes tend to suggest greater emphasis on experiential learning through field research, internships, and volunteering. How these are integrated into the curriculum is still a subject very much in transition. Whether international study is to be a discrete addition to the general education pattern, or a component of the student's academic major, or follow some other route of integration into the curriculum is still a matter of experimentation and debate.

CHALLENGES FACING STUDY ABROAD

Although the picture for study abroad is a very bright and promising one, there are many challenges that must be surmounted in order for this new area of learning to achieve its full potential. Just to name a few, one might begin with the makeup of participants. As data cited earlier demonstrate, there are imbalances with regard to the gender and ethnic makeup of participants. Women outnumber men at a considerable rate and under-represented minority students – African American, Latino, and Asian American students – still are not participating at their proportional levels in the postsecondary population.

While data on the family income levels of participants are fragmentary, judging by the institutions from which participants originate, one could surmise that low-income students are poorly represented. Large research institutions and selective liberal arts colleges are more likely to send their students abroad than are comprehensive and master's level institutions. Community colleges, where more than half of all postsecondary students enroll, send very small numbers.

Another very significant challenge is resources. To launch sound, substantive programs, institutions need both expertise and financial resources. Likewise students need travel funds to participate, although often they are discouraged from study abroad even when financial aid funds and low-cost options may be available. This issue is one that needs the support and attention not just of educational institutions but of federal and state governments, foundations, and the private sector. Neither students nor colleges/universities can build strong programs without new resource streams – especially in the current financial climate.

THE CENTER FOR CAPACITY BUILDING IN STUDY ABROAD

In 2008, NAFSA (the Association of International Educators) and A.P.L.U. (the Association of Public and Land-grant Universities, formerly

NASULGC) co-founded The Center for Capacity Building in Study Abroad to address these and other challenges. The Center will not only serve those already engaged in expansion of study abroad but also provide institutions willing to expand their study abroad, but lacking the knowledge and expertise, with the resources needed to accomplish those goals. It will focus on assisting decision-makers and policy-makers in institutions of various types and sizes, sharing the knowledge it collects and develops widely.[1]

There are, of course, many elements that need to be considered in expanding study abroad. Operational issues, such as standards, risk management, program operations, and so on are addressed in depth by organizations such as A.P.L.U., NAFSA[2] and The Forum on Education Abroad.[3] Yet, there is still a lack of widely available information on a number of topics that underpin institutional decision-making in the arena of study abroad. In late 2008 and early 2009, the Center staff attended numerous international education meetings, talked with a variety of campus leaders from institutions large and small, and consulted with the higher education associations. Out of this six-month-long data-gathering effort, there emerged a set of key institutional issues where information is still lacking, or is not yet consolidated into a form that is useful for a wide variety of institutions. Five areas stood out as needing attention, and have become the Center's focus areas for the next few years.

The first is the need for every institution to conceive and articulate a mission and goal for study abroad. Many institutions have not as yet conceived – or reconceived – their study abroad programs as an integral element of their undergraduate curriculum. As a result, campus academic and administrative leadership often has not formed a consensus on expected outcomes, optimal content, the degree to which study abroad is integral to the curriculum, and the duration and structure of study abroad. What assumptions and expectations are guiding study abroad program development?

In its past, study abroad was generally the province of students majoring in the humanities or social sciences, and in these areas it is generally a well-accepted element of the curriculum. But now that virtually every discipline must come to terms with globalization, integrating study abroad is a challenge. There is still little agreement about what should be achieved in terms of different levels of integration into the foreign community: language acquisition, appreciation of cultural differences, understanding of how the discipline is structured in the host institution, and so on. The Center aims to engage the academic community in a focused way in discussing and studying these questions in the coming years.

The second area of focus, as emphasized in Chapter 8 by Patti McGill

Peterson, is to engage the faculty as advocates for study abroad. This need follows directly from the first. Institutional commitment implies engagement, support, and advocacy from the faculty first and foremost. How does an institution gain the faculty leadership and momentum to re-conceptualize the curriculum to encompass international issues and experience in ways that meet twenty-first century demands? Answering this question is urgent and essential. Leadership from university presidents and provosts greatly increases interest and provides direction for broad-based study abroad participation, but more than any other factor, faculty support must be established. Faculty usually see their own research in international terms – keeping abreast of developing trends throughout the world and often collaborating and exchanging ideas with colleagues internationally. But many faculty do not readily accept the role of study abroad in the curriculum, and some disciplines are much more international in focus and methodology than others. These faculty often need to see firsthand what a study abroad experience can contribute and how it can be adapted to the configuration of their particular discipline. The American Council on Education (ACE) has done excellent work on this subject, in particular providing new thinking and examples of successful projects where international perspective is infused into various disciplines in its publication, *Where Faculty Live: Internationalizing the Disciplines* (Green and Shoenberg, 2006.)

Models for faculty engagement are many. Some institutions provide travel grants to faculty specifically for the purpose of gaining firsthand experience of the international dimensions of their research and teaching, to meet potential research collaborators, and to appreciate how study abroad can enrich undergraduate education. Rollins College made the news in October 2008, when its president announced a comprehensive new program to send every faculty and staff member with teaching duties abroad once every three years (Fischer, 2008.) But institutions as diverse as the University of Richmond, Maricopa Community College, Troy University, Rhodes College, Grinnell College, and many others have existing programs of a similar type – an indication that not only the largest universities can meet this challenge.

Even more commonly, colleges and universities send faculty either as instructors or as advisers with groups of students studying abroad. Michigan State University has been a leader in this arena, scheduling large numbers of its study abroad programs between May and August, engaging faculty from disciplines less represented in the traditional study abroad population, and giving them teaching and learning experience throughout the world.

In addition to offering faculty incentives directly related to study abroad programs, college and university leadership can signal support for internationalization generally by recognizing this factor in faculty job descriptions and announcements, incorporating it into tenure and promotion guidelines, and offering financial support for research projects that include international collaboration.

Faculty engagement is also the key to solving one of the often-cited impediments to study abroad: issues of academic credit. Students can be concerned that they will lose the opportunity to enroll in sequential coursework on campus, lose opportunities to work closely with faculty members, not have their study abroad coursework valued or accepted for credit, and thereby lengthen time to degree and increase financial costs. These are very real obstacles for students at any campus where study abroad is not an appropriately recognized curricular component. Faculty and administrative leaders on campus must recognize this problem and ensure that students know, as they plan their study abroad experience, how it will contribute to their progress to degree, not only in terms of general education and electives, but towards their major. Faculty advice and guidance on these points is absolutely essential. Properly structured, advising in preparation for study abroad can help students gain valuable insight with regard to their academic goals and progress overall and the relationship of their academic work to an eventual career.

The Center for Capacity Building is collecting information on different programs that have successfully involved faculty in study abroad, tracking innovative curricular patterns that encompass an international perspective, and assisting faculty and administrators working locally to advance in this work. Most recently, as an example, staff at the Center have engaged with a group of faculty from several universities working collectively to surmount institutional barriers to consortia agreements so that teaching responsibilities abroad can be shared and appropriately credited among various participating departments and universities.

The third critical issue in study abroad identified by the Center is the challenge of finance. The Center will inventory what already exists, but it is clear that this aspect of planning for study abroad expansion has not received the attention it must have. What is the range of experience in terms of costs institutions should expect to shoulder for study abroad programs and what are optimal practices with regard to "who pays" these costs? How does financing link to each institution's overall resource plan?

In surveys conducted among students and institutions to determine level of interest in study abroad, one of the most common barriers cited is cost – cost to the student and cost to the institution to provide programs. In January 2008, the College Board, American Council on Education (ACE) and Art & Science Group conducted a survey of college-bound high school students to assess their attitudes toward international study. Fifty percent of students indicated a desire to study abroad. Among students who do not wish to study abroad, the most frequently cited reason was cost.

When institutions are committed to ensuring all their students an opportunity to participate in study abroad, the college or university usually allows participants to take their institutional financial aid – along with federal and state financial aid – to pay costs. Obviously, this can impose a considerable institutional financial burden. Furthermore, as participation levels rise, these burdens become more onerous. In addition, institutions generally offer an array of different program modalities – self-sponsored, collaborative, third-party provider, exchange, faculty-led, and more. A portfolio of different types is often needed in order to give students a range of options in terms of location, duration, and disciplinary focus. Of course, resource demands differ for each of these, along with the issues of currency fluctuation, faculty participation, and risk management. Costs or resource structures that may have been manageable with small numbers of participants in a limited number of programs can become much more challenging when the portfolio of programs becomes larger and more complex. And students also find costs to be a burden when they are required to spend more for study abroad than a comparable time on-campus would require or when it extends time to degree. Institutions that rely heavily on summer study abroad often are increasing student expenses, over and above regular academic year on-campus costs of the degree, while students forego summer earnings. While federal and state financial aid can usually be used for study abroad, those depending on loans and work-study suffer.

The task the Center is embracing is to shed light on the financial structures in different types of institutions, sharing knowledge and ideas about how to most effectively and efficiently cover costs. This involves discussion of finances, comparison of portfolios and costs to identify best practices, and leadership in gaining recognition of necessary investments from states, the federal government, and private donors. The Center is issuing a white paper on this topic in spring, 2010.

The fourth challenge is the need to build an effective organization to support study abroad. What are the comparative advantages of choices for portfolios of offerings and institutional organization for support of quality study abroad offerings? How can mobilization of admissions, financial aid, academic advising, and other campus operations contribute to institutional success in expanding study abroad? The Center's agenda with regard to organization of study abroad links to, and encompasses, all three of the previous issues. As rapid changes are taking place in internationalization of U.S. campuses, the role that study abroad will play and its place within the institution is also changing. Often viewed as a stand-alone activity, it is now drawn much more directly into the academic core of colleges and universities, ideally linked to a wide array of international activities: international research, enrollment of international students, an increasingly diverse campus cultural environment, branch campuses and international programs offering joint or dual degrees, and public and community service activities with an international focus, to mention a few.

Beyond these ties to other international programs and activities, with a growing study abroad population campuses must address a variety of administrative issues: financial support for a strong organization and assistance to students so that all may participate, links with admissions and enrollment management to plan for student absence during academic terms, training of advisory staff to ensure knowledge of study abroad courses as an element of degree planning and degree checks, and development of expertise among registrar staff members reviewing international documents, among others. Virtually every academic and administrative unit on campus needs closer ties to the institution's international study programs and a deeper understanding of the goals of these programs as the number of participants increases.

Generally, this has been accomplished through high-level leadership. One might think particularly about institutions that have set numerical goals for study abroad – Goucher College now requires study abroad of every student. University of Minnesota and Michigan State some time ago set goals, strongly supported by academic and faculty leadership. Institutions also focus on participation levels by discipline, income level, ethnicity, and other factors, to ensure universal student access.

For each administrative unit on campus that links with study abroad, there is a pool of knowledge and methods that can be shared, and the Center is working to collect this information and see that it is made broadly accessible. For example, it is building a data set through campus institutional research offices that can help in refining recruitment and financial support for study abroad, informing advisers and faculty about articulation of coursework and time to degree patterns, and sharing techniques for integrating returning students and their study abroad experiences into the campus.

A fifth challenge is the need to identify capacity for the effective expansion of study abroad. Where is there emerging capacity? Given the number of students studying Spanish, what are the opportunities in Latin America? Given the increasing economic importance and expansion of higher education institutions in Asia, what opportunities lie there for those just starting to make connections? What about Africa and the Middle

East? The last priority on the Center's agenda looks beyond the internal institutional issues of U.S. colleges and universities, and focuses on where this expansion can take place internationally. What is the potential of Latin America, Asia, Africa, and the Middle East for enrolling more study abroad students? These venues have enrolled relatively small proportions of study abroad students up to this time, but they offer some of the best opportunities for the new types of experience that students need today. The most recent report from the Institute of International Education found that European countries continued to host the largest share (57 percent) of study abroad participants (Bhandari and Chow, 2008, p. 19.) But large increases are beginning to appear in other regions. In 2008, there was 20 percent growth in students going to Asia and a 19 percent increase to Africa. Latin America and the Middle East each experienced 7 percent growth. In all of these regions, more work must be done to examine new possibilities for alliances and study opportunities tailored to local strengths.

STUDY ABROAD: AN EMERGING FIELD FOR RESEARCH

The Center is not staffed to engage in significant independent research on study abroad, but it aims to identify and spotlight areas where collection of new information and engaging research effort is badly needed and to publicize research findings that are of particular importance.

As a field for research, study abroad needs more basic data. While credit-bearing study abroad experiences are reported by study abroad directors to the Institute of International Education, many students pursue learning experiences abroad outside the aegis of their institutional office. Furthermore, many institutions do not systematically track and record the study abroad experiences of their students, especially when the student enrolls via another college or university program or through a private provider program. Campus institutional research directors need to become more closely engaged in this effort, incorporating information into their data files, ensuring consistent data definitions, and tracking changes in the field. Study abroad needs to be better integrated into existing institutional research efforts. What can we say, concretely, about the value added of study abroad?

Likewise, the field needs better information on the different types of study abroad, measuring effectiveness of different structures, learning more about the relationship of learning to time spent abroad, locations, classroom work versus internships or research projects, and other content and outcome information. How can we better coordinate language instruction with study abroad? How can we track and better communicate advances in study abroad integration into all the different academic disciplines? How can institutions better articulate the value of study abroad/international alliances? And most especially, how can research help better define what we most want students to learn from this experience?

Another area that needs additional research is the educational institutions themselves. The term "internationalization" is used to describe higher education imbued with a global focus. But what does this mean in practice? What are the metrics for measuring or judging internationalization?

EXPANDING STUDY ABROAD: THE NEXT STEPS

Surveying the study abroad field, one is struck by two perceptions. First is the great vitality and energy of students, faculty, and institutions in embracing international education. Spurred in particular by the communications revolution, the "net" of globalization is reaching and connecting peoples throughout the world. And students are anxiously seeking ways of connecting directly with global environmental, economic, and health care issues in unprecedented numbers. Virtually every academic discipline finds itself impacted by international forces. The nearly daily announcement of new international academic programs, campuses, and research programs makes evident the scope of these changes. This enthusiasm is of course not universally shared as basic assumptions and practices are shaken or altered.

The second perception is the difficulty in foreseeing the ultimate shape that this global educational process will take. Extending American higher education beyond our shores in substantive ways will very much be a process of give and take. We will teach and we will learn. Certainly U.S. higher education has been a model for the world – sought after and emulated throughout the world, in part through its flexibility and capacity to change. Just as American higher education has shifted and reorganized in the past to accommodate new realities in the national economy and workforce, and just as it has integrated ever larger proportions of young people into its programs, it is beginning to reshape its form to international demands. We can expect a higher number of international students enrolling in U.S. institutions, both here and abroad, and more U.S. students not just studying abroad for a month or a semester but perhaps for considerably longer periods. In short, the present study abroad may be a step toward truly international student populations at many universities worldwide.

But in the course of such fundamental change, we must confront serious issues of goals, structure, resources, research and information. To sustain America's leadership in higher education, we must engage the higher education community in a concerted effort to enlarge these programs and gain a better understanding of how international experience will be integrated into academic programs. And at the same time, we must work closely with the private sector and with state and federal government to study and publicize the purpose and outcomes of this important emerging area of education.

NOTES

1. The Center's resources can be found at its Web site, www.studyabroadcenter.org.
2. A.P.L.U.'s and NAFSA's resources can be found at their Web sites, http://www.aplu.org and http://www.nafsa.org/knowledge_community_network.sec/education_abroad.
3. The Forum on Education Abroad's Standards can be found at its Web site: http://www.forumea.org/standards-index.cfm.

REFERENCES

American Council on Education, Art & Science Group LLC, and the College Board (January 2008), "College Bound Students' Interest in Study Abroad and Other International Learning Activities," A Special Edition of *Student Poll*.

Bhandari, R. and P. Chow (2008), *Open Doors 2008: Report on International Educational Exchange*, New York: Institute of International Education.

Commission on the Abraham Lincoln Study Abroad Fellowship Program (2005), *Global Competence & National Needs*, Washington, DC: Lincoln Commission, November.

Fischer, Karin (2008), "Professors Get Their Own Study-Abroad Programs," *The Chronicle of Higher Education*, October 31 (55)10, A1.

Green, Madeleine F. and Robert Shoenberg (2006), *Where Faculty Live: Internationalizing the Disciplines*, Washington, DC: American Council on Education.

Gutierrez, R., J. Auerbach and R. Bhandari (2009), "Expanding Study Abroad Capacity: Findings from an IIE-Forum Survey," *IIE Study Abroad White Paper Series: Meeting America's Global Education Challenge*, no.6, May, New York: Institute of International Education, pp. 6–20.

Michigan State University, "Boldness by Design." Accessed April 2009 at: http://boldnessbydesign.msu.edu/.

National Academy of Engineering (2005), *Educating the Engineer of 2020: Adapting Engineering Education to the New Century*, Washington, DC: The National Academies Press. Online at: http://www.nap.edu/catalog.php?record_id=11338.

The Wall Street Journal (2009), "Executive M.B.A. Programs Bulk Up Overseas," New York: News Corporation, April 21.

7. Creating an international experience on the domestic campus
Kathleen M. Waldron

Like many other institutions of its kind, Baruch College of the City University of New York has maintained traditional international student exchange programs with a few foreign universities. After many years of operation, however, it became apparent that only relatively few students were able to take advantage of a semester abroad. Over half of all Baruch students receive Pell grants, and most live with their extended families within the five boroughs of New York City. According to the most recent data collected by Baruch's Office of Institutional Research and Program Assessment, over 68 percent of Baruch undergraduate students were born outside the United States and hail from 160 different countries. English is not the native language of over 70 percent of all Baruch students, who speak some 112 different languages at home. Baruch currently has no dormitory space available, so there are no students in residence. Consequently, well over 90 percent of Baruch students live at home. Many students are children of immigrants and many are the first in their families to attend college. *U.S. News & World Report* ranks Baruch College as the most ethnically diverse college in the country for the last seven years and *The Princeton Review* includes the College among the top 10 percent of colleges in the country.

While increasing numbers of Baruch students are taking advantage of short-term study abroad opportunities, for a large percentage of the Baruch student body even this commitment of time and resources proves an insurmountable obstacle. In the 1990s, the College established an office to administer Baruch's exchanges and other study abroad opportunities. By 2004, Baruch was sending abroad only 200 students per year out of an undergraduate student population of over 12,000. Exchange programs existed with universities in Asia, Europe and Latin America, yet the percentage of Baruch students participating in an educational experience abroad was not growing, nor did the faculty deem it possible to mandate a curricular requirement as is done in some other colleges.

In 2004, Baruch College decided to restructure its approach to international education and develop a program more compatible with the students attending the college. Recognizing that most students lived at home, worked part-time in New York City, and often could not travel outside the United States for immigration reasons, and that the mean family income was barely $40,000 a year, the College decided to create an international experience within New York City for undergraduates who could not live and study abroad.

A proposal from the Weissman Center for International Business of the Zicklin School of Business received a generous grant from the C.V. Starr Foundation to support the creation of a Global Student Initiative. This initiative sought to build on the international diversity of the College to prepare students for work in the global economy. The Global Student Initiative, which culminated with the launch of the Global Student Certificate Program in the fall of 2005, was part of a College-wide effort to reassess Baruch's international activities and to address the goals of study abroad at a non-residential urban public institution of higher education. As the faculty discussed the Initiative, they identified preferred learning outcomes for a globally literate student. These included:

1. to foster a mindset of critical inquiry;
2. to initiate curiosity about the world as a whole rather than one target country;
3. to develop global awareness and an appreciation of the historical and cultural context of current events;
4. to develop ethical awareness progressing from an ethnocentric to an "ethno-relative" world view;
5. to gain knowledge of how to address and resolve intercultural issues;
6. to develop both oral and written language skills;
7. to foster overall cultural fluency: the ability to move easily within and between cultures.

The College conversation on international education paid particular attention to how the profile of Baruch's unique student body might affect the College's ability to achieve the learning outcomes. Baruch is home to the Zicklin School of Business, the largest accredited business school in the United States. Over 80 percent of Baruch undergraduates major in a business subject, around 20 percent major in an Arts and Sciences or Public Affairs subject. However, regardless of a student's major, at least 50 percent of all credits must be earned in the humanities and sciences.

Most Baruch students are the first in their families to go to college, and their parents are making enormous sacrifices to pay for their children's higher education. As a result, students from many families are motivated, or feel a strong pressure, to complete their degree requirements as quickly as possible. Moreover, business students in particular are keen to obtain internships during the year and especially during the summer, because such placements can frequently lead to a post-graduation job offer.

Once the seven learning goals were defined, the group decided to develop a program that would enable students who could not have a traditional study abroad experience to achieve the learning outcomes while in residence at Baruch. The result of these deliberations was the Global Student Certificate (GSC) Program.

The essence of the GSC is a planned series of directed co-curricular activities to help students discover the complex process of intercultural communication, using the very rich international environment of New York City. While the learning takes place largely outside the traditional classroom setting, the GSC Program integrates academic rigor and expectations into the events, seminars and workshops students are required to attend. The program utilizes the diverse background and skills of Baruch students as well as the unique cosmopolitan character of New York City to create a specialized learning environment that fosters multicultural exchange and appreciation. In a certain sense, the program attempts to help students realize that the intercultural skills acquired while facing the perceived disadvantages of an immigrant background (non-native English language skills, limited familiarity with U.S. society) are, in fact, an advantage in the global business world.

THE GLOBAL STUDENT CERTIFICATE PROGRAM

The GSC Program is an interdisciplinary, co-curricular program for undergraduate students aspiring to become leaders in their fields. It is designed to increase the participant's knowledge of foreign countries and cultures by combining all fields of business with anthropology, language, sociology, history, psychology, religion, philosophy, the arts and communication. It combines academic research with professional training and can be personalized to meet a student's goals. The year-long GSC Program provides on- and off-campus events featuring experts from business, government, non-profits and academia and includes globalization seminars, workshops on countries and regions, intercultural awareness training, networking experiences, leadership and volunteer opportunities and effective presentation skills workshops. The GSC Program also offers a host of networking events where students can connect with international professionals in addition to Baruch faculty and students with similar interests. At the end of the program, the student receives a Certificate that recognizes the distinct co-curricular accomplishment, as well as a notation on her or his transcript.

The GSC Program has evolved over the years and currently includes three areas: attendance at seminars and events of international focus at Baruch and outside the College; a group research project; and a portfolio of GSC-related writing. Students also benefit from a guided tour of the United Nations, visits to global corporations, free admission to leading international cultural institutions in New York City and free admission to international lectures throughout the area.

To qualify for the GSC Program, students must meet certain eligibility requirements. Students must maintain an overall GPA of 3.0 or better, be enrolled full time at Baruch College, and be a sophomore or above. To earn the Certificate, students must complete specific requirements that will allow them to accumulate nine GSC points during an academic year. The point system is a method to ensure that students earn points by engaging in certain activities from a prescribed list of alternatives.

In the 2008–09 class, all participating students are required to attend the six core GSC seminars which are taught by various academic and professional experts. Students earn six points by attending all the events. The core seminars total about 12 hours of participation throughout the year. The core seminars are:

- What is Globalization?
- Introduction to Global Governance
- Introduction to Intercultural Awareness
- Multicultural Teambuilding
- Cross-Cultural Negotiating
- Presentation Skills.

In addition, students are required to attend at least one GSC-designated event sponsored by external entities, which earns them two points. The students select a global lecture approved by the GSC faculty committee or an international cultural event in New York City. Examples are:

1. (GSC-designated global lecture) The Asia Society's presentation of "Islamic Art: Its History, Traditions and Impact Today" or the "Global Citizenship in Action? Civil Society and Accountable Global Governance" lecture offered by the United Nations University.
2. (New York City cultural event) "Kiku: The Art of the Japanese Chrysanthemum" at the New York Botanical Garden or "Traditional Music and Dance of Uruguay" offered by the Queens Library International Resource Center.

For the final GSC point, students choose one activity from the following four categories:

1. Networking Workshop led by an outside consultant with international experience
2. Visit to a global company – past visits have been to Colgate-Palmolive and New York Life
3. Study Abroad during the January Intersession – a 2–3 week organized trip
4. Visit to the Baruch College Writing Center.

International Seminars and Events

The attendance at seminars and events is planned by a full-time staff member of the College, the GSC Coordinator, Sarah Eskridge. Given the richness of New York City, students have a wide choice of cultural events to attend. Many students will custom-design their own cultural programs to focus on the themes that interest them the most but all activities are reviewed to meet the defined learning outcomes. For example, students in past GSC cohorts have worked around the theme of the environment. Others have concentrated on Islam, while others have focused on China. In 2008–09, the events recommended for GSC Program participants included:

- Petrostate, Putin, Power and the New Russia (Foreign Policy Association)
- Raks Sharki: The Magic of Middle Eastern Movement (New York Public Library for the Performing Arts)
- International Careers: NGOs and Volunteer Organizations (NYU Center for Global Affairs)
- Conversations with Alon Ben-Meir featuring Zalmay Khalilzad, U.S. Ambassador to the United Nations (NYU Center for Global Affairs)
- Jews in Vichy France (Museum of Jewish Heritage)
- Let a Hundred Flowers Bloom: Creativity and the Revolution (Asia Society)
- Kotchegna Dance Company (Kingsborough Community College)
- Networking: A Contact Sport (NY Science, Industry and Business Library)
- Mitsui Forum: What's Ahead for Futures: Commodities Trading, Global Markets and Technology (Weissman Center for International Business, Baruch College)
- International Peace Building in Semi-Independent Kosovo – Lessons Not Learned (Columbia University)

- Bharata Natyam Dance of India (World Music Institute)
- Global Citizenship in Action? Civil Society and Accountable Global Governance (United Nations University)
- Emerging Subjectivities of Urban Africans during Times of Socio-political Rupture: The Case of a South African Township (Columbia University)
- Factory Towns: Portraits of Modern China (Columbia University)
- Africa: Conversations with a Continent: Kenya (92nd Street Y)
- Atìpica Tango Band (Americas Society)
- Arjuna's Dilemma – The Bhagavad Gita Today (Asia Society)
- Music and Dance of South Indian Kathuk Ensemble (Queens Library International Resource Center)
- Art Deco in Rio de Janeiro (Americas Society)
- A Conversation on Cultural Power (CUNY Graduate Center)
- Exploring Global Identity (NYU Center for Global Affairs)
- Pakistan's Return to Democracy and Relations with the United States (The New School)
- Conversations with Alon Ben-Meir featuring Dr. Hussein Hassouna, Chief Representative of the League of Arab States to the UN (NYU Center for Global Affairs)
- German and Klavdia Khatylaev: Modern Sounds in Traditional Sakha Music (Tibet House)
- DisCanto: Traditional Music of Rural Southern Italy (College of Staten Island)
- The Culture of New Zealand (Queens Library International Resource Center)
- Duquesne University Tamburitzans (Queensborough Community College)
- *Madama Butterfly* (Metropolitan Opera)
- War Dance (Bronx Community College)
- Rome, Open City (Bronx Community College).

In addition, the College developed collaborative relationships with various cultural organizations in New York City to provide students with an opportunity to attend special seminars, lectures and talks. Examples over the past two years include: the Asia Society, the Japan Society, Ten Ren Tea House, the United Nations, and the Americas Society.

International Capstone Research Project

The GSC Program group research project utilizes a more conventional academic approach to learning about a specific country. Students are assigned a country to study and spend the year researching the business culture of that country, including the current political and economic background, specific business customs, type of government, underlying laws governing economic growth, taxes, licensing, belief systems, and any other aspect that might have an impact on doing business in that country. The cohort of GSC students is divided into teams at the start of the program each September. Each team selects a country it wishes to research and individual team members select their preferred research topic. Each team gives a 20-minute oral presentation at the completion of the program with PowerPoint visual aids. The Capstone Research Project gives students the opportunity to combine many of the skills they are acquiring in the required workshops. For example, the Multicultural Team Building workshop prepares students to work successfully in a diverse team setting, since each research group may have students from six different nationalities. The Writing Skills workshop offers instruction on grammar, editing and style, ensuring that the completed portfolio submissions are professionally written. The Presentation Skills workshop helps students deliver poised and polished presentations of their research projects to their peers at the end of the program.

The project research is overseen by Sarah Eskridge, GSC Coordinator, and each team of students has access to a cultural advisor who is a faculty member with international expertise. Each cultural advisor has been carefully selected for his or her international knowledge, personal experience of living in another country (often the country that the students are researching) and area of expertise. The cultural advisors meet with the students twice during the year to critique the presentation, both on content and format, and to give advice on areas to research in more depth. Presentations at the end of the year are made in front of a panel of fellow GSC participants, faculty, selected Weissman Center for International Business members, and the cultural advisors.

The Portfolio

In order to foster a habit of thoughtful analysis and written reflection, students write brief reflection papers on each of the GSC events they attend, as well as a review of a book on intercultural issues. Students are encouraged to move beyond a simple observation of the event into an in-depth reaction, all while practicing concise and professional writing habits. The current GSC coordinator is trained and experienced in critiquing writing, and gives individualized feedback on all submitted written work. Students are often encouraged to write two or more drafts, in order to learn how to self-critique in the future.

Students assemble all of their GSC-related writing, including the reflection papers, book review and a professional résumé, into a portfolio and submit it for evaluation by the GSC coordinator at the end of the year. In this way, they can see the development of their intercultural awareness and understanding over the course of the year. Students who successfully complete the GSC will have a portfolio of at least ten brief, polished pieces of writing, suitable for writing samples for either graduate school or potential employers, each of which should reflect the broader cultural awareness and deeper knowledge of global issues learned in the GSC Program.

BENEFITS OF THE GSC PROGRAM

The College decided to locate the program in the Weissman Center for International Business in the Zicklin School of Business. The Weissman Center for International Business is designed to enable Baruch College to respond to the global economy. Guided by an advisory council of distinguished executives, the Center's activities enrich Baruch students' preparation for careers in the global workplace by building bridges between the worlds of academia and business. Directed by Professor Terrence Martell, Saxe Distinguished Professor of Finance, the Weissman Center undertook to develop the GSC Program utilizing its existing expertise in international business and program design. The program is currently run by the GSC Coordinator, Ms. Sarah Eskridge, who reports to the Director of Study Abroad, Dr. Richard Mitten, and sequentially to Dr. Martell. The international business expertise of the many faculties participating in the Center proved invaluable to developing a program that linked to the desired learning goals. One of the early supporters of the program, Phillip Berry, former VP of the Global Workforce Initiative at Colgate-Palmolive and now co-chair of the Board of Trustees of the City University of New York, stated: "Thinking globally and acting locally is more than a slogan. From a business standpoint it requires the insight, knowledge and competency to work across national boundaries and cultures in a manner that is productive and satisfying."

Perhaps most useful was the generally accepted faculty belief that Baruch College has an obligation to prepare students to enter the world with the skills that will help them succeed. In our interconnected world and in a city like New York, where most of the students traditionally remain after completing their degrees, this means providing students with the opportunity to develop their intercultural skills. Given Baruch's highly international and frequently bi- or multi-lingual students, we expect that many graduates of the GSC Program will be drawn to post-graduate opportunities of an international nature, whether working abroad or taking their place in global institutions and corporations in the United States.

One of the unplanned but very real benefits of the GSC Program was that many students enrolled in the program prior to entering a traditional international exchange program. These students wisely realized that they could achieve a more meaningful experience by being better prepared and more knowledgeable about the country and culture where they planned to study, and being able to communicate across cultures in general. A total of 42 students have both studied abroad and participated in the GSC. Of these, 12 students participated in the GSC before studying abroad. Jenny Chan (GSC 2007–08) studied abroad in China in the fall of 2008, and says that the GSC helped her realize just how sheltered American students may be, in contrast to students from other countries. With the training provided during the GSC, she was able to be more sensitive to differences than many of the other American students participating on the same program in China, and she believed she had a definite awareness of other cultures that many other students lacked.

Students may also study abroad during the January winter intersession. During the five years that the GSC has operated, 11 students have spent the winter intersession abroad in the same year as they participated in the GSC. Even though they have not completed their GSC year at the time of studying abroad, these students benefit greatly because they are able to immediately apply the lessons they learned in the first part of the year, and they are also able to apply their experiences abroad to the GSC projects and events in the second semester. Leong Cheng (GSC 2008–09), for example, studied in Greece in January 2009 and offered the following thoughts on the relationship of his study abroad to the GSC Program:

> Living in New York, we take diversity as granted and we do not usually verbalize the difference between cultures. The GSC certainly helped me to spell out these differences in intercultural communication. A very interesting notion that the Greeks have is that there is this burden of expectation to live up to their cultural ancestors. Being Chinese myself, I can relate to that personally. I believe the GSC experience made me a better citizen of the world by educating its participants to understand the differences between multiple cultures and how to effectively engage in intercultural communication.

A student who spent the January winter intersession abroad in China, Alice Moy (GSC 2008–09), said:

> The first semester of GSC had me think more deeply about the transference, boundaries and differences in cultures. . . . I think GSC has helped me become a more open-minded, engaged citizen. Overall, I think the program was a launching point. It has helped verbalize many of the ideas and opinions I already had.

It also makes me question more about current issues, about how other countries see the U.S., issues with the UN and global governance, and the globalization of businesses and ideas. With first hand experience in Shanghai, I'm able to connect these otherwise theoretical concepts with real situations/circumstances. I now feel that I would be able to communicate these ideas and my personal experiences effectively and intellectually with others.

Another benefit of the GSC Program resulted when students returning from a traditional study abroad program desired to continue their learning experience. For many students, the study abroad period is one of intellectual awakening and self-discovery, where students often become much more sensitive to the world outside of the United States. For this reason, it is common for students to seek out international opportunities after their study abroad period, in order to prolong the experience. To date, 19 students have participated in the GSC after their study abroad experience. One of them, Hanh Nguyen (GSC 2008–09) studied abroad in France in the fall of 2007 and spring of 2008, and is currently participating in the GSC. She has a specific desire to continue learning about her former host country, and is also expanding her knowledge to other regions of the world.

CONCLUSION

Baruch College is grateful to the C.V. Starr Foundation for its continued support of the Global Student Certificate Program and to the Weissman Center for International Business Director, Professor Terence Martell, for his leadership in developing a unique program. The faculty and administration of Baruch College recognize that there is no substitute for living and working outside the United States to enhance an undergraduate student experience, yet our experience with the Global Student Certificate Program is very positive and meets the needs of the unique population of students attending Baruch College. Our location in New York City, home to so many cultural institutions, global corporations and international foundations as well as to the headquarters of the United Nations, presents a unique opportunity which we now embrace more thoroughly. Our model works because of particular factors perhaps unique to a public institution of higher education in a global city, but it is one that could be replicated by other institutions to increase global awareness among undergraduate student bodies.

8. The centrality of faculty to a more globally oriented campus
Patti McGill Peterson

Institutions of higher education in the United States are ideally positioned to respond to the call that they become more globally oriented. The primary purpose of higher education, the development and dissemination of knowledge, is not bounded by national borders. Many of the functions of universities are inherently transnational. The research function, for example, is essentially a borderless exercise. Newly developed theories of physics or fresh discoveries in anthropology move rapidly around the world, finding critics and supporters of their methodologies and conclusions everywhere. Research by its very nature must seek to establish its base and direction by understanding what related phenomena are occurring and being examined in other parts of the world. The search for a better microchip or an antifungal property for hybrid corn invites collaboration as well as competition across the globe. The ongoing debates about the effects of globalization raise the question of whether most of that collaboration is between universities and corporations in developed countries and whether developing countries are only distant by-standers and eventual consumers. No matter where one stands on these issues, the debate itself reflects how much the research function resides in the global context.

By comparison, the teaching function of colleges and universities operates in a different context. The pedagogy in our classrooms, while hopefully based on broadly informed research, does not have a global audience nor does it normally profit from an ongoing critique from scholars in other cultures. And yet the goal of having more globally oriented institutions of higher education in the United States rests heavily on a core function for colleges and universities: the teaching–learning process. The faculty's stewardship of that process is central to the achievement of the goal, but a closer examination of internationalization efforts at US institutions reveals a fundamental lack of understanding of the faculty role. Internationalization efforts, therefore, have frequently fallen short of the goal because the faculty has remained on the periphery and not at the epicenter. This issue is so critical to our colleges and universities becoming more globally oriented institutions that it warrants our concern and further investigation.

Before turning to that subject, I want to acknowledge a challenge with terminology by noting the differences in perspective of those who use "international" and those who use "global" to frame the world for further study or to discuss the processes institutions and faculty should go through to become worldlier in their orientation. My distinguished colleague, Jane Knight, author of Chapter 3, has developed a definition of internationalization that suggests that these terms should be viewed as interconnected with overlapping features (Knight, 2003.) She characterizes internationalization as "the process of integrating an international, intercultural or global dimension into the purpose, functions, or delivery of postsecondary education." This provides a helpful conceptual framework and informs the way I will use the terms as fundamentally interrelated under the umbrella of internationalization.

Yet I also need to acknowledge that the use of the terms international and global can represent, depending on how they are used, very different ways of looking at the world. International is basically about relations among nations, whether it be political, economic or educational. It reflects the basis of much of our foreign policy, the structure of many academic specialties, the focus for student mobility and the basis for international academic exchange programs such as Fulbright, which is underwritten by historic bi-national agreements. Critics of the international framework, like Thomas Bender (2006), remind us that the nation state is becoming less important in the face of cultural diasporas, environmental issues, multinational constructs for the global economy and other phenomena of globalization. Clearly the nation state in the last decade has become, in some dimensions, more important as an entity while in others dramatically less so. We perhaps need new nomenclature that acknowledges the healthy tension between these perspectives as we strive to help US institutions become more comfortably and creatively part of the larger world (Mebrahtu et al., 2000.)

Having noted those differences, I am not going to introduce new terms. The definition of internationalization above offers a good rubric for moving between "international" and "global" with the recognition that they can represent differing weltanschauungs but are each important to what I assume we can agree are principal goals – to position our academic institutions to be more globally oriented and to help our students become well educated and effective global citizens. This implies the obligation to bring multiple perspectives – international, intercultural, comparative and global – to the subject matter that we teach and to the composition of curricular and co-curricular offerings.

The other up-front caveat is that I will be aiming most of my commentary at the role of faculty members as stewards of the curriculum and the educational practices of institutions and not primarily at their role as researchers. As noted in my introduction, research activities are an important way to internationalize institutions and every field of study can profit from multicultural and comparative approaches. Graduate education, an enterprise closer to the research function than the education of undergraduates, would benefit from being developed more along these lines. I will not address this subject in this chapter but confine my remarks to the role of the faculty in assisting institutions to internationalize their academic programs primarily with undergraduate students in mind.

A TOPOGRAPHICAL VIEW

Prior to becoming Executive Director of the Council for International Exchange of Scholars (CIES), I had been a college president for 16 years. The change in venue gave me a different view. I was always concerned about the worldliness quotient of my own institution but the move meant that I got to transfer that worry to the panoply of US institutions. It prompted an article that I co-authored in 1998 with Philip Altbach entitled, "Internationalize American Higher Education? Not Exactly!" In retrospect, we were not especially positive in our critique. Basically we concluded that much was quiet on this Western front and, of those campuses that were acting on their goal to be more internationally oriented institutions, many relied on the silver bullet of study abroad or recruiting more foreign students. So-called international activities were disjointed at best. There was little evidence of what the American Council on Education (ACE) would later refer to as comprehensive internationalization. And while some were beating a drum for more opportunities for students to study abroad, almost no one was talking about providing the same opportunities for faculty, particularly those who were not area, comparative or international studies specialists.

We knew from a 14-nation study of the academic profession (Altbach, 1996) that American faculty, among the 14 countries, were seemingly less committed to internationalism. While 90 percent of the faculty in the other 13 countries believed that a scholar must read books and journals from abroad to keep up with scholarly developments, only 62 percent of the American faculty believed so. Upwards of 80 percent of the faculty in 13 countries valued connections with scholars in other countries; a little over half the American professoriate agreed. And really alarming was the indication that the American faculty were lukewarm about internationalizing the curriculum: only 45 percent said that further steps should be taken. From the vantage point of the Fulbright Program, which CIES helps to administer for the United States government, I could see other manifestations of apparent disinterest or reluctance among faculty members to become more involved with teaching in other countries, particularly in less well known destinations (Peterson, 2000). Overall, it was not a very encouraging picture. Ultimately we suggested that Americans were victims of the strength of US higher education, which helped to foster the view that everything an academic needed was right here at home.

That was nearly ten years ago. Has the situation improved? Yes, in a number of ways it has. More colleges and universities are engaged in internationalizing activities and trying to link those activities together in a more integrated fashion, particularly at the level of undergraduate education. Yet the general landscape leaves much to be desired. The Fulbright Program for faculty still faces a challenge convincing US academics that it is a great idea to spend a year in Mali or Moldova. The statistics for undergraduates remain depressed. Minuscule numbers of the total US student population study abroad. Their cross-cultural experience in those programs is often quite limited, without language facility. Even so, it is the rare institution that deliberately integrates whatever that exposure is into the student's program of study.

Only a minority of institutions have approached the issue holistically, connecting the aim of educating a future generation of global citizens with a well-thought-out curriculum at every stage of the student's experience, moving between general education and the major as well as between the local, national and global in intellectually deliberate ways. In such a curriculum every step, including study abroad, takes the student to broader cultural exposure, making the frame of reference for intelligent citizenship and its inherent responsibilities broader and more interwoven with the role of other citizens across the world. Developing the architecture for this process is the job of the faculty.

If our goal is to engage a new generation of globally competent learners, study abroad cannot be a stand-alone strategy (Peterson, 2003.) The current limitations of study abroad for traditional-age students notwithstanding, nontraditional students now represent about 50 percent of total student enrollments. These students are older, often work full-time, tend to choose a vocationally oriented program of study, and have no time to study abroad. A large portion of them are enrolled at community colleges. For the model of international education that depends upon study abroad as its key index, this group is not a likely clientele. Yet these students also need to be the object of our efforts to provide knowledge and skills for global citizenship.

This means that we need carefully crafted models to engage students, whether or not they study abroad, through more points of international and global perspective in what they study and the co-curricular opportunities that are offered to them. These models with the vision and support of administrators require teams, if not legions, of faculty to build and implement them. It should be viewed by administrators and faculty alike as an integral part of the faculty workload.

FACULTY AS AGENTS OF INTERNATIONALIZATION: THE ELUSIVENESS OF THE OBVIOUS

Students graduate, but the faculty remain and serve as the stewards of the curriculum. They can be agents of a holistic approach to a more broadly defined educational program, or they can balkanize the curriculum through a narrow conception of the academic disciplines, allowing cross-cultural scholarship to settle in tiny niches with little overall impact. As a group, they have the capacity to set a deeply embedded foundation for the international and intercultural character of an institution. They can also be fierce advocates for the status quo curriculum. I was warned early in my career that changing a curriculum is akin to trying to move a cemetery, a slow and complicated task. The question is: are we encouraging and enabling faculty to rise to the opportunity of this complicated task or are we following well-worn paths that reward insularity and unconnected departments and disciplinary fiefdoms?

There is an imbalance between the power of faculty through academic governance and their role in efforts to push the envelope on internationalization. On such issues as accreditation and quality assurance, the distribution of credits for a degree and the content of the major, the faculty have for a long time asserted their central role. When, however, we move to comprehensive efforts to internationalize academic institutions, their voices have been fainter. We need to ask why.

The question warrants a two-dimensional response: one that addresses the external factors and another that lies within academia and institutions themselves. The external forces for US faculty to be engaged professionally in other countries and other cultures are noteworthy for their paucity. Read the speeches and exhortations by government officials about the need for higher education to be a vehicle for greater understanding between people and nations in the post-9/11 world and you will see almost no references to preparing our nation's faculty to teach a generation of students to navigate this new and challenging world. The national conversation about

America's lack of preparedness to relate to the rest of the world rarely focuses on those responsible for what goes on in the classrooms of higher education. Not including faculty as centerpieces of America's readiness to relate to the rest of the world leads me to underscore the elusiveness of the obvious for those who should know better. If it were part of the discourse, I suspect that it would be an important lever to get campus leaders to think more creatively about the central role of faculty in any plans to internationalize their institutions.

Basically the public discourse has leaped over the faculty. Everybody seems to be counting the number of students who go abroad to study, whether at the undergraduate or graduate level. We know a good deal about student mobility internationally, but we know very little about faculty. If you look for information about faculty mobility, you will not find much. *Open Doors* (Bhandari and Chow, 2008), a US government sponsored publication, contains nothing about US faculty in its annual statistical review of academic mobility. Expanding the search to other international organizations, UNESCO and the OECD (some intra-EU data being the exception), I discovered that neither was collecting global mobility data for faculty. The lack of data about faculty is another sign of benign neglect in a time when we have raised the volume of the discourse about the importance of academic internationalization.

While it would help to have a more supportive external environment, we are often our own worst enemy on understanding and doing something about our internal limitations. Someone once said that we have 21st century students, 20th century infrastructure and a 19th century faculty in US higher education. It was undoubtedly a barb from a disgruntled university president who had been trying to move curricular graveyards, but it reminds us that renewal for the facilities and the faculty needs to be high on the agenda of any institution that wants to keep pace. Having a vision for the centrality of faculty for internationalization is an important step. Helping prepare them for that role requires a carefully crafted faculty development program.

Limited understanding of comprehensive internationalization on the part of campus leadership continues to be an issue for grasping this point. With many other priorities on the administrative docket, it is often hard to see the global forest when you are counting the local trees. We have seen a lot of single-mindedness about recruiting as many foreign students as can be lured and not connecting their intake to a broader plan of internationalization. We have noted previously the phenomenon of focusing on study abroad numbers as the index for internationalization. And, of course, there are linkages with foreign institutions in some cases collected in sizable numbers, but often only symbolic in nature or, if they are operative, not carefully related to an integrated plan. There is, however, usually low wattage amongst all of these activities for well-honed strategies to fully engage and support faculty in efforts to create more globally oriented institutions. It is frequently left to chance, to volunteerism, to who likes to travel or to including some as resident study abroad directors – but not to a stratagem that says everyone who teaches at this institution has a role in helping us prepare globally literate and capable citizens.

Even with clarity of vision and good intentions, many campus leaders still need to address the reward and incentive systems on their campuses to see if they support their goals. Again, we fall into the elusiveness of the obvious. If you want faculty to participate willingly, even enthusiastically, in comprehensive internationalization, tenure, promotion, leave, compensation policies and departmental practices need to be analyzed for their friendliness to things that pull faculty from their respective lairs. Internationalization efforts will require many faculty members to move to the edge of or beyond that which they were explicitly trained to do. They will also be moving often in opposition to the things that have traditionally gained them recognition in their fields and have served as the basis for the rewards they wish to receive.

Having a faculty development plan in place that provides opportunities to look at research issues in comparative prospective, to make scholarly presentations in other countries and to engage in collaborative research with colleagues in other cultures is only part of what needs to be done. The other half resides with opportunities to teach your subject matter to students in another cultural context and to consider your syllabi and pedagogical efforts through a broad cross-cultural lens. In difficult economic times this may seem like a tall order. Finding ways to leverage what is available in the institutional budget with other resources will be important.

A STIMULUS PLAN FROM THE GOVERNMENT

The United States government and its primary investors, the taxpayers, stand ready to help with a stimulus package – the Fulbright Program. Founded in 1946 by Congressional legislation, its primary crafter was Senator William Fulbright, who had been transformed by his year as a Rhodes Scholar. He knew firsthand the power of academic exchange to open thought and dialogue from his own experience in war-ravaged Europe. For him such a program was primarily about creating the educational foundations for peace and understanding by offering opportunities for students to enlarge their world through academic exchange.

The Fulbright Program can now claim status as the largest movement of students and scholars across the world that any nation has ever sponsored (Glazer, 1987.) The residual goodwill left in its wake is documented frequently in many countries around the world. It has also deposited a mother lode of international exposure and connection for the faculty of American colleges and universities who have participated in the program. While Senator Fulbright was initially focused on students and their international opportunities, the expansion of the program to faculty in its early years has had perhaps an unintended but very important internationalizing effect on US higher education in a number of ways.

In its 63rd year, the Fulbright Program offers an array of bi-national programs of exchange with over 150 countries as well as some newer multi-national opportunities. Participation is not limited by the faculty member's type of institution or professorial rank. While the majority of the grants are lecture grants, there are others that offer research opportunities and include everything from the high-profile Distinguished Chairs Program to New Century Scholars, designed to gather a group of scholars from many countries around a common research topic. With an eye to adaptability, the length of commitment varies between short-term and longer-term grants.

Our longitudinal studies of faculty who participated in the Fulbright Program (Bureau of Educational and Cultural Affairs, 2001) showed that faculty returned to their home campuses and did the following in significant numbers: could see their academic discipline more clearly in comparative perspective, made changes to the way they were teaching formerly taught courses, developed new courses on the basis of their Fulbright experience, participated more in programs for foreign students, were more active in advising students interested in study abroad and were highly likely to maintain their relationships with colleagues and institutions abroad. This sounds like a recipe for faculty being involved in comprehensive internationalization! Yet we found that many academic departments, the campus home of the academic disciplines, did not actively encourage their members to apply for lecturing Fulbrights. One frequently repeated reason was that applying for a Fulbright would be a diversion from the real work at hand – research in their discipline.

In an era when seemingly every academic institution is trying to become more global in its outlook, there is a heavy irony in the fact that the senior part of the Fulbright program aimed at US faculty and professionals has a perennial challenge of recruiting a full complement of applicants for the number of awards available. This is even more ironic when one considers the budget constraints that face many institutions. Here is a program that will actually pay for a faculty member's year abroad but is not filling its quota for a number of countries. There is something fundamentally wrong with this picture when we are purportedly deeply engaged in internationalization efforts.

In an academic version of "stick to your knitting," younger, pre-tenure faculty are steered away from Fulbright, especially lecturing grants. These are the faculty who will have the lion's share of the responsibility for moving up their institution's worldliness quotient over the next decade or so. Investing in their ability to fulfill this responsibility would seem to make a lot of sense. Wouldn't the opportunity to teach abroad be a wonderful aspect of a well-conceived faculty development plan for them? Wouldn't the possibility of teaching their subject matter to groups of students in a different culture be an enlightening process? Wouldn't the chance to spend a year in a foreign university be a possible spring board for a more robust contribution to the internationalization efforts back home? And couldn't the tenure clock be put on hold for a year while they are undertaking this venture in the name of internationalization?

THE ACADEMIC DISCIPLINES: HELP OR HINDRANCE?

One of the key questions for faculty engagement is how to allow them, without penalty, to have one foot in their discipline and another in internationalization work. The role of the disciplines in academic life is a powerful one. We essentially organize our institutions around them. Faculty, trained in a discipline, have a primary professional identity with it. The associations and publications of the discipline control standards of quality and generally the nature of intellectual discourse within the subject matter of the discipline. Within the disciplines a great deal of attention is focused on where the best research is emerging, but much less attention is paid to teaching and undergraduate education. Yet this is where most Ph.D.s are headed.

Comprehensive internationalization finds itself in the middle of this dilemma. The disciplines of graduate schools shape the outlook of faculty in myriad and conclusive ways so it is timely and important to consider their role. I commend recent efforts to examine the role of the disciplines in a report from the ACE subtitled *Internationalizing the Disciplines* (Green and Shoenberg, 2006), but I found myself being a bit of a skeptic when I visited the campus of a major research university. The institution boasted excellent departments in each of the disciplines included in the project. I asked how those departments were responding to the report's recommendations; none knew of the effort.

The project needs more percolation power. Take, for example, the 2008 annual meeting of the American History Association (AHA.) The meeting roster was impressive, overflowing with sessions on a multitude of subjects. There were opportunities for the Latin America, Asia and other area specialists to caucus. Yet it was very hard to find a session on how to teach history courses, particularly US history courses, with global perspective or how to construct the major in order to weave the student's study of history with institutional internationalization goals. The struggles of the average institution to deal with the global imperative seemed very far removed from the activities of the AHA through the lens of the annual meeting of its members.

For the 2008 annual meeting of the American Political Science Association (APSA), I used the web site's search tool for the word "international." The results were remarkable. Twenty pages of sessions were listed with the word in the session's title. Sadly, none of them led me to a single session on best practices with the APSA task force's international learning goals published in the ACE report on internationalizing the disciplines. APSA sets aside a much less well attended annual meeting on teaching and learning to consider the role of political science in the general education curriculum and the role of the discipline in helping to internationalize colleges and universities. The association is to be commended for attempting to fit the issue into the ongoing activity of its work, but it is not percolating up, as evidenced by its absence at the much more attended annual meeting. Indeed, in 2006 the group of political scientists who participated in the teaching and learning conference's session on internationalizing the curriculum put out a call to the association urging it to do the following:

- to embrace the global imperative;
- to sponsor more demonstrations of active teaching and learning practices that will assist internationalizing efforts;
- to provide an internationalizing section on the APSA web site;
- to promote discussions about how best to internationalize courses in all sub-fields of political science;
- to not surrender control of internationalizing efforts to other disciplines and professional programs.

I could find no official response to this call but we should all stay tuned.

It is important for us to acknowledge positively any effort of the disciplines to think about their comparative and global dimensions. We also need to acknowledge that the academic disciplines through their associations are not traditionally built for this effort. And while next year's annual meeting theme for the American History Association is "Globalizing Historiography," it is not necessarily a signal that the AHA will pay less attention to research and more attention to teaching or that it will challenge its members to get on board with campus internationalization efforts. Again, we need to stay tuned.

For the major disciplines the emphasis is generally not on interdisciplinary and internationalizing work on behalf of curricular transformation. Nor are they focused significantly on teaching and most particularly the teaching of undergraduates. Newly minted Ph.D.s coming out of the graduate departments of the disciplines are not being sent forth with a mandate to see themselves as integral parts of comprehensive internationalization of the curriculum. They are principally niche players, focused on getting their dissertations published and moving on to try to distinguish themselves by rules that have been laid down by generations of their predecessors. Dialogue with the gatekeepers of the disciplines may eventually bear fruit but for now, if there are going to be new rules and new expectations, it will be up to individual institutions to set them.

CAMPUS-BASED REMEDIAL ACTION

There are undoubtedly many ways to involve faculty and the academic disciplines in internationalization work. Whatever steps are taken, it is important to understand that starting with clear expectations and the willingness to change and to build new capacity will be critical to any approach. While the steps may be varied at different institutions, here are some elements that I believe are *sine qua nons* for faculty participation in internationalization efforts.

1. Internationalization activity must be driven by an institution-wide vision. The focus of the vision needs to be on students first and foremost, creating for them the best possible education that helps them locate themselves in the world and to build a base of knowledge that is comparative and global in its dimensions, both at the level of general education requirements and at that of the major.
2. All faculty in all disciplines need to support the goal. The departments should be asked, once the broader perimeters of the goal are outlined, to develop plans indicating how they will contribute to general education and shape the major in ways that reflect the goal of internationalizing the curriculum. Strategies for how to unite the campus community around this activity have been discussed in a number of places, including the ACE. The danger here is falling into routine

coordination rather than proactive leadership. This means offering creative examples of what might be done for departments that have problems imagining their contributions.
3. An additional obligation will be to integrate study abroad, internships and other co-curricular opportunities with departmental plans and the institutional vision. Cross-disciplinary planning should also be encouraged and needs to be one of the elements that departments are asked to address. This can lead to approaches such as an interdisciplinary global studies sequence that can be taken along with the major. Such approaches have the power to form the connective curricular tissue to support comprehensive internationalization.
4. Asking departments to submit their plans as part of the process may prompt extensive wish lists for expertise that needs to be added to the department before comprehensive internationalization can take place. Realistically, most institutions cannot add substantial numbers of new faculty. Assuming that we have to go with the faculty we have, it is imperative to do an institution-wide survey of faculty resources. Are any involved in ongoing collaboration with colleagues in other parts of the world? Do any have area or international studies sub-fields? How many have studied abroad during undergraduate or graduate study? Who has taught or done research abroad? What is the language competency of faculty? The answers to these kinds of questions will help us understand what the global exposure and experience has been. It is important because it is the base from which a campus can build further capacity.
5. Connecting capacity-building among the faculty to a faculty development plan that responds to priorities for the institution's internationalization goals is the keystone of this process. Such a plan will necessarily be multifaceted. It can provide opportunities for individual faculty members to bring more comparative perspective to subject matter through further study or direct cross-cultural exposure. At the group level, it can involve long-term plans for entire academic departments or foster programs for interdisciplinary teams. This is where "all of the above" is a valid expression. Choosing the right combination depends on the curricular plan. I have seen all of these approaches make significant contributions to internationalization goals. What is most important is that faculty development corresponds to what the institution wants to offer its students and the kind of disciplinary or interdisciplinary knowledge and teaching that is needed to meet those goals. Utilization of outside financial sources such as Fulbright or foundation grants should help support the plan. College and university alumni who have benefited directly from study abroad themselves are often eager to help in this area of strategic development.

6. Last but not of least importance is creating an incentive and reward system for participation in the hard work of building a more globally oriented institution. We need to take a good look at whether we are all hat and no cattle, proclaiming our desire to be more worldly but not recognizing and rewarding faculty who are helping to move the institution in that direction. The reward structure needs to undergo a complete audit and, if necessary, be revised to support the goal of internationalization.

CONCLUSION

As a parting thought, I would offer a comparative observation about higher education history in the United States. As someone who was around for the culture wars, the introduction of interdisciplinary majors, Women's Studies and African-American Studies, I recall the dire warnings. At the center of those warnings was that moving faculty beyond traditional disciplinary frameworks would surely ruin American higher education. Instead, I would venture the opinion that these developments have helped to strengthen our educational programs by integrating various facets of our pluralism as a nation into programs of study for students. We now face additional demands in ensuring that our students understand the diversity not only of their own country but also of the rest of the world. It may mean pushing the envelope of the academic disciplines, changing the ways that majors are constructed, asking more faculty to be comparative in their approach to subject matter, and rewarding what would traditionally be considered to be risk-taking behavior in academe. I commend all of these possibilities to you. The potential rewards are well worth the effort.

REFERENCES

Altbach, Philip G. (ed.) (1996), *The International Academic Profession: Portraits of Fourteen Countries*, Princeton: The Carnegie Foundation for the Advancement of Teaching.
Altbach, Philip G. and Patti McGill Peterson (eds) (1998), "Internationalize American Higher Education? Not Exactly!," *Change* 30, 36–9.
Bender, Thomas (2006), *A Nation Among Nations: America's Place in World History*, New York: Hillard Wang.
Bhandari, R. and P. Chow (2008), *Open Doors 2008: Report on International Educational Exchange*, New York: Institute of International Education.
Bureau of Educational and Cultural Affairs (2001), *Outcome Assessment of the U.S. Fulbright Scholar Program*, Washington: SRI International.

Fischer, Karin (2009), "U.S. Faculty Members Lag on Global Engagement," *Chronicle* 55, A37.

Glazer, N. (ed.) (1987), "The Fulbright Experience and Academic Exchanges," *Annals of the American Academy of Political and Social Sciences*, vol. 491.

Green, Madeleine and Robert Shoenberg (2006), *Where Faculty Live: Internationalizing the Disciplines*, Washington: American Council on Education.

Knight, Jane (2003), "Updating the Definition of Internationalization," *International Higher Education*, 33, 2.

Mebrahtu, Teame, Michael Crossley and David Johnson (eds) (2000), *Globalisation, Educational Transformation and Societies in Transition*, Oxford: Symposium Books.

Peterson, Patti McGill (2000), "The Worthy Goal of a Worldly Faculty," *Peer Review*, 3, 3–7.

Peterson, Patti McGill (2003), "New Directions to the Global Century," *Frontiers: The Interdisciplinary Journal of Study Abroad*, Fall, 189–98.

9. Internationalizing the scholarly experience of faculty
Diana Bartelli Carlin

INTRODUCTION

It is a rare post-secondary institution in the United States that does not make reference to campus internationalization in its mission statement. As a result, senior administrators crisscross the globe in pursuit of exchange partners, new sites for faculty-led study abroad programs, students, research collaborations, and international alumni cultivation. Patti McGill Peterson's Chapter 8 in this volume acknowledges the limitations of such efforts in attaining the goal of an international campus unless more effort is put into internationalizing the faculty who "own" the curriculum. Green and Olson observed that "Only when a substantial number of faculty members actively participate can the institution provide students with diverse international learning opportunities that are fully integrated into the educational process" (Green and Olson, 2003, p. 69.)

Doing so may be difficult, as Peterson indicates, but it is not impossible since the potential exists within every classroom for internationalization "as a process that prepares the community for successful participation in an increasingly interdependent world" (Francis, 1993, p. 5.) John Hudzik, the current president of NAFSA (the Association of International Educators), expressed this potential in a column for NAFSA's *International Educator*: "It is difficult, perhaps impossible, to imagine any discipline or university program that is not shaped by global forces, not able to contribute to global solutions, or better off informed by global perspectives" (Hudzik, 2009, p. 5.) Unless internationalization across the curriculum becomes a reality, the number of students who are prepared to learn, live, and work in a global society will be limited to those fortunate few who study abroad or take courses from faculty members who are committed to international education regardless of discipline.

The numbers suggest the potential for campus-wide internationalization via the faculty. An American Council on Education (ACE) study of faculty members' international activity (Saiya and Hayward, 2002) indicates that approximately 90 percent traveled outside the U.S. for research or professional meetings; however only 16 percent led study abroad groups. Thus, faculty are internationalized on some level even if realistically much activity is not consistent with Francis' definition. Faculty activity may represent research presentations at disciplinary conferences that do connect content to international or global issues or provide opportunity for cultural experiences in the foreign setting. Further, international or global perspectives gained by faculty in collaborating with international research teams, lecturing at international institutions, or attending international conferences may not be used to inform courses and be passed along to students. Because the links may not be made, currently does not imply that they cannot be made, since exposure is an important first step in internationalizing faculty scholarly activity. Making the link between faculty who are clearly internationalized on some level and the students they teach is the ultimate challenge of internationalizing U.S. higher education.

We are not alone in our search for the means, however, as some of our Canadian neighbors observed in writing about an experimental program to internationalize faculty at the University of Victoria: "A systematic study of faculty as agents of curricular change for internationalization is clearly a neglected area of research . . . [and] there has been little study of specific educational strategies to support faculty in curricular change for internationalization" (Shuerholz-Lehr et al., 2007, p. 37.) In the absence of such research, the best means available for internationalizing the faculty scholarly experience, and subsequently that of students, is to examine best practices. This chapter begins with an examination of research on the existing inhibitors to faculty international activity and then moves to an array of facilitators and practical programs to overcome the frequently cited problems of institutional and individual barriers to faculty involvement in internationalization. Many of the suggestions come from programs at the University of Kansas which were cited when the university received the Paul Simon Award for campus internationalization from NAFSA; others are from institutions with which I am familiar. Additional suggestions were found in literature searches and from projects undertaken by professional associations.

BARRIERS TO FACULTY INTERNATIONALIZATION

Three studies over a ten-year period reached similar conclusions about the role of faculty in international curriculum development. The first was conducted in 1993 by the Commission on International Affairs of NASULGC (the National Association of State Universities and

Land-Grant Colleges, now A.P.L.U – the Association of Public and Land-grant Universities.) It noted that "Administrators searching for effective vehicles to meet the challenge [of internationalizing higher education] do not recognize faculty as a major instrument for internationalization often enough" (Commission on International Affairs, 1993, p. 1.) Part of that recognition is understanding that without incentives or elimination of disincentives faculty will not provide the curriculum leadership needed. The NASULGC study revealed that "policies and procedures for leave and fringe benefits at many NASULGC institutions inhibit rather than encourage faculty international involvement. Only 16 percent of the respondent institutions, for example, reported an established practice of topping off Fulbright awards outside of the sabbatical cycle" (ibid., p. 2.) Peterson touted Fulbright awards as a means for enhancing faculty international scholarly activities that could later transition to the classroom. However, if pay cuts and other potential losses cited by the study, such as loss of retirement contributions or merit pay, stopping the tenure clock for junior faculty, or loss of funds for a department to replace a Fulbright awardee, are not addressed institutionally, then a major means of creating a globally connected faculty is reduced.

The second study was the one by Saiya and Hayward (2002) for ACE. It found that nine years after the NASULGC report many deterrents still existed:

> The ACE surveys showed that colleges and universities do not offer faculty much incentive to internationalize their courses or participate in other internationally oriented activities. Less than 5 percent of institutions overall reported that they considered international work or experience in their faculty tenure and promotion decision. In addition, fewer than one-quarter of all institutions had set aside dedicated funding for faculty to internationalize their courses or teach at institutions abroad. Less than one-third of institutions offered workshops to faculty on internationalizing their courses and less than one-fifth had opportunities for faculty to increase their foreign language skills or offered workshops on using technology to enhance the international dimensions of their courses.

Given that the study surveyed 752 institutions from community colleges to major research universities, the findings indicate consistent institutional barriers that go beyond institutional type and need to be overcome in realizing the internationalization aspect of institutional mission statements.

The third resource that addressed the barrier issue was prepared by Green and Olson (2003), also for ACE. They divided the inhibitors to campus internationalization via the faculty as falling into the institutional barriers identified by the two above-mentioned studies and individual barriers that were primarily attitudinal, such as attitudes toward international learning, personal knowledge and expertise, and cognitive competence (no connection between international research and classroom teaching.) In addition to the previously cited institutional barriers, they also emphasized a lack of resources – both financial and staffing – and disciplinary structures or standards.

In addition to the observations made above, I would add one that Hudzik touched upon in suggesting that NAFSA needs to develop "robust connections to faculty and senior campus leadership" while continuing to adhere to its "historical focus on education abroad, international student and scholars services, recruitment, admissions, and policies related to these" (Hudzik, 2009, p. 6.) The observation is this: there is often a disconnect between international offices/senior international administrators and faculty because of institutional structures creating decentralization, or there is a balkanization of international programs because leaders are not faculty members. This is not as serious an issue on smaller campuses where it is easier to have contact with a small number of faculty, but on large research university campuses the role of the international office may be unknown to the majority of faculty unless they apply for a Fulbright or are already engaged in study abroad or language and culture disciplines. Because the curriculum is the purview of the faculty and the academic deans, the institutional structures and culture may prevent linkages that can enhance international scholarly pursuits and improve the overall quality of curricular offerings.

FACILITATORS FOR ENHANCING FACULTY INTERNATIONAL SCHOLARLY ACTIVITIES

In examining numerous articles and books on campus internationalization, two things became obvious in seeking ways to overcome either institutional or individual barriers to enhancing faculty international scholarly activity: money alone is not the answer and faculty can supply much of the answer. While funding is necessary to address issues such as topping off Fulbright awards, maintaining retirement contributions and other fringe benefits for those on grants, sending faculty to international conferences or workshops, and providing sufficient staff to promote internationalization, some of the institutional problems are structural or cultural, as indicated in the previous section. The NASULGC report suggested that mission statements should include internationalization – something that is accomplished for most institutions – and that senior administrators such as the president and provost should make internationalization a spoken priority, publicly recognize faculty members who participate in international activities, encourage development of courses or seminars, and encourage collaboration with international scholars on campus (Commission on International Affairs, 1993, p. 4.)

Several of the best practice models discussed in the next sections called on faculty themselves to craft the means to deepen their international scholarly activities through creation of advisory or steering committees to develop workshops or courses. International offices need to connect directly with faculty governance bodies and with key academic leaders to share information, make resources more widely known and available, and conduct the necessary research to map international activity and locate institutional best practices that merit replication. These efforts require more time and coordination than money and less territoriality than is often common on campuses. Such approaches are not uncommon, however, and are successful in a variety of institutions. The remainder of the chapter presents tested and practical approaches to enhancing faculty international scholarly activities that address the barriers and capitalize on the facilitators.

MAPPING THE TERRITORY

It is impossible to improve a situation if the situation is not fully understood. A good starting place for any campus-wide project involving faculty is to learn what they are and are not doing. To that extent, the international programs office in collaboration with the provost's office or an academic dean's council should undertake a survey of faculty international activities. An annual survey should request information from faculty to determine who has conducted research, presented papers, lectured, or taught abroad. The survey should ask for countries where activities took place and the duration. Funding sources should also be identified. The survey should also ask whether the faculty member taught a course with international content and whether the professional activities furthered curriculum development.

If this can be done via an on-line survey and if it is sent jointly by the international office and the provost or academic deans, it is more likely to be answered. It should also be clear how the information will be used. Possible incentives include the development of lecture series using faculty international expertise; the creation of interdisciplinary research teams; providing information about external funding for faculty with an interest in a particular country, region, and research area; recognizing departments for high levels of international activity via a president's award; and connecting faculty with visiting scholars with similar interests. This information should be used in annual reports for the international office and other academic units. Mapping should also include an inventory of faculty grants such as Fulbright awards or faculty participation in programs such as DAAD's Germany Today or CCIS or CIEE professional development seminars.

Mapping will indicate if there are disciplines or schools that are not participating in international activities or if scholarly activity is confined to traditional area studies or language and culture disciplines. It will also reveal faculty who are operating internationally "under the radar screen" because they are not in traditional disciplines. In identifying internationally active faculty who are outside those usually engaged in international activity, new sources to serve on international committees or to be involved in international organizations are located. The inventory will also generate names for a speakers' bureau that can be used internally or externally and contribute to a faculty member's service responsibilities. By having a list of courses with international content, it is easier to determine how much work needs to be done to internationalize all students' campus experiences. Mapping also provides data to promote fundraising for internationalization if it is found that many faculty are privately financing their conference participation, for example. It can also identify sources of external funding that might not be known widely throughout the institution.

CAMPUS-WIDE WORKSHOPS OR SUMMITS

There is no better way to internationalize faculty than to bring them together to discuss what they are doing and what they can learn from one another. Many campuses have teaching or research summits prior to the first day of classes to share best practices and common issues that cross disciplinary boundaries. The same can be done with international issues. Bringing in an outside keynote speaker adds to the importance of the meeting. Acknowledging faculty or departmental excellence through awards given at the summit underscores the administrative commitment to internationalization. If the award is monetary as well as honorary, it further emphasizes the importance of international scholarly activity. A departmental or individual award that provides funds for curriculum development or international travel incentivizes the winner to continue and others to become engaged.

The University of Michigan-Flint provides a good example of an international summit agenda. The summit included both internal and external speakers. A keynote on the importance of campus internationalization set the stage and was followed by a presentation from a leader in study abroad. A luncheon was followed by a panel of faculty discussing their international teaching and scholarly activities, including course development and study abroad. Finally, the provost and one of the external presenters conducted a town hall to discuss the status of internationalization and what could be done to further the goal. Notes were taken and action plans were developed from the town hall.

Two outstanding examples of faculty-driven curriculum development come from the University of Oregon's School of Architecture and Allied Arts (Dewey and Duff, 2009) and the University of Victoria's Course (Re)design for Internationalization Workshop. The former is an example of how one school within a major research university mapped its international activity, addressed barriers to internationalization, and improved structures and systems. The case study is one that is easily replicated in process, although some of the actions taken may not be possible at all institutions. The University of Victoria project was aimed at the individual barriers to faculty internationalization. Using Bennett's (1993) developmental model of intercultural sensitivity, faculty participated in a 40-hour, five-day workshop. Pre- and post-testing demonstrated that perspectives regarding internationalization of curriculum can be impacted by workshops that increase the opportunity and ability to incorporate new content.

Less extensive workshop and course development models also exist. The University of Kansas has a long-standing spring seminar that provides a means for faculty to create a new course with an international focus or add a unit to an existing course. Faculty receive a stipend for participation that can be used for professional development activities that will further their international scholarly pursuits or course development. The seminar is interdisciplinary and ideas are shared among the group. Faculty apply and are chosen competitively. A second seminar on a broad international topic is also held on stop day – the last day of the semester before finals. Faculty are selected competitively and use the seminar as a way to develop a research project related to the seminar theme. Feedback from other participants enables participants to revise a proposal or a paper. Faculty are also given a stipend for participation. The stipends are provided through fundraising by the Office of International Programs. Approximately eight faculty participate in each of the seminars.

Other seminars or workshops that engage large numbers of faculty can focus on creating a study abroad course, locating and applying for grants for international research (for both graduate students and faculty), publishing in international journals, or developing international modules in an existing course. Faculty who participate in the seminars are natural leaders for these workshops, as are faculty who design and conduct study abroad courses.

SITE VISITS, CONFERENCES, AND INTER-CAMPUS COLLABORATIONS

One relatively inexpensive way to create scholarly opportunities for faculty is to host a conference that addresses global issues. The invitation list can be domestic or a combination of domestic and international. Many universities' continuing education programs assist with planning and even with financing. Many costs are recouped through registration fees. By bringing scholars to campus, a department's stature is elevated within the institution and faculty and students benefit from the papers and discussion. Proceedings further the dissemination of new ideas. One goal of such a conference should be to develop research collaborations across universities.

Conferences can also be focused on expanding long-standing student exchanges to involve faculty research. The University of Costa Rica and the University of Kansas have an exchange program that is more than 50 years old. Several years ago Kansas State University become involved in the exchange agreement. Originally designed to promote language and culture studies, the program now includes students and faculty from social welfare, journalism and mass communications, political science, education, and biology. During the past ten years, symposia were held on the UCR and KU campuses – two at UCR and one at KU. Faculty and deans from each institution and from Kansas State participated to share information about their research and to develop courses and research exchange projects. As a result of sending delegations, for example, the School of Social Welfare has developed a doctoral program for UCR faculty who want to pursue a doctorate. KU faculty have visited UCR and have studied social welfare practices in Costa Rica to better understand what their students will need and to locate models that are potentially useful in their work, especially issues related to immigrant populations.

Site visits to exchange partners by faculty and academic administrators that are led by an international administrator are an excellent way to expand research and teaching collaborations beyond traditional student exchanges. They can also expand the number of students participating in study abroad programs by introducing faculty from programs not previously involved in study abroad to the research and curriculum offerings at a partner institution. They are also a good way to develop new partnerships. By using the mapping project, an international office can determine whether multiple faculty have independent contacts at the same university or at universities in a country or region where the institution wants to develop new programs. Faculty with similar research interests and strengths that dovetail those of the potential partner can participate in a visit and assist the international office in determining whether a partnership is viable. Often international institutions at which alumni teach are good targets for such visits since there is already a relationship and trust established as well as potential research collaborations.

Nurses have developed a model site visit program that involves nursing faculty from multiple universities. The collaborative program with Russian nurses occurs biennially and involves a cruise between Moscow and St. Petersburg with stops at small villages, large cities, and universities to examine how nursing is taught and practiced in Russia. The nurses "exchange ideas, develop knowledge and experience, increase tolerance and sensitivity, form new friendships, and contribute to professional advancement" (DiFazio et al., 2009, p. 94.)

Professional associations also have the means to bring faculty from multiple universities together to advance scholarly collaborations. The National Communication Association (NCA), my disciplinary association, has sponsored conferences in numerous countries for scholars from the U.S. and a host country. I participated in conferences in Finland and Mexico. The latter was co-sponsored by a Latin American communication association and involved faculty from several countries. Both conferences involved the usual exchange of papers, but the papers were focused on the state of research within the discipline in each country, and discussions regarding research collaborations took place. The Finnish conference was preceded by a visit to Russia and included a meeting with faculty from several Russian universities who were interested in forming a Russian Communication Association. Russian scholars who attended the meeting later participated in the annual NCA meeting in the U.S. and through meetings at the conference did form the Russian Communication Association. Active research and teaching exchanges and scholarly publications were produced from the initial visit by a member of the NCA staff and eight faculty from as many universities. Other disciplinary associations have and should develop similar projects.

One of the more complex outgrowths of site visits and conferences is the development of joint or dual degree programs. This is a subject on which an entire chapter could be written. Currently the Council of Graduate Schools is conducting research to develop best practice models for such programs. The advantages of joint and dual degrees extend beyond the students who earn two degrees or receive credit at two institutions to the faculty. Faculty exchanges and faculty research projects typically develop out of these collaborations. Often faculty can take advantage of laboratory equipment or contacts at the partner institution to further their own research.

PREPARING FUTURE FACULTY

If universities are to achieve their internationalization goals and if faculty are prepared to take full advantage of the globalization of research and scholarly publishing, then graduate students need to be prepared to assume international roles immediately upon entering the professoriate. Preparing Future Faculty programs were started by the Carnegie Foundation and the Council of Graduate Schools in the 1990s. A large number of research universities participate. While the initial idea was to prepare graduate students for positions in a range of institutions from community colleges to doctoral research universities, many institutions are now adding an international component. Virginia Tech has an exemplary program that takes advantage of existing exchange partners and a Virginia Tech campus in Europe. The dean of the graduate school arranges for an interdisciplinary group of students to visit European institutions to learn how research and teaching are done and they also meet with representatives of higher education associations to learn about the Bologna Process and higher education reform in Europe. The program is short-term study abroad but the long-term impact is that a group of future faculty is internationalized.

Another way to internationalize graduate students headed for the academy is to provide funds for their research activities. International and graduate/research offices can combine forces to fund summer research or dissertation research projects that have international foci. The National Science Foundation has recognized the growing globalization of scientific research and has added an international component to the GK-12 program that enables graduate students to work with K-12 teachers and students to develop new ways to teach math and science. The grant program includes funding for students to do summer research abroad and to learn how math and science are taught in other countries. The PIRE (Partnerships for International Research and Education) is another NSF program that encourages international research collaborations and potentially joint and dual degrees. Both faculty and graduate students participate in this program. FIPSE/Atlantis is a joint U.S. Department of Education and European Union program that promotes faculty research collaborations and joint and dual degree programs. There are other NSF grants that promote international partnerships.

It is important for international offices to work with graduate and research offices in the early stages of developing grant proposals to ensure that the necessary exchange agreements are in place in case the grant is received and that issues related to acceptance of three-year Bologna degrees is clarified. The chief international officer should be familiar with the Federal grants that include international opportunities and work with research administrators to prepare faculty to deal with the issues related to international agreements and also to help identify potential partners. This is where the mapping project can be useful. It is important for faculty to know before they pursue opportunities provided by granting agencies whether or not agreements exist or need to be negotiated. Thus, it is advisable that the international office prepare a directory of all international agreements that is updated annually or each semester and contains all of the provisions of the agreement. Such a directory should also include the step-by-step information for arranging an agreement or an addendum to one for a specific research or teaching purpose.

CONNECTING WITH VISITING SCHOLARS

Many universities have visiting scholars on campus who are part of major programs such as Fulbright or the Junior Faculty Development Program. Other scholars are sponsored by their universities or by their countries. Although a faculty member on the U.S. campus may be an official mentor for purposes of meeting funding agency or university requirements, many visiting scholars have few opportunities to connect with the larger university community. Once again, the mapping project can be useful. If possible someone in the international office should examine the data base of faculty members to determine who has connections with faculty at the institution or region from which the visiting scholar is coming or who has similar research interests. A social gathering with faculty who share interests could be arranged by the international office. Many visiting scholars are willing to lecture in classes or conduct brown bag sessions.

This past semester I had two visiting scholars who audited my speech-writing class. They were active participants in the class and related what we were discussing to practices in their countries. Thus, my students and I both learned from their presence. One of the scholars was with the Junior Faculty Development Program (JFDP) and her mentor and I are going to work on grant projects with her to help her develop curricula at her university. This will expand our activities in the region and further develop relationships between the universities. This type of activity is common among participants in the JFDP, which is an excellent program for internationalizing faculty and promoting scholarly exchanges.

PUBLIC RELATIONS BASICS

In highly decentralized universities it is possible that many faculty are not aware that there is an international office and what its purpose is. Thus, it is important for international educators to let the university community know that they are partners in their international scholarly activities. One of the best ways to "advertise" faculty-oriented programs such as workshops, seminars, funding, or study abroad leadership is to create a brochure that is distributed to all faculty listing all of the services and programs provided by the international office. Links to the on-line forms for travel money or scholarly grants for internationalization, the directory of exchange agreements or manuals for bringing visiting scholars to campus should all be included. Very little paper is shared with faculty now and it is likely to be noticed, especially if the first page makes it clear that this is something to benefit them. It does not have to be expensive – a legal size tri-fold with two colors should suffice and it can be run on an office printer. The main thing is to get something to faculty. New faculty can be invited to lunches with international administrators and staff (usually this is best done in their second semester once they are settled in) and the brochure can be used as a starting point while the services the international office offers are described. If the lunch can be held in a conference room in the international programs suite, it creates a presence for new faculty that might take years otherwise for them to develop.

Shared governance is a fundamental precept of U.S. universities and curricular changes typically require faculty governance for acceptance. Thus, it is important for international educators to understand the faculty governance process and engage it to fill slots on task forces and committees. In fact, if the governance structure can create an international subcommittee to be the official liaison to international programs, the likelihood is greater that there will be advocates for curricular changes or adoption of new programs that require governance approval. Any initiative to promote campus internationalization must involve faculty input and leadership. It is best to have committees chaired by faculty and programs developed with faculty input rather than having someone from the international office lead the project.

Another way to let faculty know what is available to assist them with their scholarly pursuits is to visit departmental or school meetings and make a brief presentation about international programs and the types of workshops that are available to faculty. This needs to be every few years since programs and faculty change and not everyone will have attended a new faculty luncheon.

Information sharing is also important across the campus to avoid duplication and to promote collaboration. The international office can serve a convening function by creating an advisory council composed of faculty from each school or college on campus. Each academic dean would appoint a person to the council which would meet several times a year to share information about internationalization projects within the school. The council is also a way for the international office, especially in large, decentralized universities, to know about initiatives taking place outside of the international office umbrella and to share those programs with other units.

CONCLUSION

The 2002 ACE report found that "The majority (67 percent) [of the faculty surveyed] believed it was the responsibility of *all faculty* to provide undergraduates with an awareness of other countries, cultures, or global issues" (Saiya and Hayward, p. 10.) It is likely that the percentage is even higher today with the increased emphasis on internationalization by senior administrators and accrediting agencies. The report also found that over one-third of the faculty agreed with the statement that "The more time spent teaching students about other countries, cultures, and global issues, the less time is available for teaching the basics" and 25 percent "did not believe it was a necessary component of U.S. education" (ibid, p. 10.) Because faculty are most intent on doing those things for which they are rewarded, the advice from past studies regarding promotion and tenure and other institutional barriers cannot be overlooked. Without the institution connecting international scholarly activity to those responsibilities that faculty are expected to undertake, all of the best practices in the world will not increase faculty participation in international activities, and subsequently the majority of students will not have an international experience while on campus.

A majority of the best practice models described in this chapter directly link internationalization to teaching, research, and service. As a result, there should not be a conflict between the traditional reward structure and international activities. In fact, many of these programs greatly enhance faculty opportunities for scholarly productivity. Furthermore, faculty resistance to teaching "skills" necessary for students to survive in a global economy can be redefined as creating and disseminating knowledge within disciplinary structures that enable students to make critical judgments and adjust to cultural variables in ways that will serve them in an increasingly diverse United States as well as in the larger world. The key to campus internationalization is indeed the faculty, but that key will only be turned if and when internationalization is seen as a hallmark of the 21st century university just as development of general education was of the 20th century one. By promoting campus conversations with faculty at the center, support for internationalization activities, and appropriate rewards, faculty scholarly international activity will grow on campuses and the goal of providing an international education for all students will be a reality.

REFERENCES

Bennett, Milton J. (1993), "Towards Ethnorelativism: A Developmental Model of Intercultural Sensitivity," in R. Michael Paige (ed.), *Education for the Intercultural Experience*, Yarmouth, ME: Intercultural Press.

Commission on International Affairs (1993), *Internationalizing Higher Education Through the Faculty*, Washington, DC: National Association of State Universities and Land-Grant Colleges (ED 364 169.)

Dewey, P. and Stephen Duff (2009), "Reason before Passion: Faculty Views on Internationalization in Higher Education," *Higher Education*, 58 (4), 491–504.

DiFazio, R., M. Boykova and M.J. Driever (2009), "International Education: Developing Site Visit Guidelines to Enhance Understanding," *The Journal of Continuing Education in Nursing*, 40 (2), 91–5.

Francis, Anne (1993), *Facing the Future: The Internationalization of Post-Secondary Institutions in British Columbia*, Vancouver: British Columbia Centre for International Education.

Green, Madeleine F. and Christa Olson (2003), *Internationalizing the Campus: A User's Guide*, ACE Center for Institutional and International Initiatives, Washington, DC: American Council on Education.

Hudzik, J. (2009), "Reshaping International Education," *International Educator*, May/June, 4–6.

Saiya, Laura and Fred M. Hayward (2002), *Mapping Internationalization on U.S. Campuses*, Washington, DC: American Council on Education.

Schuerholz-Lehr, S., C. Caws, G. Van Gyn and A. Preece (2007), "Internationalizing the Higher Education Curriculum: An Emerging Model for Transforming Faculty Perspectives," *Canadian Journal of Higher Education*, 37 (1), 67–94.

10. Bringing international students to campus: who, what, when, where, why and how?

Charles E. Phelps

My use of the standard list of traditional journalistic questions is more than whimsical; each of these questions deserves a good answer in terms of bringing international students to our US campuses. I hope to accomplish that goal for you by the time you finish reading this chapter. I will, however, divert from the sequence suggested in the title. By the end, I hope to have accomplished the goal of helping readers think about numerous issues associated with bringing international students to campus. Let us begin with the underlying logic of having international students on campus.

WHY? (WHY SHOULD COLLEGES AND UNIVERSITIES SEEK INTERNATIONAL STUDENTS?)

The most obvious answer to this question focuses on the core educational mission of your school. How much does diversity matter in your educational mission, and what do you mean by "diversity"? If the word mostly means bringing under-represented US populations to your campus, then thinking about international students may not make much sense for your school.

Including international students in your definition of diversity has multiple positive benefits. First, of course, it can enrich the experience of all students at your campus, not to mention the horizons of faculty and staff. As the world becomes increasingly international in trade, travel, communication, and mass media, students' familiarity with other cultures will help them understand and interpret the increasingly global world in which they live. The different perspectives brought by international students can also broaden everybody's perspectives on social and ethical issues at the forefront of many campus discussions and courses.

Internationalization can also bring important legal protection to other diversity efforts on your campus. Following the important US Supreme Court rulings about collegiate admissions (See Grutter v. Bollinger), many colleges and universities have adopted educational mission statements that speak to the values of diversity, thus providing an important legal buttress for all aspects of diversity-related recruiting. For example, at the University of Rochester, following an extensive campus discussion, the faculty endorsed and the trustees adopted a statement of educational philosophy that illuminates this issue. It says (in part):

> Our University's distinctive heritage . . . leads us actively to seek out and include persons from diverse backgrounds and origins who carry with them their own valued and important perspectives. . . . [we believe that] productive inquiry best takes place when individuals can explore and share their experience and thoughts as equal members of our community, uninhibited by prejudice or discrimination. Thus, our pursuit of excellence requires that we create and support a community of faculty, students and staff who together and individually enhance diversity and who strive to make themselves and our community ever better.[1]

This statement of educational philosophy forms the backbone of the institution's diversity-related recruiting, and that recruiting embodies diversity on many dimensions, including race, gender, ethnic and international origin, regional and cultural background, and abilities of different types. But if diversity only includes recruitment and support of individuals from traditional under-represented minority groups within the United States, then your efforts can run afoul of relevant Supreme Court rulings. Thus expanding your diversity vision to include international students can help protect your legal ability to achieve more traditional diversity goals.

The second reason is that the world around us contains some extraordinarily talented students. If you succeed in finding and attracting them, the quality of your student body will rise, an asset to their fellow students, to your faculty, and for your institution's reputation, both immediately (in terms of "class profile" and its effect on recruiting subsequent students) and later as they become successful alumni.

The third is that many international students come without need of financial aid. Thus (crassly, perhaps) attracting international students sometimes achieves the dual goal for admissions officers of both increasing class quality and reducing the "discount rate" (foregone tuition.)

The fourth reason is that it is worth remembering that international students bring not only the benefits of diversity to our campuses, but also intellectual power and insight. International students and faculty (mostly hired after receiving doctoral training in the US) bring a wealth of expertise to our student bodies and faculties in colleges and universities all around the country. For example, one analysis at the University of Rochester shows the importance of international student participation. In patent disclosures (the first step to patent filing in all universities) over a recent period of five years, 42 percent of all inventors listed on disclosure forms at the University of Rochester were not US citizens, and more than half of the graduate students on patent disclosures were from other countries. Since 2000, roughly one third of all patents granted to the University of Rochester have had at least one foreign inventor involved (Jacobs, 2005, p. 6.) The same patterns will surely appear in journal publications, scientific reports and conference presentations, and other forms of scholarly communication. In other words, we are missing out on a lot of valuable brain-power if we do not fully involve international students in our educational processes.

WHERE AND WHO? (WHICH STUDENTS, FROM WHERE AND TO WHERE?)

The answers to the questions "from where?" and "to where?" have very different implications. To answer these questions, I will turn to recent data on the sources and destinations of international students in US colleges and universities.

From Where?

As the data in Table 10.1 show, international students in recent years have come (for the most part) from a relatively small handful of countries, most predominantly China, India, South Korea and Japan, with Taiwan sandwiched next on the list by US neighbors Canada and Mexico.[2] The top eight nations (through Turkey on the list in Table 10.1) account for over half of the total international student population in the United States.

Many of these international students come to the United States for graduate and professional studies, but an increasing number will come for undergraduate education. The most obvious reason is population growth and rates of completion of pre-collegiate education throughout the world, providing students who create an important opportunity for US higher education.

The world's educated population is growing at a remarkable rate, primarily arising from growth in pre-collegiate education in the Asian sector (most notably, China and India.) China now has the largest population in the world at 1.3 billion, growing at an annual rate of 0.6 percent. India has

Table 10.1   Leading places of origin for international students

Rank	Place of origin	2004/05	2005/06	Percent of total (2005/06)
1	India	80 466	76 503	13.5
2	China	62 523	62 582	11.1
3	Korea, Republic of	53 358	58 847	10.4
4	Japan	42 215	38 712	6.9
5	Canada	28 140	28 202	5.0
6	Taiwan	25 914	27 876	4.9
7	Mexico	13 063	13 931	2.5
8	Turkey	12 474	11 622	2.1
9	Germany	8640	8829	1.6
10	Thailand	8637	8765	1.6
11	United Kingdom	8236	8274	1.5
12	Hong Kong	7180	7849	1.4
13	Indonesia	7760	7575	1.3
14	Brazil	7244	7009	1.2
15	Colombia	7334	6835	1.2
16	France	6555	6640	1.2
17	Kenya	6728	6559	1.2
18	Nigeria	6335	6192	1.1
19	Nepal	4861	6061	1.1
20	Pakistan	6296	5759	1.0
	Rest of world	161 070	160 444	28.3
	World total	565 039	564 766	100.0

Source: International Educational Exchange Network, http://opendoors.iienetwork.org/?p=131534

the second largest population at 1.1 billion, growing at about 1.6 percent per year.[3] These trends will make India the most populous nation in the world within just a few years. Between them, these two nations already have three-eighths of the world's population. While these nations are not as affluent as the United States and Europe on a per capita basis, together they create about two-fifths of the world's Gross Domestic Product (indicating purchasing power.) Moreover, their inflation-adjusted economies are growing rapidly: 8 percent for China, 4 percent for India, versus 0.4 percent for the US. While other sectors of the world's economy are also important, the size and growth of these two economies makes them a key focal point for higher education in the United States.

To put this into more vivid perspective, consider a simple example: by recent estimates, nearly one-third of India's population of 1.1 billion people is in the under-14 age group, and this population segment is growing rapidly (22.7 births per 1,000 people.) India has a median age of less than 25 years. By contrast, China, because of restrictive policies, has a much lower birth rate (13.5 per 1,000) and has only 20 percent of their population in the under-15 age group, with a median age of about 35 years. Thus India has about 0.35 billion in the "K-12 pipeline," while China has "only" a bit over 0.25 billion in the same age group. In terms of potential college attendees, India already leads the world, and their lead will grow with their relatively high birth rate.

To re-frame this more towards higher education, each single-year age cohort (for example, age 18) in India now has about 24 million people in it. About half of all children in India complete secondary education, and about 10 percent (a rate that grows through time) enter post-secondary education.[4] Thus, in very round numbers, India currently has about 12 million 18-year olds with at least some secondary education, and 2.5 million of them enter some form of post-secondary education.[5]

These numbers will grow through time, probably fairly rapidly, through two forces. First, the inherent population growth rates in India will lead to increases in the size of each age cohort. Second, and possibly of even greater importance, as the wealth of Indian citizens rises (that is, as the globalization of the economy in general accelerates), more and more of them will seek college education for their children. Higher education is a luxury good: as income rises, the demand for college education rises at an even higher rate.

By contrast, the US college-age population is static at best and by most demographic forecasts will be shrinking through time as the second-generation "baby boomers" work their way through the educational system. Most forecasts show the number of high school graduates in the United States falling slightly in the coming years, more notably so in the Northeast and less so in the South and West. In (again) very round numbers, the United States has about 4 million people in the age-18 cohort, almost all of whom are enrolled in secondary school, and about 3 million (70–80 percent, depending on the measure) enrolled in post-secondary educational programs of some sort. US colleges and universities grant about 2.7 million degrees annually.

Comparing these data, we see that the "college-attending" population in India already almost matches that of the United States, and India will soon have more students attending post-secondary educational programs than we do as their college participation rates grow from the current 10 percent level to higher levels. And their relative size will grow through time because of differential population growth rates (1.7 percent versus 0.9 percent.)

Table 10.2 Post-secondary schooling participation (percent)

	1985	1995	2005
China	2.9	5.3	20.3
India	6.0	6.6	11.4
USA	60.2	80.9	82.7

Source: http://devdata.worldbank.org/edstats/cd1.asp

China has a somewhat different situation. The age-18 population cohort in China is "only" about 18 million people, and it grows more slowly than India's because of government policy to restrict childbearing. However, the rate at which Chinese citizens attend secondary education and beyond is not only high but appears to be growing rapidly. By recent World Bank estimates, about 75 percent of current Chinese children enroll in secondary school and about 20 percent enroll in post-secondary education. Thus this year, China will have about 3.6 million 18-year-olds in post-secondary education, already more than the number entering post-secondary education in the United States. And China's rapidly growing economy (6–8 percent "real" per year by World Bank estimates) will accelerate the rate at which Chinese youths attend post-secondary educational programs.

To punctuate these college-attending growth rates, consider the time path of proportions of age cohorts attending post-secondary schooling in these three countries through time (see Table 10.2.) While I repeat myself here, I wish to emphasize again that these proportions will surely grow considerably in these growing economies; wealth fuels both the ability and the desire to attend post-secondary school, and we can only expect that these rates will rise rapidly through time. By comparison, current levels of post-secondary schooling participation in other representative developed nations include (in rank order) South Korea (90 percent), Sweden (82 percent), Russia (71 percent), Canada (62 percent), Israel (58 percent), France (56 percent), Japan (55 percent), Turkey (51 percent), and Germany (46 percent.) I would not be at all surprised to find China appearing somewhere on this list within a quarter century, perhaps sooner.[6]

Aggregating data from other nations would make the same point more broadly, but with less dramatic numbers. The potential college-attending population is large, growing, and (unless global investments in higher education facilities far exceed my understanding), US colleges and universities probably will stand to gain more than to lose from globalization of the world of higher education, at least in the coming decades, particularly our larger post-baccalaureate degree-granting institutions.

To summarize this, global growth in the number of students seeking post-secondary education will make the overall market for higher education grow. If the US can avoid disturbing normal flows of students (as occurred in the immediate post-9/11 era) our higher educational institutions should find growing possibilities for enrolling international students.

The lesson drawn here arises from centuries of observation of international trade. When one nation produces something more effectively than others, they tend to specialize, out-producing their internal demands and exporting to the rest of the world. Only artificial trade barriers can impede these flows. These trade flows arise more readily in manufactured products and commodities (ore, grain, and so on) than for services, particularly for services requiring the individual buyer to participate in person (haircuts, restaurant meals, education, and surgery, for example.) The United States can continue to be a major and growing exporter of educational services unless we make it so difficult for foreign scholars to come here (for instance, through immigration control) that they turn elsewhere for their highest educational attainment.

One advantage we have in the United States is hard for many other nations to replicate: the world has about 0.4 billion native English-speakers, and about an equivalent number who have English as a second language. Some estimates say that a quarter of the world's population has at least minimal competence in English. Thus education carried out in English will have a natural attraction to scholars from around the world. Some universities now growing in other nations have partnered with US universities, and many of them actually have instruction in English, no matter what the native language of the country.

To Where?

Most international students come to the United States to attend either large university-type schools or schools in large cities. In slightly rounded numbers, data show that about half of the total (which now reaches almost 15 million international students) attend doctoral or professional master's level programs, and about half are in undergraduate or AA degree programs. By definition, the graduate and professional students attend our larger and more comprehensive universities. The remaining half – those attending undergraduate or AA programs – nevertheless still flock to larger universities, eschewing small college environments. Of that undergraduate half, about 60 percent study in doctoral-granting institutions and another 17 percent in masters-granting institutions.[7] Thus, only about one out of every eight international students studies at the undergraduate level in an undergraduate-only institution. This distinction is particularly striking when one notes that these same doctoral- and masters-granting institutions account for only 30 percent of institutions and 43 percent of students overall.[8] Thus the "density" of undergraduate international students is twice as high in doctoral- and masters-granting institutions as in undergraduate-only schools.

While no data exist to verify this, I conjecture that those undergraduates studying in small colleges do so selectively in schools providing nearby access to larger cities, since this would increase their chances of finding relevant ethnic and cultural communities and resources to assist them in adjusting to their new country. I will elaborate on this issue of international students finding a "community" they can call their own in a later section.

WHEN?

The question of "when" pertains to timing of creation or expansion of your international profile. For some college and university leaders the answer will be "never" since they will conclude (and rightly so, in some cases) that a major endeavor to increase international enrollment is not to their school's comparative advantage.

For those who envision an expansion in their international presence, my advice would be "as very soon as financial conditions permit." I phrase this with particular focus on current financial conditions because of the major economic downturn that enveloped the world of higher education, and indeed the entire world, in 2009 (as I write this chapter.) But there are advantages to moving rapidly.

First, as described in a previous section, the opportunity seems to be on the rise in nations such as India, China and others. The population of college-eligible students will increase rapidly for years to come. Eventually those nations will develop their own resources to hold onto their best students, but until then, the time is ripe. *Carpe diem!*

Next, entering another country with a major recruiting effort takes time and resources, but all the more so as the field gets crowded. This seems much like an activity to which there are considerable returns for being a "first mover." To the extent that international students become informal sales agents, first movers have an immense advantage, since when their students return home for summers or other academic breaks, they will often return to their secondary school and talk about their experiences. If they have had good experiences, they become your first-line sales force. First movers capture the second generation of these informal sales forces, and similarly for later generations.

Finally, as you graduate international students and they return to their home country, they not only become another type of sales force but can also serve as interviewing agents to assess the skills and attitudes of prospective students. I discuss these issues more in the "How" section.

WHAT? (WHAT DO THESE STUDENTS STUDY?)

Describing what international students study is relatively simple at the graduate level: they primarily study in engineering and science fields. Table 10.3 shows the relevant data for doctoral studies (showing US citizens as a percent of total student enrollment.) In the fields of engineering, nearly seven out of every ten doctoral students are international. At the other extreme, in the humanities and in education-related doctorates, only one-eighth are international students. Less than a third of all social science doctoral students are international, and although the data are not available to show this readily, most of these concentrate in the most mathematically focused disciplines, particularly economics, where international students dominate in many programs. Interestingly, even within the sciences, international students show a clear preference for physical (as opposed to life) sciences.

Table 10.3 *US citizens as percent of earned doctorates in the US, by field and country of origin*

	1985	2005
All doctorates	74.7	60.9
Physical Sciences	67.3	48.0
Life Sciences	76.4	63.5
Physical + Life Sciences	72.4	56.9
Engineering	38.5	31.2
Sciences + Engineering	64.4	49.7
Social Sciences	79.4	70.3
Humanities	83.5	82.5
Education	85.6	82.5

Source: National Science Foundation, Survey of Earned Doctorates, 2006.

While I know of no data to demonstrate this, I conjecture that undergraduate choice of majors closely resembles these doctoral-level data. International (and first-generation American) students have a high propensity to select majors that will provide immediate labor-market entry into relatively high-paying jobs, most particularly engineering and business. Liberal arts education in the United States stands distinctively apart from education elsewhere in the world, and in many ways we can view the ability to diversify our intellectual pursuits during college as a wonderful byproduct of the level of wealth we enjoy. Studying the humanities is a luxury, not affordable to many students and their families from overseas.

In addition, studying the humanities in an arts and science setting is probably less productive for international students than for American students. First, their competence in English is likely to be weaker than that of their American counterparts (although not always, to be sure.) Second, they simply do not have the common background usually assumed (like the air we breathe) in most studies of literature and the arts. Think how many common phrases in American English do not translate well. Idiomatic language acquisition is always the most difficult part of language study. Literature, in particular, is filled with idiomatic references.[9] Thus, even students demonstrably competent in English as a second language often miss idioms and references in literature and the arts. Recognizing this, they may turn more to subjects of study where the lack of cultural commonality has less importance – namely mathematics, the sciences and engineering.

HOW? (HOW TO RECRUIT, RETAIN, EDUCATE, SUPPORT, AND CELEBRATE INTERNATIONAL STUDENTS)

Now we get to the meat of the issue. What steps can a college or university take that produce a successful international student presence? Although the precise ways each school will undertake these steps will be unique to their setting, all successful programs will have common elements. I discuss these below together with some options that each school might think about in creating its own manifestation of a good international student program.

Recruiting
Schools that simply post a few pages on their web sites to attract international students will have little success. A more concerted effort will yield higher dividends. Here are some issues to think about.

English language competence
How important are written and verbal competencies in English? And how can schools assess this? Obviously, the Test of English as a Foreign Language (TOEFL) provides a basic level of information about each

student, but only in written English. Class work is conducted mostly with verbal communication, so the ability to comprehend spoken English may be more or less important, depending on the field of study. Technical fields may actually be easier for international students, since the language of mathematics is relatively common across all societies and technical terms tend to have similar sounds in many languages.

If the student will enter a graduate program and be expected to teach, there are also issues raised about spoken language competence. If students speak with heavy and difficult accents, they may fare poorly as teaching assistants in the United States, which in turn (in some settings) hampers their ability to garner financial aid (which often depends on teaching participation.) Only an in-person interview, preferably face to face, can judge this aspect of communication skills. Some graduate programs rely on personal interviews conducted either by a recruiter sent specifically to the country or by alumni of the program who live in the home country of the applicant, or through consortium interviews, if available. The advent of internet-based video conferencing may improve these issues considerably in the future. Certainly internet telephone services such as Skype are now widespread around the world, and any school or program wishing to assure itself of English language competence can readily achieve a telephone-based interview at a minimum.[10]

Financial aid
Financial aid differs greatly for undergraduates versus graduate and professional students. Many colleges and universities admit international students only as full pay, although we can expect to see changes on this horizon as colleges compete for desirable international students. At the undergraduate level, colleges might seek out successful international alumni and ask them to endow scholarship funds for "successor" international students (most desirably from any nation, but probably a more successful "pitch" if the students come from the alumni's home nations.)

At the graduate level, a completely different series of hurdles emerge for international students. First, many graduate programs in the sciences fund their doctoral students with training grants (in the biomedical sciences via the National Institutes for Health and in physical sciences and engineering via the National Science Foundation) – grants for which international students are not eligible. Thus, international students may migrate more into laboratory-assistant jobs that are not so restricted and do not require as much language fluency.[11]

In the social sciences and humanities, most graduate fellowships do not rely upon external funds, but commonly have explicit requirements for teaching roles for the students. If the graduate student's spoken English is weak, this raises significant conflict within the department and the institution, since assigning weak-language students as teachers harms the undergraduate mission but keeping these students out of the classroom ostensibly harms part of the graduate program mission, which includes preparation of the graduate student for teaching roles after they graduate. (The best remedy for this, of course, is a direct assessment of the verbal English language skills of prospective students before offers of admission are made, as the previous discussion about English language competence outlined.)

Travel and visas

Although we think of international students as travel-savvy automatically, that sometimes will overstate their skills and experiences. The biggest pitfalls relate to visas, the rules by which they are issued, and the many ways they can lapse (hence preventing reentry into the country if the student has returned home for a period of time.)

The most common visa status for students is F1. It is generally issued to students who come to study full-time in an academic program or to study English as a second language. For students entering vocational training, the M1 visa is relevant. (The J1 visa is used in two ways that normally affect US universities: for post-doctoral fellows and for visiting scholars.) When a student is admitted, the college or university files an I20 form with the Immigration and Naturalization Service (INS), stating the details of the student's admission (program, expected time to degree, and so on). If any of these details is to change, a whole raft of work emerges for both the student and the school.

Students can run afoul of their visa status in innumerable ways, and a good collegiate program will be alert to help head these problems off – proactively and with every international student. Most importantly, students must study on a full-time basis: three quarters or two semesters per year and with a normal course load (as defined at your school) for full-time status. While students can sometimes keep their student status with a part-time load, it is a complicated process that should not be done at the last minute.

Because the F1 visa is an entry document, some international students run into trouble when they drop to part-time status and return home for a visit, only to discover they can not re-enter the United States if their school has (properly) notified the INS of the change in status. So it is very important to keep track of international students' full-time situations and head off problems associated with going to part-time work load.

Similar issues arise if the student changes degree programs, either laterally (by changing, say, from an MS in Biochemistry to an MS in

Bioengineering), upward (from an MS to a PhD) or downward (from a PhD to an MS or MA.) If the student intends to transfer to another school, even more complications arise. All of such program changes require filing of federal forms (I20 or DS2019), well in advance of the program change.

If the conditions permitting the issuance of an F1 visa change or lapse, the student has only a 15-day grace period to remain in the US. (The J1 visa allows a 30-day grace period.) So if the student falls to part-time status or changes programs without filing proper forms, they lose their approved-visa status within short periods (15 or 30 days.) These are issues best headed off in advance with help from the institutional international student office.

Finally, students on F1 or J1 visas are limited in their hours of employment to 20 hours on campus. (This is linked to the desire to have these students maintaining full-time student status, and may have a tinge of job protection built in as well.) After 9 months of study (and submission of appropriate forms by both the school and the individual), they can work off-campus, but the 20-hour limit still holds (40 hours during summers or other extended school breaks.)

On-campus Support and Nurturing

An attractive and effective international student program will pay a lot of attention to the "care and feeding" of international students at every level and in every school or segment of the university or college. Many universities combine these services into a central Office of International Education (or some similar unit), but many of the relevant functions (such as student's academic standing within a doctoral program) are best monitored at the departmental level. An effective collegiate program will link together all relevant groups and sources of information.

Some of the things I have come to understand during my 13 years as Provost of the University of Rochester may not be wholly apparent to many educators (faculty and staff.) Thus I will attempt to catalog next some potential pitfalls in academic and campus support for international students.

Understanding US norms about academic honesty
Many international students have (at best) a weak understanding of normal American perspectives on academic honesty, particularly relating to plagiarism. Citation standards differ greatly from culture to culture. A good international student program not only provides this information to students upon their arrival at the school but reinforces it regularly through time.

Understanding the US health care system

The United States stands uniquely among developed nations in not having universal health insurance. Students coming from other countries may have very different life-histories regarding access to health care. Thus, mandatory student health fees or the need to purchase separate health insurance may seem quite alien to many of these students. Most US colleges and universities require that students maintain health insurance in addition to paying student health service fees. This bifurcation of financial responsibility will likely confuse many international students. Good communication (at a minimum) will likely pay high dividends in avoiding problems. This is obviously best done before a major illness occurs. Students with families (primarily graduate students) have special issues to deal with, since international students and their family members are not eligible for US programs such as Medicaid and the Supplemental Children's Health Insurance Program (SCHIP.)

Smoking cultures

Most of the United States has rules about public smoking that are far more restrictive than those of other nations. Collegiate campuses sometimes impose even more restrictive smoking rules than are required by local or state law. These laws and rules may create confusion and anger among international students who view their rights to smoke as having been violated. We evolved into these rules slowly over a period of decades, but most international students will have been thrust into them abruptly. Thus, communication with international students before they enter and discussion after their arrival may help them understand both why we have these rules and how they can satisfy their smoking urges within the boundaries of the rules. Your student health services may help as well by offering smoking cessation programs specifically tailored to international students' concerns and issues.

A sense of community

Few of us like to be lonely. Many things fend off loneliness, but the most important for many international students is a group of at least several students who share their culture, history, food preferences, language and religious beliefs. This has myriad implications for international student recruiting and support.

I discussed previously how international students strongly migrate towards larger academic PhD and master's degree-granting institutions rather than independent four-year colleges, even when studying as undergraduates. The reason almost certainly hinges not so much on the reputation of these institutions as the ability of the international students to find a relevant community into which they can blend. A small college in a remote village in New England, Ohio, North Dakota, Oregon or Florida will be unlikely to provide such a community to the international student. While many wonderful academic opportunities exist in relatively rural and remote sites, they probably are not the right cup of tea for many international students.[12]

One solution to this problem, even for relatively small colleges, is to concentrate their international student recruiting in one or a few countries overseas. This has multiple advantages, including decreased recruiting costs, but primarily it allows the formation of a meaningful community of people of common heritage.

Some students from other nations bring special needs, including (often intermixed) dietary and religious preferences. People from some religious and/or cultural backgrounds will not eat meat (or some types of meat), and hence need access to special diets. They may wish to have dedicated areas for religious observance. A welcoming international program will recognize these needs in advance and deal with them appropriately.

Religious holidays bring another confounder to the table. Particularly for students who practice religions that are uncommon in the United States find their religious holidays out of sync with standard American holiday schedules. While they may be happy to have extra time off for traditional American holidays, they may find that nobody knows about or recognizes their own special days. It is especially important to inform faculty members about appropriate policies and behaviors in such situations. For example, a faculty member who schedules an exam on (say) a Bahai', Muslim or Hindu holy day may do so inadvertently. A faculty member who refuses to allow a makeup exam for such a student has created an important barrier for that student's success and/or willingness to return to campus the following year.

The downside of having clusters of international students from the same country is that they may begin to form cliques (or more extremely, enclaves or ghettos) that shut out others. This obviously defeats the purposes of international student participation in student body composition if it occurs *in extremis*. What can collegiate administrators do about this? First, the campus culture should make it clear that all student groups – international and otherwise – are and should be open and inclusive to all. Also, faculty and staff who serve as advisors to student groups should be taught how to spot the formation of cliques and inwardly-turning clubs and how to help guide them back into the open.

Dining and dietary rules
Jewish Kosher and Muslim Halal dietary rules are similar, both requiring slaughter of animals according to prescribed patterns and prohibiting

the eating of pork (and the meat of some other animals.) Local religious representatives can advise on how to prepare food in campus facilities that meets the requirements for followers of their religions.[13] Also, many followers of other faiths (for example, Hindu) are vegetarians of various degrees of strictness. While most campuses now offer vegetarian foods, attention to these preferences and advertising their availability is essential for attracting a diverse international student population.

Celebrations of diversity
Having created an internationally diverse student body, a college can further benefit all students by finding ways to celebrate that diversity. Many collegiate web sites tout their international student body composition, but sometimes with deliberately obscuring language. For example, one web site I found says that the student body of 1100 has "students from 29 countries." This could mean genuinely international – or only fewer than 3 percent of the student body. Another web site counts "international students and US citizens who were raised overseas," which may include (for example) children of military families who were raised on overseas military bases. While such students may have a different perspective on life than those who have not had such experiences, they do not bring the same kind of cultural diversity to a campus that true international students do.

On-campus celebrations of diversity can take many forms. One approach I have long admired was adopted by the William E. Simon Graduate School of Business at the University of Rochester some years ago. The Simon School has a very diverse MBA student body, drawing literally from around the world, with international students representing a significant fraction of each incoming class. The Simon School celebrates that by having students from each nation host a "culture day" at which they appear in traditional garb from their country, prepare and offer samples of traditional cuisine, and on some occasions even perform traditional dances from their home countries. This approach has helped bring these diverse international cultures together and has proven popular and effective for years.

On larger undergraduate campuses, clubs with specific ethnic, regional, or religious foci can perform the same function, and even more so since they can meet regularly. Parties, dinners, dances, and slide-show "tours" of their homelands can help other students learn about each others' cultures and histories. These clubs serve a dual purpose of creating a "critical mass" feeling of mutual support by students who have come to the United States to study, hence helping to ward off loneliness as well as providing mutual support mechanisms for students thrust into new and sometimes difficult situations. If your campus is not large enough to support such groups, it may be useful to think about ways to create them. These types of clubs, however, have diminished value if they become mere enclaves of students who have the same background. Collegiate administrations can encourage an open environment for such clubs in many ways, and such encouragement can only enhance the true values of campus diversity.

The obvious solution is to find ways to aggregate students into larger clusters that make sense. In a small college environment, for example, a consortium of local colleges might help create such groupings by providing transportation services for students to meet regularly from campus to campus for (say) students from South Korea. This can provide a "Korea Club" that no single campus could otherwise support. Students in such clubs can provide the same "outreach" activities on multiple campuses as single-school clubs can provide on their own campus.

Failing that opportunity (for example, in a relatively remote rural college), you can consider aggregating by homeland geography, hence creating (for example) a "South and Central America Club" or a "Pacific Rim Club." While not identical in purpose or function to clubs with specific country designations, these aggregated groups can in many ways serve the same functions as the "pure" form.

Ethnic tensions
Ethnic or geo-political tensions created politically or historically overseas can sometimes spill over into international communities within our campuses. Some recent or contemporaneous overseas tensions that can emerge on campus include China versus Taiwan, Israel–Arab tensions in the Middle East, China versus Tibet, Catholic versus Protestant tensions in England and Ireland, and the like. If students bring these overseas tensions to campus, it cannot help but affect campus environments. In some ways, of course, this can be just the sort of positive tension that makes our campuses so lively and intellectually interesting, but they can bring real risks as well.

One phenomenon emerging occasionally is that campus students of all origins take up a "cause" from an overseas conflict (sometimes sparked by the presence of international students from the embroiled region.) Sometimes these even turn into sit-in demonstrations, building takeovers, or classroom disruptions. Often these student events "demand" that the administration take a particular stance on a contemporaneous overseas event.[14] Advance planning and thinking about how to deal with these issues will be useful, and advance warning from your student-life services may provide enough time for sufficient planning to avert a messy situation. Simply asking your international student and student affairs staff to keep their ears open for brewing disputes among various segments of your student body may be the simplest preventive medicine available.

Another important issue with international students arose after the World Trade Center destruction on September 11, 2001. As the news emerged about the terrorist attacks, accompanied by immense uncertainty about what else might transpire, it soon became apparent in news reports that the attacks were carried out by militant Muslims. This immediately spilled over into campus environments where some Muslim students (both domestic and international) who wore traditional Muslim garb became (on some campuses) targets of abuse or hostility, either directly face to face or indirectly (for instance, via graffiti.) Some Muslim students in that situation feared for their own safety and sought protection from campus officials. Responses varied, but included faculty-led discussions about Muslim beliefs and traditions, interfaith prayer vigils, and (sometimes) personal escorts for the concerned students until things calmed down.

These events have occurred before (for instance, treatment of Japanese-origin people at the outbreak of World War II) and probably will in the future. The best medicine, again, is preventive: think about how to deal with such issues in the broader context of free speech versus "hate speech" codes on campus, rules (and enforcement thereof) for sit-ins, classroom discussions, and the like. These complex issues are in many ways at the very core of what colleges and universities seek to achieve, but as they boil over into more conflicted situations, the learning values diminish and the disruption costs increase. Every campus will have its own approach to handling these things, and thinking through campus responses in the broader context of speech and behavior protocols is probably the best approach.

Special Issues in the Sciences

Restricted materials and "deemed exports"
Involving international students, post-doctoral fellows, and visiting scholars in laboratory sciences brings another set of potential pitfalls, most of which the relevant department admitting the student or post-doc may understand only poorly. Most of these issues center on access to materials or to specialized knowledge that might be considered dangerous to our national security.

A whole host of biological and chemical substances, for example, as well as technology that might be used to create them have the potential to create harm. The government rules list not only chemical and biological materials but also missile technology, nuclear technology, and a general class called "national security." This last issue – access to technology – creates a whole raft of issues for the collegiate world to worry about – the so-called deemed export. The rules that pertain here differ (as one might expect) for (say) scholars and students from Great Britain versus those from Cuba or North Korea. A whole list of materials require an export license. In addition, particularly with regard to technologies (and software source codes) that might be used to create harmful things, the mere exposure of a person to either the technology or even the instruction manual can be considered a "deemed export." Thus, the Department of Commerce considers a uranium centrifuge to have been exported to a "country of concern" (Group D on the Department of Commerce list) or a country deemed to support terrorism (Group E) if an individual from the said country sees the manual of operations for the technology, or computer software source code, or even attends a talk describing the technology.[15]

Most universities conducting research in these areas have this process well under control, but research institutions should regularly audit their processes, including a review of the country of origin of students and other scholars studying within their environs.

Funding
Although previously noted, it is worth remembering here that foreign nationals are not eligible for some types of training grants that regularly support PhD students and post-docs in laboratory and other sciences. Those with "Green Cards" can apply for many other sources of research funding, but the training grants are more commonly restricted. Thus when an institution opens its doors to international students in these areas, they normally must provide internal resources to support stipends for the students.

Epidemic or pandemic diseases arising overseas
Another complicated problem, which "comes with the territory" of international students is how to deal with suddenly emerging epidemics overseas of virulent and dangerous disease outbreaks. These have arisen repeatedly in the recent past – for example, Ebola, severe acute respiratory syndrome (SARS), avian flu and others – and will again in the future. A swine flu epidemic arising in Mexico in early 2009 has the potential for a worldwide pandemic infection in future years. The immediate issue arises when a virulent outbreak has just occurred before known travel of students (or their families) from the infected area. Collegiate campuses have special concerns about having people with such highly contagious and virulent viruses present because of the special living conditions on campus. Students live together in dorms, attend classes with large numbers of people closely

packed into tight seating ("classrooms"), assemble in large public events (sporting events, graduation ceremonies), and interact regularly in food service areas, sometimes serving as food handlers.

Campuses can choose among many ways to deal with these issues, ranging from travel bans (that is, simply telling the students to stay home),[16] to quarantine upon arrival to "regular observation" upon arrival, to doing nothing (and many gradations and combinations in between.) Student health service doctors and nurses should be actively involved in thinking about these issues, both because they will be on the front line dealing with them and also because they have access through their associations of student health service providers to advance thinking and preparation for such events.

After Graduation

We should not forget our international students the moment they receive their diplomas. They can serve as important resources for future international programming goals in several ways. In the immediate term, of course, as they return home, they will inevitably interact with potential new students. The ways they have been treated and the overall perceptions about their time in the United States will determine what they tell future students. Those who have had a positive experience and who express an interest and willingness to do so can serve immediately as informal ambassadors of our programs.

International alumni can also, with proper guidance, provide an on-site interview resource to help the admissions officers understand more about the interests, talents, personality and English language skills of prospective students. As with any alumni interview group, these alumni are used more effectively if given proper training and instruction, including what to say (and what not to say!), interview report forms, and perhaps even mock-interview sessions with role-playing.

Ultimately, of course, international alumni will succeed in their careers to a greater or lesser degree, and those who succeed more may become important donor prospects for the alumni development officers. Probably the most important thing to do now to make this succeed is to establish mechanisms whereby to keep in touch with international alumni in the future. This is more difficult for international students than domestic students, but also often very difficult to do for graduate programs (particularly PhD programs) where the initial contact information may well be the department from which the students received their PhD or perhaps even their thesis advisor. Finding a way to keep contacts alive will ultimately sow the seeds for future development successes.

CONCLUDING REMARKS

Internationalization of campus student bodies creates dividends in many dimensions, beginning with fundamental campus goals such as providing all students on campus with a diverse and exciting intellectual and social experience and ending with opportunities to engage international alumni in further recruiting endeavors and development efforts, perhaps focused on supporting subsequent internationalization of the campus.

The time is ripe for energizing our campus efforts, even in difficult budget conditions. First movers will retain a permanent advantage as the population of potential students is rising rapidly, particularly in India and China, and the domestic supply of undergraduate education in those foreign lands will likely lag the growing demand for decades to come.

Since early in the 20th century, the United States has dominated international competition in higher education – more so than almost any other sector of our economy. While other nations seek to expand their roles in providing international education (particularly those on the Pacific Rim such as India, China, Australia, and Singapore), the United States can remain dominant and successful – unless we fail to undertake appropriate efforts to woo international students to our shores.

> On the plains of hesitation,
> Bleach the bones of countless millions,
> Who, at the dawn of victory,
> Sat down to wait
> And waiting – died!
> (George Cecil, 1928; also variously attributed in modified versions to Omar Khayyam, John Dretschmer and Adlai Stevenson)

NOTES

1. For the entire statement, see http://www.rochester.edu/diversity/philosophy.html.
2. Much of this section replicates material from an earlier essay I wrote for TIAA-CREF about international competition in higher education of interest. That essay can be found at http://www.tiaa-crefinstitute.org/articles/Globalization_of_Higher_Education.html. The tables in this chapter were used in that 2007 essay.
3. Source for all country-specific economic and population growth data in this chapter: www.worldbank.org/data/countrydata/countrydata.html.
4. World Bank EdStat is the source for these and comparable data on participation rates.
5. Recall from Table 10.1 that the U.S. has about 75,000 students from India, probably less than 1 percent of the post-secondary school attendees in India.
6. All data on schooling participation from http://devdata.worldbank.org/edstats/cd1.asp.
7. Data source: International Educational Exchange Network, *Open Doors* (2006) *Report*

on *International Educational Exchange*, available at http://opendoors.iienetwork.org/?p=131534.
8. These data count the number of institutions classified by the Carnegie Foundation as "exclusively undergraduate two year," "exclusively undergraduate four year," and "very high undergraduate." If one includes the Carnegie Foundation classification of "high undergraduate" these numbers fall to 18 percent and 17 percent respectively.
9. One of my favorite examples is the title of a wonderful short story in the science fiction genre by Poul Anderson, who (despite his non-traditional American name) was born in Pennsylvania. A detective from the future narrates this story, written in 1961, relating a conversation in a bar where the detective and another man discuss time travel, and the hypothetical issues of police work if time travel were to exist. Only at the end do we realize that the detective is indeed a time traveler, and has been sent to capture a fugitive from the future, who (we learn at the end of the story) is the other man at the bar. At the end, the detective drugs the fugitive, travels through time with him and drops him in front of the city gates just before Troy is sacked. The title of this short story? "My Object All Sublime." Those not familiar with Gilbert and Sullivan will never catch the "hidden" title – "to let the punishment fit the crime." The verses of the song contain yet another subtle play on words, saying "My object all sublime, I shall achieve *in time*, to let the punishment fit the crime," the perfect fit for a story about time travel.
10. This does not necessarily ensure that the person speaking on the phone is the true applicant. Video conferencing provides further assurance on this front, and in-person interviews are even better.
11. I know of one case where an entire US university laboratory operates using only Mandarin language.
12. *U.S. News & World Report* lists only 40 "liberal arts colleges" as having more than 5 percent international students. See http://colleges.usnews.rankingsandreviews.com/college/liberal-arts-most-international.
13. For Muslim-acceptable food products, the Muslim Consumer Group, based in Illinois, provides guidance.
14. A very recent example would be the Israeli incursion into the Gaza Strip in early 2009.
15. The list of Group E countries currently includes Sudan, Syria, Cuba, and Iran. North Korea was removed in July 2008.
16. UC Berkeley, for example, banned students from affected nations during the 2003 SARS epidemic. This affected about 500 students from various Asian nations.

REFERENCES

Grutter v. Bollinger, http://www.law.cornell.edu/supct/html/02-241.ZS.html, and Gratz v. Bollinger, http://www.law.cornell.edu/supct/html/02-516.ZS.html.

Jacobs, Bruce (2005), "The Tangible Contributions of International Graduate Students: An Alternative Approach and Some Evidence from the University of Rochester," *Council of Graduate Schools Communicator*, 38 (4), May.

11. Reinventing higher education in a global society: a perspective from abroad

Gowher Rizvi and Peter S. Horn

The arguments for global education are obvious and compelling but nonetheless warrant restating. In an interdependent global society, the distinction between home and abroad has largely vanished. Information technology, radio and television have shrunk the world. Not only do we live in a global economy and society, but it is also a very complex, interconnected and interdependent world. All countries, big and small, must cope with the realities of a global society. It is no longer possible to differentiate between national and international, home and abroad, or local and global. Home and abroad are no longer separate categories. No country is an island entire of itself. The United States is a part of the global community, and it cannot shirk away from problems in faraway regions even if our own direct interests may not be directly at stake. Therefore, the challenge for colleges and universities, both in the United States and around the world, is to prepare and equip students as global citizens.

In this chapter we argue that colleges and universities, faced with the challenges of the new knowledge-based global society, must reinvent themselves and rethink their roles and purposes.[1] Can we redesign our curriculum so that we can continue to impart the benefits of a liberal arts-based education but at the same time create room for global experiences without increasing the academic burden on the students? How do we make global education an integral part of the student experience? How do we integrate a global perspective into our curriculum? In a complex global world how do we build knowledge that both encompasses multiple disciplinary perspectives and at the same time draws from comparative experiences of different societies? And finally, we have to tackle the seemingly daunting challenge of making quality education affordable and accessible for all academically able students irrespective of their ability to pay for it. We will argue that, in a knowledge-based society, every individual is an important resource and society cannot let that precious resource go to waste. Harnessing human capabilities is not just a case of equity and social justice – and both of these are important – but a matter of survival and national and global economic security.

A LIBERAL HIGHER EDUCATION AND THE TRAINING OF THE MIND

The purpose of higher education is to discipline students' minds: to enable them to solve problems and teach them how to learn. A liberal arts-based education not only trains and disciplines the mind, but also inculcates in the students the power of rational reasoning and gives them the analytical tools needed for lifelong learning and the pursuit of a profession. A disciplined mind can distill information, formulate questions, sift through evidence, marshal arguments, separate the trees from the woods, organize the facts cogently, explain a phenomenon, and draw conclusions based on the evidence. It inculcates in students the habits and joys of lifelong learning. A liberal arts education equips individuals with the tools to seek the truth that will free them from ignorance, superstitions, prejudices, narrow-mindedness and bigotry. These "portable" skills and disciplines of the mind have an enduring value and will enable students to cope with the changing demands and challenges of life.

There are certainly other prominent models of higher education, such as the research-based university, that produce graduates who function at such a level, but that is not necessarily their core objective. And it is not the case either that the models are mutually exclusive. But, in short, a liberal arts education bestows upon students a disciplined, inquiring mind that can be put to use in any field of human endeavor. Such a mind may be the most valuable asset that higher education can inculcate in students irrespective of whatever they choose to do after graduating.

Colleges and universities around the world emulate the range of models present in the US, and while it is more typical of private, well-supported institutions, liberal arts education remains sought after internationally given its emphasis on disciplining the mind and equipping students with lifelong learning skills. And it is true that the other models with more of a focus on vocational skills are frequently emulated abroad as well.

Globalization has major ramifications for what we teach our students, what experiences we offer them while they are at the universities, and how we build knowledge that will enable us to better understand the global world. The challenge for the colleges, therefore, is not only to continue to train and discipline the minds of the students through higher education, particularly in the traditional liberal arts, and to provide them with the

TRAINING GLOBAL CITIZENS

As global citizens our students will have to traverse many worlds and operate at many different levels. They must at the same time be at home both here and abroad. They should be able to transfer from one society to another effortlessly, be capable of communicating in multiple languages, and be able to work in institutions and organizations that are international, diverse and multicultural.[2] No less importantly, they should be able to understand diverse perspectives born out of differing cultural and geographic experience. And as global citizens our students will compete not only with those in the United States but also with the best and the brightest around the world. There will be no room for mediocrity in a knowledge-based economy.

We have to capture every "teachable moment" by creating a total learning environment so that students imbibe as much from their surroundings – their friends, clubs, societies and dining halls – as they do from their professors, classes, lectures, seminars, laboratories and tutorials. It is therefore vital that what is offered in the formal academic curriculum is supplemented by opportunities and experiences on the campus that will expose the students to the world outside. In other words, we have to replicate a microcosm of the world outside within our own universities. We must let the world into our ivory towers.[3]

Colleges must adapt the curriculum to train students to be global citizens who will need to be much more acculturated with the larger environment in which they will live and work. Today global education and international exposure is no longer an add-on or an optional part of the curriculum and college experience. Rather, global education must be an integral part of the core experience – academic and extra-curricular – that colleges and universities offer to every student throughout the entire period of their college life. There must be a compulsory global education requirement for the successful completion of the degree. The international immersion programs through the junior year or semester abroad schemes – traditionally the staple method of exposing students to outside societies and culture – are important[4] but not sufficient in themselves. The training of our students as global citizens will require continuous and integrated experience of international issues and culture throughout their entire life on the campus.

The global experience is not a discrete or a separate part of the education of the students. Rather it must be interjected into the everyday life of the students by bringing to the campus a diverse and international community of students and faculty. This will involve creating a learning environment in which the students can experience and understand the outside world while still in the college; it will entail creating opportunities, facilities and programs to give students a firsthand experience of the world outside their borders.[5]

To prepare students as global citizens we have to train them to understand that diverse groups of people presented with the same set of evidence will often reach different conclusions. Very often there is no right or wrong answer. Our view of life and the world is often subjective and is shaped by our cultural, geographic and societal experiences. That is why we strive for diversity in our campuses. It offers the students the opportunity to test their own assumptions with fellow students and scholars of different nationalities, religions, languages and socio-economic backgrounds. It is the failure to understand and respect each other's perspectives and assumptions that often contributes to global misunderstandings, tensions and conflicts. To make the university truly diverse, we have to recreate a microcosm of the world at large, and we must make our colleges the destination of choice for students, visiting faculty and scholars, practitioners, distinguished lecturers, writers, filmmakers and so forth. Colleges and universities should take advantage of the enormous human resources in their neighboring areas to tap into the rich pool of international expertise from the diplomatic community, international organizations, the government, corporations, the courts, the rich array of civil society and development agencies, think-tanks, newspapers and, of course, immigrant communities. In addition to hosting distinguished visitors, colleges should provide global exposure through international film, music, literary and cultural festivals and international cuisine.

Integration of the global perspective in the curriculum is necessary but not enough for producing global citizens. The learning must go beyond the confines of the campus; the students must have the opportunity of experiencing the world firsthand through studying, working and living abroad. Most American and European colleges are trying to enrich the experiences of the students by bringing foreign students into their campuses. Some colleges have set a target of recruiting up to 10 percent of foreign students. Other colleges are setting up campuses abroad to give their students international exposure. Still other colleges are forging partnerships with distant universities so that their students can study and experience other societies and ways of learning.[6]

While more students are availing the opportunities of study abroad or partaking in exchange programs with other overseas colleges, there will be students who are unable to take advantage of these opportunities for financial or other reasons. We have already argued that overseas experiences are important but that global education cannot be confined to travel abroad or limited to one part of the college experience. Colleges must bring the world to the doorsteps of the students so that they can continuously experience global education. The integration of the global perspective into our curriculum must be accompanied by experimentations in the classroom as well. The experience in the classroom – both faculty teaching and student discussions – is often and understandably circumscribed by our shared experience, assumptions and outlook. Not surprisingly we see the world from our perspective. The challenge for us is to enrich our perspective by understanding other perspectives and points of view.[7] How do people view us, and how do they view themselves?

Some institutions have responded to the challenge of introducing global perspective into the classrooms through use of information technology to set up virtual global classrooms. Some institutions are experimenting in global classrooms where the faculty and the students from a number of institutions in different parts of the world use technology to bring the faculty and students together virtually into a single class, in real time; they follow a collaboratively designed single course and participate as a single class. The faculty are often drawn from all participating institutions. They teach jointly, but each faculty member is discretely responsible for a particular lesson or segment of the course, and they use a variety of pedagogic techniques. The students at all the sites are able to see and hear the faculty and each other on the screen in real time. Questions and class participation are heard and seen by all the students, and questions and comments can be directed to a faculty or to a student in any of the institutions. All the students have a common curriculum and readings, and all have the same assignments, which are done in small groups drawn together from all the institutions. The global classroom is designed as an additional element in the global education and experience of the students.[8]

The experiment in the global classroom holds enormous promise. If the experiment is successful, the students can participate in global classes throughout their college experience. The global classroom experience can be much more integrated to the total curriculum – as opposed to an isolated or one-off experience like the study abroad. Students have the benefit of being taught by faculty from multiple institutions and can experience different pedagogic approaches and perspectives on a daily basis. Furthermore, the global classroom can be cost effective while offering both flexibility and choice. It also has enormous attraction for faculty as it exposes them to the outside world through the experience of teaching a course jointly with faculty of other institutions and backgrounds.

REDESIGNING THE CURRICULUM

Let us now turn to the question of the curriculum. International exposure and experience certainly matter, but ultimately it is the academic content of the courses that remains at the heart of the college's mission. We have to rethink what we teach the students and revisit both the curriculum and the pedagogic approaches through which we impart instruction. One of the great challenges for colleges in the twenty-first century will be to devise curricula that will be innovative and imaginative and that will reflect the changed circumstances of our global society.

The academic work that our students do must provide them with the analytical and empirical tools necessary to comprehend the global society. This means that colleges and universities have to integrate, to the greatest extent possible, a global perspective in as many of the courses in the curriculum as is feasible. It is no longer sufficient to create or add a number of courses that are labeled as "international" or "foreign." That will be more of the same and will not be adequate in a global world where the demarcation between local and international, national and global, and home and abroad has ceased to be a useful analytical or conceptual tool. The creation of "majors" and "minors" in Global Studies may be an intermediate step to fully globalizing the course contents. Anything to advance a student's global knowledge is a step forward in making them global citizens and enhancing their employability. In many colleges even engineers, doctors, architects and teachers are opting to take global options both to gain exposure and to enhance their employability. The more innovative colleges now offer the students an opportunity, irrespective of their majors or specializations, to earn a certificate in global studies.

One of the real challenges for the universities will be to devise a curriculum that will be innovative and imaginative, reflect the changed circumstances of the twenty-first century, and have a pedagogy centered on students. In a global world based on the knowledge economy[9], the skills and versatility required for success in life and business are much more demanding. Addressing the challenges of today's world will require a move away from old-style pedagogy. The pedagogic choices in the new curriculum must invariably be student-centered ones in which various teaching instruments – lectures , tutorials, seminars, case studies, simulation, role playing, student-led discussions and problem solving, student projects, films and videos, peer group learning – will have to be experimented with and adapted to make learning interesting, participatory, reflective and creative.

In too many colleges today, the students are forced to reside in the silos of their own discipline, unaware of and unconcerned with other disciplines and approaches. Even in the best traditions of liberal arts programs, the emphasis on majors and concentrations tends to narrow the exposure of the students to other relevant bodies of knowledge.[10] The new curricula will have to reflect that concern and move away from traditional "disciplinary" training. In the last fifty years, colleges have experimented with inter-disciplinary, cross-disciplinary and multi-disciplinary approaches to training undergraduates but have met with limited success, and it will require versatility and knowledge drawn from diverse disciplines to study and understand the big challenges confronting our world.

In a world of high specialization, the focus of the academics on their "parent discipline" is perfectly understandable: it is through specialization, often narrow specialization, that scientific advances have been made and the frontiers of knowledge advanced, and it is impracticable to expect the members of the faculty to be equally familiar with more than one discipline or sub-discipline. At the same time, it is obvious that "academic specializations" of the faculty have not served well either the students or the employers who hire the students. No one has yet found a perfect solution to the challenges of specialization versus broad-based general education. Education without depth is probably no more useful than in-depth knowledge of one subject without familiarity with a large number of other useful bodies of knowledge. Nor is there any easy answer as to how to fit in the short space of graduate and undergraduate degrees both the demands of an academic program and the competing demands of the employers to train the students in skills needed for the professions.

While the challenges are enormous, the problems are not insurmountable once we are in agreement on the necessity of training global citizens and on the role that higher education will play in preparing students for the new global society. No academic program can ever hope to teach a student all the subjects that are necessary in their lifetime, and even the most broad-based liberal arts education is constrained by how much and how many different subjects can be effectively imparted in four years. Besides, knowledge is changing and growing constantly, and very often what is learned in colleges becomes dated before long. The purpose of the college is not to prepare students for a particular profession – these are skills that many students will acquire on the job and in any case many of them will change jobs and professions many times in their lives – but rather to discipline their minds, enable them to solve problems, and teach them how to learn. These "portable" skills and disciplines of the mind have an enduring value and will enable the students to cope with the changing demands and challenges of life.

The faculty and the students, by and large, understand the importance of creating new courses and curriculum material that genuinely integrates the international perspective in everything that is taught. But this is more easily said than done. First, this is a labor-intensive process and will require each faculty member to review, revise and redo his or her courses. Very often this will require rewriting lectures, securing new teaching materials, and writing new case studies. Second, in some cases, it may require faculty to undertake fresh studies and retool their own research. Changes of such magnitude can only be done gradually and over a period of time. And third this will require additional resources that are scarce in the best of times and particularly difficult to obtain in stringent times.

The provosts, deans, and departmental chairs will have to be strategic and opportunistic to implement the changes. Most of the changes will happen when faculty vacancies occur or new faculty positions are created. The appointment of every new faculty position affords an opportunity to rethink the direction in which the provost and deans want to take their college. No position should be filled automatically and mechanically; rather each faculty vacancy or new appointment should be viewed as a strategic opportunity of to achieve the desired objective of adding to the international expertise of the faculty. Academic leaders must also consider other innovative and novel mechanisms for augmenting the global expertise of the faculty. Colleges should consider tapping expertise in the government and the private sector through appointments of professors of practice. Colleges should tap distinguished statesmen, diplomats, chief executive officers, judges and public servants as adjunct faculty to give the students insights into the world of practice.

In addition to effecting these changes through recruiting new faculty or replacing those retiring or otherwise departing, colleges will need to provide faculty with sabbaticals and leaves of absence from their teaching to develop new curriculum material and courses. In the interim, colleges will need to use visiting scholars and adjunct faculty with international expertise to fill the gap. This will be a long process, but it is the most effective way to create a curriculum with a genuinely global perspective.

An important part of becoming global citizens is to be able to converse and conduct business in multiple languages. Not surprisingly, graduates with multi-language fluency are increasingly the most sought-after by employers competing in a global marketplace. It is common for European and Asian students to emerge from college fluent in several major languages. In India, students are fortunate in that they grow up with several languages including English. Indeed, proficiency in English has given Indian students a huge advantage in a global society where English has emerged as the language of business. Colleges and universities in any country cannot afford to produce graduates disadvantaged in this regard. It should be a condition of graduation that every student demonstrates a fluency in one or more foreign language. Institutions in the US are cognizant of this and are establishing language centers using technology to teach foreign languages. Colleges and universities must make foreign language teaching a priority as part of their globalization efforts.

KNOWLEDGE BUILDING IN A GLOBAL SOCIETY

In the challenging environment of the new millennium, we have to move beyond disciplines to a "post-disciplinary" era by equipping students with a body of knowledge that will enable them to deal with the big issues and questions of our times from the perspectives of different disciplines and diverse methodologies. It will require versatility and knowledge drawn from diverse disciplines to study and understand the big challenges confronting us. Take, for example, the question of the environment. It is one of the big challenges of our time, but it is certainly not capable of being understood or addressed by environmental science alone. Environmental challenges call for the understanding not only of the earth and environmental sciences but also of history, human rights, governance, resource management, sustainable economics and development studies, just to name a few. In other words, the undergraduate students, instead of specializing in a particular discipline, will focus on a large problem facing the society and seek to study and understand the problem simultaneously from diverse perspectives and academic disciplines. Colleges will need to ensure that the courses and concentrations are designed around problems and issues rather than disciplines. Questions like environmental degradation or global warming, making democracy work in plural societies, or poverty or social justice are not confined to any one country, nor are they problems only for developing societies. Students will have to learn and understand these large issues of the twenty-first century in a comparative framework and see if some of the solutions found elsewhere have any resonance with their own experience and problems at home.

Globalization has also profoundly impacted the way in which we conduct research and build knowledge. We have earlier argued that the problems and issues of the twenty-first century are complex and not capable of being understood through the prism of a single discipline. Our knowledge building must not only involve drawing on the corpus and insights of multiple disciplines but must also be empirically tested against both the local and global experience and perspectives. Most of the major challenges of the twenty-first century – population explosion, genocide and forced large-scale migration, the scarcity of food, water and energy, deforestation, environmental degradation and global warming, cross-border and global terrorism, public health issues such as epidemics like HIV/AIDS or bird flu, trafficking in women and children, and so on – are global and transnational issues. They can neither be resolved within the borders of a single country nor studied or understood in isolation from the rest of the world. In the twenty-first century, credible knowledge can only be built through a two-way exchange of experience and information, through collaborative and comparative research, and based on mutual respect.

No college or university in the world, no matter how large, good or rich, has all the resources and expertise to address all the big problems confronting our world today. Most, if not all, of the problems listed above are transnational and largely located outside the United States and Europe. Moreover these problems are, by their very nature transnational and not capable of being addressed in a single country. The scholars in the West, in order to remain on the cutting edge of research, will have to work in places outside their homes and will have to collaborate with scholars in distant places. In other words knowledge building will have to be both transnational and collaborative. This offers a huge opportunity for colleges and universities to team with scholars around the world and address the big problems of concern to society.

Finally, in the field of knowledge building we have to be mindful of another important consideration. The West no longer has a monopoly of knowledge production nor are the developing societies any longer content to be uncritical consumers of Western knowledge. Knowledge in the twenty-first century will have to be collaborative. It has to be built through a two-way exchange of information, experience and ideas. It must tap into knowledge systems of other societies and cultures. And it must be based on a relationship of mutual respect and reciprocity. The earlier "extractive" relationships whereby scholars collected material, data and samples and returned to their home institutions to publish and patent their ideas are no longer acceptable.[11] Scholars undertaking field studies in other countries and societies will have to abide by certain ethical standards and codes. They must be willing to share the benefits of the research with the host societies and, most importantly, since much of this work will be done collaboratively, they must acknowledge the intellectual ownership of the local partners.

EXCELLENCE AND ACCESS IN HIGHER EDUCATION

We have earlier argued that colleges and universities are the engine that will drive the global economy, as well as country-specific economies, in a knowledge-based global society. It follows that in a world where skills are scarce every individual must be harnessed to develop his of her full human potential. As we transform the mouths to feed into hands and brains that are productive and creative, our youth become our most valuable economic resource. The two biggest challenges facing colleges and universities in the twenty-first century are the questions of excellence and access. In other words, how do we build and maintain world-class colleges and universities and at the same time ensure that quality higher education is affordable and accessible to all academically qualified students irrespective of their socio-economic backgrounds, not just to the academically brilliant or the financially well-off?

Not surprisingly in most developed and developing countries there are effectively two systems of education: one for the haves and one for the have-nots. Those who can afford to pay for education have access to quality education and the professional and financial success that typically results from such higher education. The same can often not be said about those who cannot afford to pay. This happens despite the fact that there is no evidence to suggest that intelligence is disproportionately concentrated in any socio-economic group.

Most elite colleges and universities in the United States continue to draw their students disproportionately from the upper income groups in the society; the children from the top 5 percent of the income distribution occupy a disproportionately large share of seats in the Ivy League and other top US institutions. Historically, public higher education in the United States was primarily focused on ensuring equitable access but, with a number of honorable exceptions, was often faced with resource scarcity that challenged its ability to maintain quality. The United States is not alone in having a disproportionate share of seats in the better institutions occupied by students from advantaged backgrounds. Furthermore, many of the brightest students in other countries, especially those with the ability to pay, choose to leave their home country and study abroad at better-quality institutions than often exist at home.

But the issue is more nuanced in the United States than often found elsewhere. There is no lack of higher educational opportunity for the socio-economically disadvantaged but academically brilliant and gifted individual in the United States. Rather, the challenge is that most of the very poor, especially among ethnic minorities, are so far behind on all measures of academic preparedness and even academic ambition that they do not get the chance for a college education. The issue in the United States is not the lack of opportunity for the poor but academically brilliant, but for the poor and academically average and below average.

To pursue excellence without equal access is not only socially reprehensible but also not worthy of our societal endeavors. But it is not only an issue of social justice; it is also a matter of practical economic necessity. In a knowledge-based economy, a large number of academically qualified students effectively denied access to higher education because they cannot afford the cost represents a large pool of potentially productive resources that individual countries and the global society at large can no longer afford to waste, especially in a world where in many countries the fertility rate is declining, the population is aging and the proportion of productively active persons in the economy is declining. Making quality higher education accessible to all those capable of benefiting from it is economically incumbent on society as a whole.

There is also a strong academic reason why bright students from disadvantaged socio-economic backgrounds should have access to quality institutions – it is in the best interest of all students who attend the colleges and universities. Colleges and universities prepare students for life; and it is important that they reflect, in a microcosm, the realities of the world. To create such a learning environment colleges must recruit a genuinely diverse faculty and student body, which is not easy. Meaningful diversity must include socio-economic diversity in addition to gender, race, religion and nationality. There must also be room for ideological and intellectual nonconformity. Empirical and pedagogical evidence suggests that students learn best in such diverse institutions. It enables the students to learn from each other, to test their ideas and assumptions with those who come from different experiences, and to become aware that people presented with the same evidence often come to different conclusions. The experience of international and multicultural dormitories, classes, and sports clubs helps students to develop interpersonal skills and prepare them for the global world into which they will be entering.[12]

PAYING FOR EXCELLENCE AND ACCESS

Unless access to quality higher education around the world is guaranteed, a societal commitment to create an even playing field will never become a reality. Financial aid (loans and grants) for socio-economically disadvantaged but capable students, not just the academically brilliant and gifted, should be treated as a fundamental right. Financial aid should be both means and merit based – it must not be a quota system, nor should it in any way lower the academic rigor and requirements for the socially and historically disadvantaged groups. However, the means test should not be mean. The purpose of financial aid is to create an even playing field in which all students have equal opportunity to develop their fullest potential and creativity.

In India, the New Delhi-based Foundation for Access and Excellence has demonstrated not only that talent resides in the most disadvantaged groups of Indian society, but also that institutions with the vision to admit them have also benefited academically. It requires a commitment, an understanding of the academic value of diversity, and an enlightened self-interest to seek and target students from historically disadvantaged groups.

In the United States, some wealthy private universities like Harvard have clearly understood the pedagogical value of diverse students and have set aside a percentage of the income from their endowment for bursaries for disadvantaged students. Some public universities like the University of Virginia have done likewise through programs such as Access UVa.[13] Not only has Virginia reached out to disadvantaged groups, but in the process it has raised its own academic standards. To remain academically competitive and to attract high-quality students, other colleges must follow suit.

The Ford Foundation marked the new millennium by making a grant of 350 million dollars to establish an International Fellowship Program targeting the academically brilliant but economically and socially disadvantaged students for post-graduate study. The Foundation has developed an extremely sophisticated and calibrated selection process: the "dual tripwire." The application of each candidate is filtered through two separate lenses – academic and socio-economic. Only those candidates who can successfully cross the "dual tripwire" – that is, demonstrate a record of academic brilliance and a verifiable evidence of disadvantage – are allowed to move forward in the selection process. The success of the International Fellowship Program has convinced many institutions to enhance their efforts to recruit students from deprived areas around the world.

If society is serious about its commitment to making quality education accessible to all deserving students irrespective of their financial circumstances, it shall need to think outside the box. It cannot, and must not, hide behind financial constraints. Once we accept that no student who has been accepted for admission on merit will be denied access for reasons of financial disabilities, the concern for social justice must inform all financial and academic planning. This entails the need for greater cost sharing among students and their families from personal resources, various levels of government from the power to tax, borrow and lend, and colleges and universities from their resources.

To the extent that all students benefit from a diverse experience on campus, it is fair for tuitions to reflect the expense of such a benefit in the same way as they reflect the other costs of providing the education experience. College administrators, in determining the level of tuition, should factor in the cost the university incurs in providing a diverse, multicultural and international environment. Individuals and society should view the cost incurred in promoting diversity – like the cost of education itself – as an *investment* rather than as an expenditure.

Once we begin to take the view that expenditure on education is an investment, and grasp the huge returns higher education produces, it should be possible to think of funding access to quality higher education through numerous innovative ways. Higher education can certainly compete with other societal needs (primary education, health care, infrastructure, and so on) for funds in government operating budgets, but that competition is intense as other needs are often deemed of greater immediate importance. In today's knowledge-based economy such an outcome may be not just short-sighted but suicidal. But it is the political reality.

We are not aware of any form of investment that will benefit government and society more over a very long period than investing in higher education. That benefit should be viewed not only in terms of an investment return but also socially and ethically. It is important for governments to realize that investment in higher education increases both personal income and national output, therefore increasing a country's tax-base in the long run.

CONCLUSIONS

The challenges posed by globalization for the colleges are immense and extend far beyond study abroad programs and adding international courses to the curriculum. We must rethink the entire experience that colleges offer to the students. Our students will be competing for jobs against global competition and will be pitted against the best around the world. We have to prepare them to be both global citizens and to be globally competitive. We will need to revisit what is taught, how it is taught, how colleges will continue to build knowledge, and how they will meet the challenges of providing quality education in a knowledge-driven economy. Tinkering on the edges will not suffice. Fundamental rethinking is required and the colleges must join with the society in an open debate.[14] It is a challenge for our entire higher education system.

Colleges are the engines that will drive our societal prosperity, and it is no exaggeration to claim that the success of our society rests upon their success. Quality, innovation and excellence will be the hallmark of successful colleges. Knowledge and scholarship are benchmarked by global standards and colleges will be judged accordingly. In a global world the colleges, the faculty and the students cannot be sheltered behind national walls or work in isolation from the rest. To be competitive, universities, like the market, must attract the best faculty and students, and they must provide world-class facilities, libraries and laboratories.

In a world where market orthodoxy reigns supreme, colleges are under pressure to provide students with skills for gainful employment through vocational training. This is based on a fundamental misunderstanding of the role and the purpose of undergraduate teaching in liberal arts institutions. Colleges must not succumb to the market pressures. It would, in fact, be futile to do so. No academic program can ever hope to teach a student all the subjects that are necessary in their lifetime and even the most broad-based liberal arts education is constrained by how much and how many different subjects can be effectively imparted in the four years of college. Besides, knowledge is changing and growing constantly, and very often what is learned in colleges becomes dated. The purpose of the college is not to prepare students for a particular profession or to impart vocational training; many students will acquire the skills they need on the job, and in any case many of them will change jobs and professions many times in their lives. If statistics are to be believed, all those graduating this year will on average change professions 3.7 times, and no one really knows today what different professions these students will try in their lifetime. And while liberal education is not about imparting vocational training, it does give the student the analytical tools needed for the pursuit of a profession.

Faced with the challenges of globalization, most institutions and organizations – corporations, governments, manufacturers and the media – have had to reinvent themselves. Colleges are no exception, and like other institutions, they too are changing. The question of reinventing colleges has not been as explicitly discussed because they are, in some ways, different. While deliberative faculty self-governance of the colleges and the need for faculty consensus has made changes invariably slow, it is also a source of the colleges' strength. It has enabled them to resist many passing fashions or changes for the sake of change. While colleges cannot escape from addressing the challenges posed by globalization, they must build on the strong foundations and traditions and firmly preserve their distinctive liberal arts traditions.

NOTES

1. John C. Scott, "The Mission of the University: Medieval to Postmodern Transformations," *The Journal of Higher Education* 77, no. 1 (January/February 2006.)
2. Marvin Bartell, "Internationalization of Universities: A University Culture-Based Framework," *Higher Education* 45, no. 1 (January 2003.)

3. Arnoud de Meyer, Patrick T. Harker and Gabriel Hawawini, "The Globalization of Business Education," in *The INSEAD-Wharton Alliance on Globalizing: Strategies for Building Successful Global Businesses*, ed. Hubert Gatignon and John R. Kimberly (Cambridge: Cambridge University Press, 2004), pp. 107–109.
4. Karen Fischer, "Short Study-Abroad Trips Can Have Lasting Effect, Research Suggests," *The Chronicle of Higher Education*, under "Today's News," http://chronicle.com/daily/2009/02/12191n.htm (accessed February 20, 2009.)
5. Susan Frost and Rebecca Chopp, "The University as a Global City," *Change* (March/April 2004), 44–50.
6. Various models of institutional internationalization are described in De Meyer, Harker and Hawawini (see note 3), pp. 107–113.
7. See Nadine Dolby, "Encountering an American Self: Study Abroad and National Identity," *Comparative Education Review* 48, no. 2 (May 2004.)
8. Farleigh Dickinson University has been a pioneer in creating global classrooms; see J. Michael Adams, "Think Globally, Educate Locally," *New York Times*, June 20, 2004, and Sierra Millman, "A Course Teaches the Concept of Global Citizenship," *The Chronicle of Higher Education* 53, no. 41 (June 15, 2007), 6.
9. See Ulrich Teichler, "The Changing Debate on Internationalisation of Higher Education," *Higher Education* 48, no. 1 (July 2004), 10–14.
10. See William R. Brody, "College Goes Global," *Foreign Affairs* 86, no. 2 (March/April 2007), 126–9.
11. The internationalization of Australian colleges especially reflects these goals of mutual benefit and equal exchange; see Anthony Welch, "Going Global? Internationalizing Australian Universities in a Time of Global Crisis," *Comparative Education Review* 46, no. 4 (November 2002), 433–71.
12. Janet Smith Dickerson, "The Impact of Increasing Diversity in Higher Education or, The Teacher's Gift: Permission to Go Home," *Proceedings of the American Philosophical Society* 142, no. 2 (June 1998.)
13. University of Virginia Student Financial Services, under "AccessUVa," http://www.virginia.edu/financialaid/access.php (accessed May 21, 2009.)
14. See Harold T. Shapiro, *A Larger Sense of Purpose: Higher Education and Society* (Princeton, NJ: Princeton University Press, 2005.)

12. American higher education in an increasingly globalized world: the way ahead

D. Bruce Johnstone

Although this chapter is the last in this volume and purports to peer into an uncertain future, it is by no means a summary as such. The participants in the 2008 TIAA-CREF Institute conference, "Higher Education in a Global Society", as well as the other scholars who contributed chapters to this volume all speak with authority as well as individual perspectives and different personal and scholarly approaches to the underlying theme of American higher education in an increasingly globalized world. I shall seek neither to summarize nor to synthesize. Rather, I shall take advantage of my co-editorship to make some concluding comments, informed by the rich insights of these chapters as well as by my own perspective as a scholar of international comparative higher education finance, governance, and policy and further by my varied administrative experiences as a vice president for administration of a leading private research university, president of a public comprehensive college, and chancellor of a large public system.

Without rehashing the definitional complexities of "globalization", "internationalization", and related terms, and without intentionally venturing into the stew of competing political and economic ideologies and the conventional academic critiques of Anglo-American economic, cultural and linguistic hegemony, I begin simply by recognizing the greatly increasing cross-border mobility of ideas, commerce, scholars, scholarship, and students. In short, our discussion of higher education in an increasingly globalized world begins with the observation and celebration of the increasing mobility and interconnectedness throughout the world of what colleges and universities everywhere do – which is to teach, credential, discover, communicate, conserve, criticize, and serve.

This increasing mobility and interconnectedness of higher education is driven by many forces, including deliberate governmental policy (on the part of most countries), the inquiring minds of scholars and students, the special interconnectedness of science and the increasing interconnectedness of commerce, and the extraordinary advances in technology and transportation that have so diminished former barriers of time and distance.[1] The terms of trade increasingly favor goods and services with high knowledge content and thus favor nations with advanced technologies and advanced systems of higher education. That the international language of both science and commerce is English serves to further privilege institutions and scholars in English-speaking countries, especially the United States. These are privileges for which we should feel neither guilty nor apologetic, but which do burden us with responsibilities both to assist in the spread of knowledge and in the expansion of higher educational capacity elsewhere and to recognize and respect the strengths of higher educational systems, universities, and scholars in other parts of the world and to learn from them.

Finally, as all of our contributors have suggested, the increasing importance of knowledge and increasing scholarly mobility and international interconnectedness are mutually reinforcing. Successful scholars gain reputation, publication opportunities, students, research grants, and consulting contracts – all of which gain more recognition, reinforcing the cycle of reputational quality. Thus, although globalization in the sense of its larger impacts on economies and cultures and its association with the ascendance of markets and competition will undoubtedly continue to be a subject of political and ideological contestation, this increasing mobility and interconnectedness of the institutions of higher education and of their scholars and students is happening and is generally encouraged virtually throughout the world.

THE INTERNATIONALIZATION OF AMERICAN HIGHER EDUCATION

Higher education in the United States seems by many measures to be astride the higher educational world. US universities are named as 13 of the top 20 and 25 of the top 60 places in THE's "World University Rankings" (*Times Higher Education Supplement*, 2008.) We claim some 30 percent of the world's scientific publications (OECD, 2007.) We received in 2008 20 percent of the world's higher educational students studying outside of their home countries (Institute of International Education, 2009.) Such measures, however, portray the *dominance* of US higher education, arguably a function of our immense size, relative wealth, and economic and cultural hegemony, but do not necessarily signify a higher educational system adapting to an increasingly globalized world.

However, the question underlying the conference that launched this volume and the one that most of the contributors were asking is whether – and more importantly how – US higher education can become more internationalized. That is, how do our undergraduate curricular requirements, the curricula of our many majors and post-baccalaureate degree programs, our provision of learning outside of the classroom, our selection of students and receptivity to their prior learning, and the search for and selection of our faculty and academic leaders become genuinely more international, more globally accommodating, and more receptive to – and when appropriate learning more from – the way education beyond the secondary school is carried out in the rest of the world? Or, posed in the spirit of global competition, how do we avoid simply resting on our 20th century laurels and on our historic dominance – still looking competitive, but losing ground to a surging European higher education area that is aggressively seeking to restore its 19th and early 20th century preeminence under the banners of a more united Europe and the agendas forged in Bologna and Lisbon, not to mention the surging universities of China and India?

As in most arguments framed by the posing of extremes, the truth lies somewhere in the vast middle. Global awareness in both undergraduate and graduate curricula is almost certainly increasing in American colleges and universities, as is study abroad and the interconnectedness of American scholars with international counterparts. However, the American citizenry continues to be largely ignorant of, and uninterested in, the world outside its borders except as a source of threats or of exciting places to visit. The challenge to American higher education to impart far more global awareness is important and immense.

The weakest link in the genuine internationalization of American higher education continues to be the lack of second language facility on the part of American undergraduates and American faculty sufficient to study and conduct serious research in another language. The increasing English language facility of students and scholars from other countries provides an easy way out for the tens of thousands of students and scholars from other countries seeking to study in the United States, as well as for the American faculty member seeking an international sabbatical experience and for the US undergraduate seeking a more or less casual semester or summer of study abroad (too often simply in another English-speaking country.) In fact there was probably a greater number – and undoubtedly a greater proportion – of US faculty and graduate students capable of serious study and research in a language other than English 50 or even 100 years ago than today.

There are signs of improvement, particularly in resurgent numbers of US high school students taking a foreign language in school and especially in the numbers studying Chinese, Japanese, Arabic and other languages beyond the perennial standards of French and Spanish (American Council on the Teaching of Foreign Languages website, 2009.) Nonetheless, the extent of genuine second language facility of American college students sufficient to spend a year or more of serious study in a non-English-speaking country is still far less than it should be. The long slippage of the once ubiquitous foreign language expectation for college admission and the even more serious decline of the requirement of a second language for college graduation must take a significant share of the blame for the scarcity of American undergraduates capable of spending a year abroad in serious study. And with English language scholarly journals dominating the world of scholarship, especially in the sciences, with English language graduate-level seminars (again, especially in the sciences) becoming part of advanced doctoral studies throughout the world, and with the demise of the one-time American Ph.D. requirement for reading knowledge of two languages other than English, American university faculty have limited facility to conduct serious research in another language (unless their dissertation and long-term research agenda so require.)

While we are almost certainly doing a little better in the internationalization of the American undergraduate experience than in our recent past, most of the rest of the world is doing so very much better. Thus, there seems to be a widening asymmetry in much US higher educational academic exchange, both of students and of scholars, with students from other countries frequently seeking entire degrees and scholars typically seeking serious collaborative research, while American undergraduates are frequently seeking a brief study abroad experience that is only marginally related to their undergraduate concentration, and American faculty too often seem to be seeking a sabbatical experience for rest and scholarly refreshment. A 2008 white paper of the Institute of International Education reported that the greatest room for growth in study abroad opportunities for American students, from the perspective of potential host countries, was in longer-term programs, including full degree study opportunities, although US students continue to avail themselves primarily in short-term study abroad programs (Guitierrez et al., 2008, cited in Blumenthal and Guitierrez, 2009.) And in any event, the proportion of US students experiencing study abroad, while increasing and while undeniably important for those fortunate enough to participate, is still minimal, reaching only an estimated 1.3 percent of total US enrollment in 2005 (Salisbury et al., 2009, p. 120.)

While American educators will go on hoping for more second language facility on the part of American students, the increasing ubiquity of the English language means that the asymmetry in second language acquisition is here to stay. But the American way of higher education finance may also contribute to the asymmetry of academic exchange between the United States and the rest of the world. American colleges and universities, public and private alike, are generally more (and in comparison with Europe far more) dependent on tuition fees, which may or may not be lost if the American student enters into a study abroad experience that is not an integral part of an already paid for semester or two (implying full degree credit for the experience.) This tuition dependence undoubtedly makes American colleges – especially at the undergraduate level and especially if they are minimally selective – particularly receptive to international students from families who can pay the high US tuition fees, but also similarly reluctant to lose a semester or two of tuition for credit-bearing courses from their own students taken elsewhere.

If the study abroad offered to the US undergraduate can be offered as an integral part of an academic semester, then the already paid tuition fee – particularly at a US private college – can be a major source of income for support of the experience, even generating a kind of profit that can, in turn, support some of the additional costs such as a US faculty advisor, travel expenses, and scholarships for those students who are on scholarship anyway, and perhaps even cover the fees for some of the international students who may well be unused to tuition fees and whose families may on average be less affluent than their American exchange counterparts.

However, while the export of US higher education in the form of international students coming to US colleges and universities – to the financial tune of some $15.54 billion in the 2007–08 academic year (Institute of International Education IIENetwork) – is significant for the financial health of many US institutions and for the US balance of trade, and is fully consistent with the commercial dimension of the globalization phenomenon, it does not in itself signify much about the more fundamental goal of educating American students for an increasingly globalized world.

LEARNING FROM EACH OTHER

It would be a mistake to judge the success of internationalization simply by numbers or proportions of US students going abroad to study. Part of the globalization phenomenon is the potential for a rich cross-fertilization of ideas and policies. In the case of higher education, a goal of the presumably greater internationalization that is made possible and even inevitable by increasing globalization is the degree to which colleges and universities and national systems of higher education – including those in the United States – can learn from, as well as enrich, each other.

In the arena of mutual influence, the exchange – for example, between Europe and the United States and much more so between the United Sates and the non-European world – is also, like the exchange of students, asymmetrical, with continental Europe moving in a direction more nearly resembling the United States (and the UK) than the United States taking on policies or attributes of European higher education. Much of this European movement has been codified by the so-called Bologna Agreement reached by the education ministers initially of 29 European countries meeting in that academically historic Italian city (growing to include some 46 countries by 2009), as well as by the supra-national European Community meeting in Lisbon, where the European heads of state and leaders of governments resolved to enhance the prestige and the scholarly productivity of what they termed a European Higher Education Area (Van der Wende 2009.) The participating European countries would accomplish this by:

- moving (within a defined time frame) away from the former European long first degree, which was largely examination based, predicated on a somewhat indeterminate time but usually six to seven years in duration, roughly equivalent in program content to an American masters degree, which had little or no room for either curricular experimentation or changes of program, and which effectively locked the student into his or her university of initial matriculation except for a year or so in another university, either in-country or in another country;
- moving toward a three-fold degree structure, beginning with a bachelors degree of either three or four years' duration, followed by a masters degree of one or two years, and finally a doctorate that would be closer to an American Ph.D. in its greater emphasis on a prescribed set of courses preceding the dissertation.

Student mobility in this new European arrangement was to be greatly encouraged (particularly in contrast to the former examination-based long first degree) by modularizing the program: in effect, granting the bachelors (and perhaps the masters) degree based on an accumulation of courses with prescribed credits and transparent curricular content that could move with the student – not unlike the way that American students transfer institutions in very large numbers and take their course credits with them.

Bologna, Lisbon, and subsequent agreements were decidedly top-down – from ministers and heads of governments to universities – with varying degrees of enthusiasm and compliance from faculty, elected rectors, deans, and students. At the same time, the very great dependence of most European universities on their central governments, which have vastly more financial leverage over the universities than does the US central (Federal) government – in addition to the generally insignificant role played by private universities – as well as the relatively much greater authority over the terms and conditions of faculty appointments via the civil service status of most European faculty gives the European ministers, on the whole, considerably greater leverage over their universities than the US federal government and even more than most US state governments.

In other ways also, universities and higher educational systems in Continental Europe and much of the rest of the world are adopting measures associated with US higher education. Most striking is the acceptance of the need for non-governmental revenue, partly from the tentative and still deeply contested acceptance of tuition fees. Even the Nordic countries, while still the last worldly bastion of free higher education for their citizens (and perforce for all other EU citizens), are reluctantly moving toward tuition fees for non-EU students. The UK from 1997, the Netherlands and Portugal soon thereafter, Austria from 2000, and even a few of the German states by the year 2009 charge tuition fees that are exceptionally small by US public university standards but that represent a monumental departure from past practices (Marcucci and Johnstone, 2007.) Also, increasingly emphasized and much less contested, but still difficult to realize, is the successful tapping of alumni and other sources of philanthropy by public universities and colleges as in the United States (Johnstone, 2005.)

Public universities (and to a somewhat lesser extent other four-year public colleges) in the United States have, by international standards (albeit differing by state), a great deal of institutional autonomy. Coupled with the American public governing board, which places a kind of buffer between the institution and the state government, and the corresponding tradition of the strong American university president, chosen by this board and frequently from outside of the university, public colleges and universities in the United States have considerably more institutional autonomy and active management than public universities in most other countries. Again, universities and other institutions of higher education in Europe are adopting similar models of what has been called New Public Management (NPM) – in part to cope with the extraordinary and incessant rise in higher education costs everywhere, and the need to make the kinds of reallocation decisions that are exceptionally difficult to make in a European higher educational governance system in which the university head is totally beholden to the faculty (and frequently to politicians.)

A final example of influence moving to Europe from America – which critics would label the encroachment of Anglo-American policy on

Continental European higher education – is the slow, uneven and still deeply contested acceptance of competition among the public universities of a nation. Although Continental European universities always differed somewhat in their academic reputations and their attractiveness to students, these differences traditionally were not to be accentuated or encouraged – and most certainly not by governmental policies. Aggressive competition for students or for professors brought such rebukes from the faculty and generally from the political left as "marketization" or "commodification" and making the already favored even more so. At the same time, the failure of the German universities to come even close to the American or British universities in the so-called league tables of top universities led the German government to begin in 2008 the contested selection of a small number of German universities for special revenue enhancement – and their avowed differentiation and elevation in status as well as affluence.

The lessons to be learned are not all one way, however. Under the previously mentioned Bologna and Lisbon strategies, European public systems and individual universities, as of 2009, have been moving deliberatively toward what are termed Qualification Frameworks: the specification of learning outcomes by degrees, levels, and disciplines in order to further within-EU student mobility and the transparency of higher educational offerings. Clifford Adelman, a former higher education analyst for the US Department of Education's National Center for Educational Statistics, in a study entitled *The Bologna Process for U.S. Eyes*, reiterated some concrete suggestions for change in US higher education practices following Europe and the Bologna process, including:

- developing detailed and public degree qualification frameworks for state higher education systems, and, for all institutions, following the Tuning model in students' major fields;
- revising the reference points and terms of our credit transfer system;
- expanding dual-admissions "alliances" between community colleges and four-year institutions;
- refining our definition and treatment of part-time students;
- developing a distinctive version of a diploma supplement that summarizes individual student achievement.

(Adelman, 2009, p. x)

Table 12.1 summarizes some of these lessons to be learned, including lessons we can learn from Europe and elsewhere as well as lessons that much of the rest of the world – for good or for ill – seems to be taking from the examples of higher education in the United States.

Table 12.1 *Internationalization of higher education: learning from each other*

Critical problem or need	What the US can learn from higher education in other countries	What other countries can learn from US higher education
1. Austerity: the need for adequate revenue that increases with increasing costs and provides incentives for non-tax revenue, efficiency, and quality	Most OECD governments are more generous and consistent on tax support of universities (but weak on non-tax revenue, on financial flexibility, and on management.)	US public institutions suffer from dependence on erratic state government aid but gain greatly from non-tax revenue: tuition, philanthropy, and grant and contract overhead.
2. Inefficiency: the need for greater institutional productivity and efficient resource allocation	Greater austerity in many countries has led to an appearance of economy, but not necessarily to efficiency, although UK and Netherlands provide good exceptions.	US traditions of institutional autonomy, professional management (including strong presidents), and examples from private sector tend to force efficiencies.
3. Uneven or inadequate teaching: the need for more rewards for good teaching	Learning expectations may be higher. Separation of teaching from examining may bolster good teaching. Minimal student mobility, little competition for students, and low or no tuition may discourage good teaching.	US traditions of student mobility along with strong non-university institutions, competition, transferable credits and widespread use of teacher evaluations all support teaching.
4. Assessment policies and instruments that measure learning and other outcomes	Considerable activity and some progress in Europe via Bologna in *qualifications frameworks* to stipulate learning outcomes by degree, level, and discipline. UK provides rigorous (albeit controversial) research assessment exercise.	The US provides an often criticized but seemingly effective and mainly non-governmental accreditation process. States and systems freely experiment with linking outcomes assessments and annual budgets.
5. Diversification: the need for different tertiary sectors that meet	Short-cycle institutions in some countries within universities. Bologna stipulations of learning	US community college tradition of combining so-called terminal programs

Table 12.1 (continued)

Critical problem or need	What the US can learn from higher education in other countries	What other countries can learn from US higher education
diverse local and student needs, but that do not limit accessibility	outcomes may further linkages, but non-universities are weak in many countries.	with transferability of community college credits toward bachelors degrees
6. Inequalities by social class and ethnicity: the need for more equitable access to and participation in higher education	Emphasis is on free or very low tuition fees and other forms of student welfare, although potential students from disadvantaged backgrounds are still lost to the system.	High tuition fees may be barrier to some, although extensive financial assistance, affirmative action, special counseling and remediation, and access institutions help.
7. Barriers to international student mobility	Europe traditionally had little student mobility, but Bologna-inspired quality assurance, the European Credit Transfer, and *tuning* may change this.	Course credits and ease of transfer plus mainly portable student aid greatly encourage and ease transfer and mobility.

THE WAY AHEAD

I will conclude by offering some thoughts on the way ahead, not, as I made clear in my introduction, purporting to summarize the excellent chapters of this book or of the 2008 TIAA-CREF Institute conference on higher education in an increasingly globalized world, but merely as concluding observations on a rich and timely theme.

1. Globalization, however defined, is primarily a function of modernity and technology. While governmental policies can encourage or impede the effects of globalization, many of its effects, both positive and negative, are beyond the reach of policy.
2. Globalization profoundly affects nearly all of our modern social institutions, probably none more than universities (and most other institutions of higher education.) Because of their central role in the advancement, transmission, and preservation of knowledge – all of these activities being supremely international – universities and other institutions of higher education are central players in the process of

globalization. Faculty impart (or fail to impart) global awareness to their students. Faculty analyze and critique the process of globalization at the same time as they live the process in their scholarship and teaching.

3. The United States, for all its extraordinary economic, cultural, political, and military reach, is in many ways an insular nation. As a nation, we have long been largely ignorant of the world outside our boundaries except as places to visit, or countries with which to trade, or cultures to fear or resent. This is true of the average US citizen; unfortunately, it is also true of too many of our elected leaders.

4. Therefore, it is incumbent on our institutions of higher education – meaning both public and private and including all types of post-secondary institutions as well as all levels of prestige or selectivity – to impart greater global awareness to our students, as well as to those beyond our curricular reach through our scholarship and service to the wider society.

5. A major barrier to greater global awareness in the United States is our weakness in second languages (other than among those who were born outside of the United States into another language.) Greater second language facility must begin in middle and high school, and be reinforced by language requirements for college graduation – and in selective colleges and universities, through the reintroduction of meaningful second language expectations for entry.

6. Global awareness must then be strengthened through one of the finest and most valuable of American higher educational traditions: the general education requirement, which is expected in one form or another of almost all US Baccalaureate graduates and which transcends specialization and vocational preparation. Within this general education requirement, which typically takes between one-quarter and one-third of the four-year Baccalaureate experience, can and should be significant global and international learning. Community college education, despite the limitations of fewer curricular hours, less academic selectivity, and more vocational pressure, must also find ways to impart greater global awareness to its students.

7. Similarly, but depending on different higher educational decision-makers, greater global awareness must be brought into most, if not all, of our collegiate upper division majors or concentrations, as well as into all or most graduate, or post-Baccalaureate, curricula.

8. Study abroad should grow and be integrated into curricular expectations of the undergraduate general education requirement and/or the upper division majors or concentrations. Special efforts must be made – with support from states as well as from the federal

government – to eliminate financial barriers to study abroad and to broaden the socio-economic base of study abroad participation.

9. All of this, of course, requires above all the powerful support of the faculty – which in turn highlights the need to encourage and reward learning and scholarship as well as curricular development that is genuinely international. This goal begins with the criteria for appointment, promotion, and the awarding of tenure, which are the most important coins of the scholarly realm. Faculty also need access to library resources, telecommunications, and sabbatical leave opportunities that further scholarly growth in international learning.

10. While appointment and promotion decisions generally begin with the faculty, these sought-after steps in academic careers are ultimately dispensed by academic leaders: chairs, deans, provosts, and presidents and chancellors. Their decisions send powerful signals about those scholarly traits that are to be valued. In addition, new academic ventures, majors, degree programs, and partnerships all require revenue; and budgets are the purview of institutional leadership. In short – and in full recognition of the primacy of the faculty in all good institutions of higher education – academic leaders have the opportunity to make a difference in the greater internationalization of their institutions.

11. At the level of state government, public college and university budgets must respond to quality, as evidenced in part by international activities, and must recognize the appropriateness of curricular and scholarly activities that are international.

12. At the level of the US federal government, core federal programs such as the Fulbright programs must continue to be supported and to grow. Unnecessary and time- and resource-consuming barriers to international student entry must be eased.

13. Finally, in these and other ways, the United States must continue to hold onto its position as the premier academic destination for both students and scholars from other countries as well as being a model for the various traditions – including academic freedom, integrity, and accountability, shared governance, a concern for teaching and learning, and a devotion to more equitable access – that, in the end, account for this primacy.

I could go on, but this list has perhaps served its purpose. I have attempted to illustrate some of the many ways by which our colleges and universities can rise to the challenges posed by our increasingly globalized world. If we as scholars and academic leaders fail to do so – resting instead on the extraordinary scholarly record of the American research university, the fortuitousness of our native English language, or the uniquely American tradition of the undergraduate general education requirement – we can be sure that other countries, already more internationalized than we are in very many ways, will step forward to claim the privileged position and the attendant advantages we have had for so many years. Let us rise to this challenge.

NOTE

1. As I was drafting this chapter, a very personal example came in the form of a new book, edited by one of the contributing authors to this volume, Jane Knight of Canada, containing chapters from 12 of us who were Fulbright New Century Scholars, in a Fulbright program initiated under the leadership of another contributing author, Patti McGill Peterson. The Fulbright Program is an example of international mobility and scholarly interconnectedness by governmental policy – mainly of the United States, but with support from some 155 Fulbright partner countries. The scholarship originated in a collaboration of scholars from (in alphabetical order) Australia, Brazil, Canada, Egypt, Korea, Morocco, Oman, Poland, South Africa, Uganda, the United Kingdom, and the United States. What brought us together in this essentially voluntary effort – other than the facilitating governmental policies – is what we do as university scholars. And what made the solicitation and collection of these chapters possible from scholars in 12 countries and made possible the editing and production of the book in the brief span of several months is the technological miracle of e-mail and attachable documents.

REFERENCES

Adelman, Clifford (2009), *The Bologna Process for U.S. Eyes: Re-Learning Higher Education in the Age of Convergence*, Washington DC: Institute for Higher Education Policy.
American Council on the Teaching of Foreign Languages website, June 2, 2009, http://www.actfl.org/i4a/pages/index.cfm?pageidTikmew.
Blumenthal, Peggy and Robert Guitierrez (eds) (2009), *Expanding Study Abroad Capacity at U.S. Colleges and Universities*, New York: Institute of International Education, IIE Study Abroad White Paper Series Issue Number 6, May.
Guitierrez, Robert, Rajika Bhandari and Daniel Obst (2008), *Exploring Host Country Capacity for Increasing U.S. Study Abroad*, New York: Institute of International Education, IIE Study Abroad White Paper Series Issue Number 2, May.
Institute of International Education (2009), *Atlas of Student Mobility*, "Global Destinations for International Students at the Post-Secondary (Tertiary) Level, 2008." Downloaded 6/1/09 from http://atls.iienetwork.org.
Institute of International Education IIENetwork, "Economic Impact of International Students." Downloaded 6/1/09 from http://opendoors.iienetwork.org/.
Johnstone, D. Bruce (2005), "A Political Culture of Giving and the Philanthropic

Support of Public Higher Education in International Perspective," *International Journal of Educational Advancement*, 5 (3), 256–64.
Marcucci, Pamela N. and D. Bruce Johnstone (2007), "Tuition Policies in a Comparative Perspective: Theoretical and Political Rationales," *Journal of Higher Education Policy and Management*, 29 (1), 25–40.
OECD (2007), "OECD Science, Technology and Industry Scoreboard 2007," Paris: Organisation for Economic Co-operation and Development. Downloaded June 3, 2009, from http://www.oecd.org/.
Salisbury, Mark H., Paul D. Umbach, Michael Paulsen and Ernest Pascarella (2009), "Going Global: Understanding the Choice Process of the Intent to Study Abroad," *Research in Higher Education*, 50 (2) 119–43.
Times Higher Education Supplement (2008), "World University Rankings." Downloaded June 3, 2009, from http://www.topuniversities.com/.
Van der Wende Marijk (2009), "European Responsiveness to Global Competitiveness in Higher Education," Berkeley: Center for Studies in Higher Education, Research and Occasional Paper Series CSHE 7.09.

Index

Notes
 individual universities are listed by their location

access, to education 37–9, 166–8
 and ability to pay 63, 171, 194–5
 and cross-border education 57, 63
 in developing countries 164–6, 194
 and financial assistance 195–7
 need to improve 194–5, 209
accountability 34, 38–9, 211
accreditation
 'accreditation mills' 65
 articulation arrangements 49, 51
 course credits 21, 38, 51, 207, 209
  for study abroad programs 23, 118
 and cross-border education 48–54, 58, 63–5, 67
 quality and recognition 52, 58, 63–5, 138, 209
 'rogue' education providers 48–50, 65, 67
Adadolu University, Turkey 32
Adelman, Clifford 207
administration, of universities/ institutions
 autonomy, advantages of 208
 barriers to internationalization 110–11, 119–20, 151
 international program offices, role of 97–8, 152–3, 158–60
 organizational structure
  in Europe 151, 206
  in US universities 35, 208
Africa 26, 53 *see also* South Africa
Air, University of (Japan) 32
Altbach, Philip 136–7
alumni, international 181
American Council on Education (ACE) 117–19, 136

 report on internationalization of education 142–3
 study of faculty role in internationalization 148–51, 160
American History Association (AHA) 143–4
American Political Science Association (APSA) 143
Apollo Group 44, 53
Arab Open University 53
Arizona State University 70
articulation arrangements 49, 51
Asia 26, 30–31, 44 *see also* individual countries
Association for International Educators (NAFSA) 148–9
Association of Public and Land-grant Universities 149–50
Australia 29, 44, 53, 100

Bahrain Education City 59
Baruch College, City University of New York
 ethnic diversity of 9, 124–6
 financial assistance for 125
 Global Student Certificate Program 9, 125–33
 study abroad programs, involvement in 9, 124
Bayh-Dole Act 1980 (US) 79
Bender, Thomas 135
Bennett, Milton J. 154
Biopolis, Singapore 72
Blumenthal, Peggy 202
Bohm, A. 44
Bologna Process, for creation of EU Higher Education Area 109–10, 157, 205–9
borderless education 43
brain train/ brain drain 15, 27, 54–5, 62
branch campuses 27, 43–5, 53, 58, 65–6

branding, of universities 64–5
Broad, Molly Corbett 4
business
  education as tradable service 46–7, 55, 62–3
  as education providers 50
  influence over higher education, in US 18
  research, role in 72–3, 79–80

California, University of 112
campuses
  branch campuses 27, 43–5, 53, 58, 65–6
  diversity, need for 8–9, 195
  as world microcosm 187–8, 195
Canada 25–6, 44, 149, 167
Canizares, Claude 4–5
Capaldi, Elizabeth D. 5–6, 80
Carnegie Mellon University 7, 44
  Computer Emergency Research Team (CERT) programs 85, 87–9
  corporate partnerships 53
  domestic partnership programs 101–2
  overseas course/ degree programs
    advantages of 108
    central administration body, role of 97–8
    Department of Defense collaborations 85, 87–91
    doctorate programs 103
    establishment of 94–7, 98–103
    funding implications 93–4
    historical development of 92–3
    locations of 84, 86, 88–91, 103–6
    masters programs 98–103
    problems encountered 85, 106–7
    in Qatar 84, 103–6
    reasons for 84
    technology, use of 95
    undergraduate programs 103–6
  Software Engineering Institute (SEI) programs 85, 87, 90–91
Castells, Manuel 15
Center for Capacity Building in Study Abroad 8
  establishment 115–16
  issues identified for attention 116–21

Central and Eastern Europe 30
Chile 44
China
  distance learning 32
  enrollment/ participation trends 6, 25–6, 164–7
  international students from 164–7
  private universities in 44
  research collaborations 78–9
  research funding in 71–3, 78–9
Chinese University of Hong Kong 112
Cloete, Nico 15
Columbia University 44
Commerce Control List 76
Commission on the Abraham Lincoln Study Abroad Fellowship Program (2005) 110
communication skills, of international students 171–3
community colleges, US 20, 31, 38, 115, 210
comparative education 42–3
conferences, internationalization
  advantages of 149, 151, 155–6
Cornell University 105
corporations *see* business
Costa Rica 44, 155
Council of Graduate Schools 156–7
cross-border education
  and access to education 57, 63
  challenges to 62–6
  course accreditation/ recognition 48–54, 58, 63–5, 67
  cultural issues 42–3, 56–7, 174–7, 187, 195
  definition 43, 46
  drivers for 54–6
  education hubs/ cities 44–5, 52, 56, 60–62
  education providers
    business as 50
    new/ alternative providers 50–51
    provider mobility 48–9, 52–4, 66–7
    traditional providers 49–50
  impacts of 57–8
  intellectual property, of courses 52
  international trade implications of 46–7, 52, 55, 62–3
  language, impact of 57

Index

mobility
  categories of 47–8
  of labor 54–5
  program mobility 48–9, 51–2, 66–7
  for nation-building 55–6
  national security issues 57, 76–7, 179–80
  quality and recognition 52, 58, 63–5, 138, 209
  rationales for 54–8
  taxation issues 19, 52, 106–7
  trends in 47
Crutcher, Ronald A. 8
cultural issues 57
  academic honesty 174
  celebrating diversity 177–8
  dietary requirements 176–7
  differences in student focus 187, 195
  ethnic tensions 178–9
  intercultural sensitivity, developmental models of 154
  and international research collaborations 77
  multicultural education 42–3
  religious differences 176
  sense of community, need for 175–6
  smoking, attitudes towards 175
curriculum
  faculty-led change to 148–9, 154
  for global citizens 186–92, 211
  interdisciplinary education 34, 142–5, 189–90
  relevance of 65–6

Dalton, D.H. 79–80
Defense Advanced Research Project Agency (DARPA) 78
degrees, domestic
  offering outside home nation (*see* Carnegie Mellon University)
Denmark, Technical University of 112
Department of Defense (now Homeland Security), collaborations with Carnegie Mellon University 85, 87–91
developing countries
  globalization, impact on 18–19
  US education as model for 27
DiFazio, R. 156
diseases, control of epidemics/ pandemics 180–81
distance learning 28, 31–3, 43, 51
  effectiveness of 32–3
diversity, of students 11
  balance, need for 162–3
  celebrating, methods of 177–8
  differences in focus of 187, 195
  underrepresentation in study abroad programs 115
double/ dual degree arrangements 27, 51, 156
Dubai 44
Duke University 112

education cities/ hubs 44–5, 56
  Carnegie Mellon role in Qatar 84, 103–6
  failures of 45
  incentives for 52, 54
  other descriptors for 59
  rationales and expectations 60–62
education providers
  businesses as 50
  and cross-border education 48–9
  definition 47
  provider mobility 48–9, 52–4, 66–7
  rogue providers 49–50, 65, 67
education services
  in cross-border education 48–9
  trade in 46–7, 55, 62–3
elite academic systems 25–7
English *see under* language
enrollment, global trends 19, 25–6, 29–30, 38, 166–8
ethnic diversity, underrepresentation in study abroad programs 115
European Higher Education Area 205
European Union
  higher education policies
    access to education 39
    Bologna Process (creation of EU Higher Education Area) 109–10, 157, 205–9
    European Credit Transfer 209
    financial challenges 29, 206
    lessons to be learned by US from 21, 208–9
    Qualification Frameworks 207–8
    and student mobility 205–7

Lisbon Accord 2007 72, 205
New Public Management (NPM) 206
research collaborations, opportunities for 72
university organizational structure 151, 206
Everyman's University, Israel 32
exchange programs 114, 155
Export Administration Regulations (EAR) 76

faculty
  academic career paths 37
  as ambassadors 11
  character of, trends in 36–7
  and collaborative research agreements 75, 156
  curriculum change by 148–9, 154
  development programs for 139
  exclusion from policy-making, impact of 138–9
  Fulbright Program 137, 140–42, 150–51
  function of 134
  funding 151, 157–8
  interdisciplinary education 34, 142–5, 189–90
  international mobility of 139
  internationalization
    and academic disciplines, balancing 142–5
    ACE study of involvement in 148–51, 160
    barriers to 149–51, 154
    conferences/ summits, advantages of 149, 151, 153–6
    and curriculum redesign 191–2
    development methods 153–6
    guidelines for better 10, 144–6
    importance of engagement in 9–10, 138–40
    incentives for 23, 118, 139–40, 145–6, 150, 152–3, 208, 211
    and institutional structure 151
    missed opportunities for 142–4
    role of 8, 148–51, 160–61, 190, 210
    site visits, advantages of 155–6
    study of 136–7, 152–3
  support/ training for 66, 158–60
  views on 136–7
  part-time, increase in 36–7
  power of, shifts in 36
  Preparing Future Faculty programs 157–8
  research focus of 36
  study abroad programs, engagement in 113–14, 116–18, 148–9
  and visiting scholars 158
financial assistance, for students
  importance of 195–7
  for international students 163, 172–3, 180
  programs for 196
  for study abroad programs 115, 210–211
  types of 48, 124
  in US 20–21
financial markets, 2008 crisis in
  and globalization 1, 17, 22–3
first movers 170–71, 182
flow, of educational/ academic talent see brain train
Ford Foundation 196
foreign students and faculty see under faculty; students, international
France 26, 29
franchise programs 27, 43, 48–9, 51
Fulbright Program 137
  advantages of 140–42
  establishment of 140–41
  recruiting challenges of 141–2
  topping off 150–51
funding see also financial assistance; tuition fees
  for domestic degrees offered abroad 93–4
  for faculty training 151, 157–8
  for international research collaborations 70, 74–5, 79–80
  for research in China 71–3, 78–9

General Agreement on Trade in Services (GATS) 55, 62–4
George Mason University 45
Georgetown University 44, 105
Georgia Tech 112–13
German University, Cairo 53
Germany 26, 29, 31, 35, 167

global citizens, training students to be 186–8
global classrooms 188
global education 42–3
  advantages of 19, 125, 184–5
  in domestic institutions (*see* Baruch College)
  and global citizens 186–8
Global Education Index (GEI) 43
global schoolhouses 45, 59
Global Student Certificate Program (Baruch College) 9, 125–33
  benefits of 131–3
  Capstone Research Project 129–30
  corporate supporters of 131
  curriculum 126–31
Global Student Initiative (Baruch College) 9, 125
Global student mobility 2025 report 44
globalization
  advantages, for commerce 16–17
  definition 14–16, 45–6
  disadvantages 17–19
  and financial markets, 2008 crisis in 1, 17, 22–3
  and global issues 70–71, 192–3
  and government policy, whether beyond 16–17, 209
  and higher education
    advantages of 19, 125, 184–5
    challenges for 190–92, 197–8, 210
    consequences of 22–3
    disadvantages of 18–19
    implications for 3, 15–16, 18–19, 185–6
    influences on 200–201, 209–10
    massification 27–8
    role in internationalizing US 12–13
  and internationalization 15–16, 46, 67, 135
  nation state, impact on 135
  research focus 134, 192–3
  sources of wealth under 17–18
  and taxation 19, 52, 106–7
  whether function of technology 16
Goucher College 120
government policy
  and international research, promotion of 73–5
  protectionism 17
  whether globalization is beyond 16–17, 209
Greece 98–9
Green, Madeleine F. 117, 142, 148, 150–51
Guaglianone, Daniel 8
Guitierrez, Robert 202

Harvard University 44, 112, 196
Hayward, Fred M. 150, 160
health care, for international students in US 175
Held, David 15
Hibernia College 53
higher education, generally *see also* cross-border education
  academic systems
    changes to 33–5
    types of 25–8
  attitudes towards, changes in 28–9, 38–9
  challenges to 43–5
  demand for, increases in 19–20, 43–5
  distance learning 28, 31–3
  elite education 25–7
  enrollment, global trends in 19, 25–6, 29–30, 38, 166–8
  financial challenges 28–9
  and globalization
    challenges for 190–92, 197–8, 210
    implications of 3, 15–16, 18–19, 185–6
    influences on 200–201, 209–10
    and massification 27–8
    mobility and interconnectedness, increasing 200–201
  governance, traditional model of 33–4
  institutional growth 33–5
  internationalization 134, 143–4
    descriptors for 42–3
  managerialization 28
  mass education 25–8
  massification of 3–4, 25–8
  new institutions, development of 30–31, 38
  portable skills gained from 185, 190
  purpose of 28, 38, 134, 184–6, 190, 196–7

as a tradable service 46–7, 55, 62–3
universal education 25–6
higher education, in US
  access and affordability 194–5
  administrative structure/ power in 33–5, 208
  attractiveness to international students/ faculty 20–21
  business influence over 18
  challenges for 202
  community colleges 20, 31, 38, 115
  competition with foreign institutions 11
  enrollment/ participation trends 25–6, 166–8, 201
  and globalization, role in internationalizing US 12–13
  lessons to be learned from other countries 12–13, 21, 208–9
  as model for the world 27, 122, 185
  private educational institutions in 30–31
  research university league table rankings 19–20, 80
  second language, need for 3, 12, 23, 191–2, 202–3, 210
  study abroad programs 110–111, 113, 203
  superiority and dominance of 2–3, 11–12, 136–7, 201, 211
Higher education in a global society, TIAA-CREF Institute conference, 2008 1–6, 8–11, 200
Hill, C.T. 81
Hong Kong 59, 112
hubs *see* education cities
Hudzik, John 148, 151

incentives
  for education cities/ hubs 52, 54
  for faculty to promote internationalization 23, 118, 139–40, 145–6, 150, 152–3, 208, 211
India 6, 25–6, 33, 164–6, 196
Indianapolis, University of 53
Indonesia 30
Institute of International Education 121, 203

intellectual property
  and cross-border programs 52
  and international research collaborations 74, 79
intercultural sensitivity, developmental models of 154
international education
  providing in domestic institution (*see* Global Student Certificate Program)
International Education City 44
International Fellowship Program (Ford Foundation) 196
international program administration offices
  faculty awareness of 158–9
  public relations 158–60
  role of 97–8, 152–3
international research collaborations 4–5
  corporations, role in 72–3
  cultural issues 77
  and economic development 77–80
  funding for 70, 74–5, 79–80
  global focus of 36, 70–71
  government policy, role of 73–5
  historical background to 73–4
  legal and regulatory issues 75–7
  opportunities for 70–72
  reasons for 70–75, 77–80
  role of faculty 75
  US involvement in 74, 79–81
international teaching/ research summits, advantages of 153–4
international trade, implications for cross-border education 46–7, 52, 55, 62–3
International Traffic in Arms Regulations (ITAR) 76
International Virtual University 53
internationalization
  conferences/ summits, advantages of 149, 151, 153–6
  definition 15–16, 42–3, 46, 135
  and faculty
    and academic disciplines, balancing 142–5
    better focus, guidelines for 144–6
    governance 158–60

incentives for 23, 118, 139–40, 145–6, 150, 152–3, 208, 211
missed opportunities for 142–4
and globalization 15–16, 46, 67
mission goals for 151–2
strategies for 46
Internationalization and trade in higher education: opportunities and challenges (OECD) 56
Internationalizing the disciplines 142
internships 8, 114–15
Israel 32, 167
Italy 26–7, 29

Japan
   Carnegie Mellon partnerships in 101
   distance learning 32
   enrollment/ participation trends in 26, 37, 167
   faculty scholarship trends 36
   international students from 164–5
   private education in 30
Johns Hopkins University 45
Johnstone, D. Bruce 206
joint degree arrangements 27, 51, 156
Junior Faculty Development Program (JFDP) 158

Kalamazoo College 8
Kansas, University of 149, 154–5
Kapur, Devesh 6
Kerr, Clark 33
knowledge, increasing importance of 17–18, 193
Knowledge Village, Dubai 44

labor force
   as driver for cross-border education 54–6, 58–62
   educating, importance of 17–18
   global, characteristics of 8
laboratories 28, 33, 211
Lambert, Leo 3
language
   and cross-border education, impact of 57
   English
      asymmetry of 203–4
      competency in, of international students 171–3
      as first language, advantage of 168, 211–12
     second, need for in US education 3, 12, 23, 191–2, 202–3, 210
Latin America 26, 30–31, 36, 44
Laureate Education 44, 53
legal and regulatory issues 107
   export controls 57, 76–7, 179–80
   intellectual property 52, 74, 79
   for international research collaborations 75–7
   national security 57, 76–7, 179–80
   taxation 19, 52, 106–7
Li, Zhang 6
libraries 28, 33, 211
lifelong learning 1, 18, 43, 63, 185–6

McPherson, Peter 3, 8
managerialization, of higher education 28
Marcucci, Pamela 206
Marginson, Simon 15–16
marketing, of universities 64–5
mass academic systems 25–6
Massachusetts Institute of Technology (MIT) 5, 79, 112–13
massification, of higher education 3, 25–6
   challenges to 3–4, 28
   implications for organization and governance 26–7
Mexico 44
Michigan-Flint, University of 153–4
Michigan State University 112, 117, 120
Minnesota, University of 111–12, 120
Monash University, Australia 53
multicultural education 42–3
multiversity, definition 33, 105–6

Nanyang Technological University of Singapore 112
National Academy of Engineering 113
National Communication Association (NCA) 156
National Science Foundation 70, 73–4, 157
national security, and cross-border education 57, 76–7, 179–80
Netherlands 34, 44, 53

New Delhi Foundation for Access and Excellence 196
New Public Management (NPM) 206
New South Wales, University of 45
New York, City University of *see* Baruch College
New York University 44–5
New Zealand 29
non-profit educational institutions 30–31
Northwest University 44, 105

Office of Foreign Assets Control (OFAC) 76–7
Olson, Christa 148, 150–51
Open University, UK 30
Oregon, University of 154
organizational structure
  autonomy, advantages of 208
  as barrier to internationalization of faculty 151
  as barrier to study abroad programs 110–111, 119–20
  in Europe 151, 206
organized research units (ORUs) 34

Panama 44
Papadakis, Constantine 8–9
Partnerships for International Research and Education (PIRE) 157
Paul Simon Award for campus internationalization (NAFSA) 149
Pennsylvania, University of 6, 112
philanthropy 20–21
Philippines 30
Phoenix, University of 31, 53
plagiarism 174
Portugal 100–101, 103
Preparing Future Faculty programs 157–8
private initiative education 44–5
  development of 30–31
  enrollment trends 29–30
public relations 158–60
Puerto Rico 44
Purdue University 112–13

Qatar 44, 59–60, 84, 103–6
qualifications
  Qualification Frameworks (EU) 207
  quality and recognition of 58, 63–5

quality assurance
  and cross-border education 52, 58, 63–5, 138, 209
  'rogue' education providers 49–50, 65, 67

racial diversity, underrepresentation in study abroad programs 115
recession, protectionism during 17
recruitment, of international students 171–4
regulatory issues *see* legal and regulatory issues
Rensselaer Polytechnic Institute (RPI) 112
research *see also* international research collaborations
  global focus of 134, 192–3
  research competency 71–2
  research universities, changing role of 31
  US place in global R&D rankings 72, 79–81
Rhode Island, University of 113
Rochester, University of 163–4, 177
'rogue' education providers 49–50, 65, 67
Rollins College 117
Russia 167

Saiya, Laura 150, 160
Salmi, Jamil 15
Schoenberg, Robert 117, 142
Shanghai Jiao Tong university league tables 19
Shuerholz-Lehr, S. 149
Singapore 45, 72, 102, 112
Sirat, Morshidi 15
site visits, internationalization advantages of 155–6
smoking, international students' attitudes towards 175
South Africa 32, 99–100
South Carolina, University of 10–11, 112
South Korea 30, 36, 102–4, 167
Spanier, Graham 10
students, generally
  access to education, trends in 37–9, 166–8, 194–5

Index

brain train/ brain drain 15, 27, 54–5, 62
demand for education 37–8, 165–6
diversity 11, 38
  balance, need for 162–3
  celebrating, methods of 177–8
  differences in focus of 187, 195
  underrepresentation in study abroad programs 115
education hubs, expectations of 60–61
financial assistance 20–21, 48, 115, 195–7, 210–211
as global citizens 186–8
indebtedness of 18
mobility
  barriers to 209
  in European Higher Education Area 205
nontraditional students, trends in 38
views on purpose of education 38
students, international
  academic honesty, standards of 174
  advantages of 162–4, 181–2
  age, trends in 169–70
  as ambassadors 4, 170–71, 182
  attracting, reasons for 162–4
  attractiveness of US to 20–21
  communication skills of 171–3
  community/ cultural needs of 175–7
  dietary needs of 176–7
  and epidemic/ pandemic diseases, control of 180–81
  and ethnic tensions 178–9
  financial assistance for 163, 172–3, 180
  first movers 170–71, 182
  forming cliques 176
  health care for, in US 175
  integration in domestic campus 10
  international alumni, role of 181
  and national security 179–80
  numbers studying abroad 10
  places of origin, trends in 164–8
  recruitment issues 171–4
  religious needs of 176–7
  and restricted materials/ deemed exports 76–7, 179–80
  smoking, attitudes towards 175
  study destinations 168–9
  study type/ subject trends 168–71
  support issues 174–7
  travel issues and visas 173–4
study abroad programs
  academic value of 8, 210
  challenges to 115, 122, 211
  course credits 23, 118
  destinations for US students 113, 121
  direct enrollment programs 114
  duration of programs 113
  examples of 111–13
  exchange programs 114
  expansion potential of 120–21
  faculty
    faculty-led programs 113–14
    role in program development 116–17, 137–8, 148–9
  financial support for 23, 118–20, 211
  government policy goals
    in EU 109–10
    in US 110–11
  integration of 145
  internships 8, 114–15
  issues for attention 116–21, 123
  mission goals for 116
  problems facing
    finance 118–19
    organizational structure 110–11, 119–20
  research into, need for 121–2
  student attitudes towards 118–19
  and student diversity 115
  trends in 27, 109–11, 122, 137
  unrealistic nature of 8–9, 124
Sweden 29, 167

Taiwan 30, 78
taxation, and cross-border education 19, 52, 106–7
technology
  and distance learning 28, 31–3
  global classrooms 188
  and role in globalization 12
Test of English as a Foreign Language (TOEFL) 171–2
Texas A&M University 44, 53, 105

Thailand 32–3
TIAA-CREF Institute
  Higher education in a global society, conference 2008 1–6, 8–11, 200
Times Higher Education Supplement, university league tables 19, 201
transnational education 43
Trow, Martin 25–6
Troy University 53
tuition fees 57, 196–7
  dependence on 204
  in Europe 206
  and globalization 18
  paid by foreign institutions 11
  in UK 29, 206
  in US public sector 20–21, 204, 209
Turkey 32, 164, 167
TV University, China 32
twinning programs 27, 43, 48–9, 51

UNESCO (United Nations Educational, Scientific and Cultural Organization) 73
United Arab Emirates 44–5, 53, 59
United Kingdom 26, 208
  as destination for US students 113
  educational policies 27, 29
  Open University 30

United Nations 73–4
universal academic systems 25–6

validation arrangements 49, 51
Victoria, University of 149, 154, 196
Virginia Commonwealth University 44, 105
Virginia Tech 157
virtual universities 43, 51, 53, 188
visas 173–4
visiting scholars 158

Waldron, Kathleen 9
Washington, University of 112
Washington University in St Louis 11
Weill Cornell Medical College 44
Western Europe 26, 31, 34 *see also* European Union; individual countries by name
Wilson-Oyelaran, Eileen 8, 10
women, student enrollment trends 38
Wrighton, Mark S. 11

Yale University 112
Yodof, Mark 5

Zakaria, Fareed 2–3
Zicklin School of Business *see* Baruch College